William Edward Armytage Axon

Stray Chapters

in Literature, Folklore, and Archaeology

William Edward Armytage Axon

Stray Chapters
in Literature, Folklore, and Archaeology

ISBN/EAN: 9783744772174

Printed in Europe, USA, Canada, Australia, Japan

Cover: Foto ©Andreas Hilbeck / pixelio.de

More available books at **www.hansebooks.com**

STRAY CHAPTERS

IN

LITERATURE, FOLK-LORE, AND ARCHÆOLOGY.

STRAY CHAPTERS

IN

LITERATURE, FOLK-LORE,

AND

ARCHÆOLOGY.

BY

WILLIAM E. A. AXON.

JOHN HEYWOOD,
DEANSGATE AND RIDGEFIELD, MANCHESTER;
AND 11, PATERNOSTER BUILDINGS,
LONDON.
1888.

PREFACE.

THE following pages will be found to contain Essays and Papers upon topics connected, more or less closely, with history, literature, bibliography, folk-lore, and statistics. These stray chapters have for the most part already appeared in periodicals or in the transactions of societies, and they are now brought together in the hope that their variety will be held to excuse the absence of that connecting thread which is rightly looked for in a formal treatise upon a definite subject. The author of a volume of miscellaneous papers has a special difficulty in framing a suitable designation for the offspring of his pen. Few would expect to find an essay on the work of a librarian where Mr. John Fiske has placed it—in a volume entitled *Darwinism, and Other Essays*. This difficulty has pressed even upon great writers. There is a volume of De Quincey, which contains essays on Pope, Theory of Greek Tragedy, Literature, French and English Manners, Charles Lamb, Philosophy of Herodotus, Plato's Republic, Sortilege and Astrology, and Notes on Walter Savage Landor. To this delightful *olla podrida* De Quincey gives the title of *Leaders in Literature, with a notice of some errors affecting them*. This might, with as much and as little propriety, have been given also to any of the other volumes of his writings. De Quincey felt the situation, and puts forth an ingenious plea in mitigation of censure. He says: "The difficulty of framing titles for books—such as shall adequately indicate their separate purposes and functions, whilst at the same time offering some colourable air of novelty, is sufficiently understood. But the full pressure of that difficulty as it sometimes exists, and as, in fact, it exists in the case immediately before us, is but imperfectly appreciated. Where certain elements have been from the first intended to take their station side by side in the same volume, they will have been trained artifically beforehand into a fitness for co-membership in a whole. But the difficulty is prodigiously aggravated when the separate parts, that are suddenly and unexpectedly required to cohere into a systematic whole, arose originally upon casual and disconnected impulses, without any reference to final convergement, or any reference whatever to a central principle. The difficulty in extreme cases of this nature ripens into an impossibility.. Where there are absolutely no points of logical contact, it becomes a mere fantastic chase after a rainbow to pursue any comprehensive title such as can override the whole. In a case of that nature some indulgence may be reasonably challenged ; and a dispensation from that rigour of logic which would otherwise govern the case."

The puzzle which the modern writer has to solve is one that he inherits from a somewhat remote antiquity, and if his solution is not always a happy one, he may console himself by thinking that his predecessors were not more fortunate. Aulus Gellius called his book of miscellaneous essays and annotations *Attic Nights*, because the reading on which they were founded and the arrangement of them constituted his business and amusement during many long winter nights which he spent in Attica. He cites, but only to ridicule, some of the titles employed by the essayists of his day. "These authors having got together a various, mixed, and as it were, immethodical kind of learning, have for this reason studied to give their books refined and dainty titles." As examples, he cites : *The Muses, Silvae, Minerva's Robe, The Horn of Amalthea, Honey-combs, Pastures, My own Readings, Ancient Readings, Flowerets, Inventions, Lights, Tapestries, Pandects, Helicon, Problems, Manuals, Small Arms, Memorials, Practical Hints, Leisure Amusements, The Parterre, The Orchard, Commonplaces, Miscellanies.* "For my own part," he says, " and suitable to my own capacity, without care or study, and as some may think rudely enough, I have called my book *Attic Nights* from the place where it was written and from the circumstance of its being in the winter ; thus yielding the palm to others in the dignity of my title, as the work itself is obviously inferior with respect to the labour and embellishment of style." It will be seen that of the titles cited by

Aulus Gellius some are still in common use, whilst others may fairly be regarded as obsolete. No divine of the present day is likely to call his lucubrations *The Coverlet* or *Patchwork*, although the *Stromata* of Clemens Alexandrinus may have a place of honour on his bookshelf. Ben Jonson not only called his short detached essays *Underwoods*—a name revived by Mr. R. L. Stevenson—but gave the not very inviting name of *Timber* to his observations on men and manners.

The classical *Meadow* is modesty itself when contrasted with *Meadows of Gold and Mines of Gems*, the title given to El-Mas'udi's historical encyclopædia. The Oriental taste in this matter is somewhat extravagant, and often the last thing to be gathered from a title is the nature of the book to which it is applied. The Arabic dictionary of Medjd-ed-din Mohammud ben Yakub el Feroozabady is called *The Ocean*, whilst that of Butrus al Bustâny is known as *The Ocean of the Ocean*. If this title is appropriate, then still more so is that of the abridgment of it, which is called *A Drop from the Ocean*. The *Fables* of Bidpai or Pilpay are ethical essays cast in the form of anecdotes and apologues. Some of them are found in *The Five Books* (Pantschatantra). The Arabic version is called *The Book of Kalilah and Dimna* (the names of two jackals); one Persian translation is known as the *Lights of Canopus*, another as *The Touchstone of Knowledge;* a Latin imitation is styled *The Other Æsop*, whilst the Latin translation by John of Capua is *The Directory of Human Life*. An Italian version is called *The Government of Kingdoms;* the Turkish version is entitled *The Imperial Book*, which in Spanish becomes *The Political and Moral Mirror for Princes, Statesmen, and all Class of Men*. Another Spanish version is *Examples against the Deceits and Dangers of the World*, and from this Firenzuola is thought to have derived the substance of his *Discourses of Animals*. Doni translated the Latin version into Italian as *Moral Philosophy*. Here are at least a dozen different titles for what is substantially the same book, and it cannot be said that any of them are very appropriate. Those who frequent the shady nooks of libraries will readily remember scores of such instances. A well-known case is that of Caxton's *Game and Play of the Chess*, which has very little to do with that amusement, and is in reality an anecdotal treatise on ethics. Guido Colonna wrote *De Regimine Principum*, which was translated into French as *Miroir Exemplaire*. It was adapted to the names of the chessmen by Cessoles, whose *Liber de moribus hominum et officiis nobilium super ludo scacorum* has been translated into most of the European languages. Here an inappropriate title made the fortune of the book.

In England we have had a long series of essayists, from Bacon downwards. Owen Feltham called his essays *Resolves*, and ends each with a formal resolution. Arthur Warwick styled his *Spare Minutes ;* Francis Quarles revived the classical *Enchiridion*. Dr. John Brown was not the first to call his book *Horae Subsecivae*. Few authors are so frank as Southey, whose *Omniana* has for its second title *Horae Otiosiores*, which, in the English form of *Hours of Idleness*, was selected by Byron for his early verses. Perhaps the most whimsical book of miscellanies ever written is that to which Southey gave the name of *The Doctor*. The framework into which he has fitted the gleanings of his prodigious reading is even more artificial than that employed by Athenæus, whose immense store of information as to classical dietetics, manners, and literature is thrown into the unreal form of a conversation at a *Banquet of the Learned*. A claim might have been made upon the *Anatomy of Melancholy*, as a book of essays compacted together by an artificial method. Amongst the periodical essayists there are few with titles that are really appropriate, although use has blunted our perception of the fact. *Tatler, Spectator, Rambler, Lover, Babbler, Looker-On*, and *Peeper*, are not names indicative of a polite philosopher making observations on literature and manners. Nearer to our own time authors have not been more successful. Knox's *Winter Evenings*, Drake's *Noontide Leisure*, Lowell's *My Study Windows*, are evidences of the difficulty. Mr. J. A. Froude's *Short Studies on Great Subjects* are open to the double objection that they are not all short, and they are not all on great topics. William Hazlitt calls one of his volumes *Winterslow*, from the name of the village where it was written, whilst *The Plain Speaker* and *The Round Table* are the titles given to other collections of his miscellaneous papers. "Cuthbert Bede" is not likely to have any invasion of his *Rook's Garden.* A provincial volume appeared some years ago, entitled *Spice Islands passed in the Sea of Reading.* A book popular with our grandfathers was *The Lounger's Commonplace Book.* It is rarely that an entirely original or completely appropriate title can be found, and the reader may think that these *Stray Chapters* have been suggested by the *Stray Leaves* of Dr. John Scoffem. Such is not the case, however, in spite of the resemblance.

It may, of course, be urged that the easiest way of escaping the difficulty above-mentioned is that of forbearing to add another to the many volumes of miscellaneous literature already in existence. To this the reply is that the writer, having always had a strong taste for that section of libraries, old and new, thinks it probable that the taste is one shared by many others. Men in this busy age have not always time for elaborate treatises, and yet have a keen interest in even the byways of literature and archæology. Some of the brief papers in this volume will, it is hoped, appeal to their sympathy and favour. I may put in the plea of Aulus Gellius to his readers, "that if they shall find what they long since knew, they would not despise it as trite and very common; for what is there in literature so abstruse but that many men knew it?"

With respect to three of the papers, I have, since they were in type, received the following letter from the Rt. Hon. W. E. Gladstone:—

Hawarden Castle, Chester, September 21, 1887.

Sir,—I have to thank you for these most interesting papers. As regards the longest of them—that on the population of the year A.D 2000—it happened very singularly that I had, a fortnight before, sent off an article of my own to be published in an American periodical (*Youths' Companion*) on the same subject. I will endeavour to obtain a copy for you, but your paper is rich and mine poor on the literature of the subject. With respect to the colour-sense, I have not been able to follow up the discussion. My assertion, however, is more limited than you suppose. I have affirmed nothing, except about the Homeric Hellenes. Dr. Benisch, a learned Rabbi, was inclined to some similar affirmation as to the Hebrews at some date. Mr. Darwin was good enough to send me Dr. Krause's Review, but I found he dissented on grounds analogous in principle to those on which Galileo was condemned. I have no title to dogmatise, but I have a very strong impression that poverty of nomenclature cannot explain the matter so far as Homeric Greece is concerned, for this reason, that its nomenclature for sensible objects is so rich. I sent Mr. Darwin a paper on "The Homeric Epithets of Motion," which are so many and so diversified that we cannot, I think, translate them, except (in part) by the aid of paraphrase.

I remain, Sir, with many thanks,

Your very faithful and obedient,

W. E. GLADSTONE.

W. E. A. Axon, Esq.

I have to thank the Company of Stationers for allowing me to reproduce some papers from *Companion to the Almanac,* and the proprietors of other periodicals for permission to include here some of the articles now reprinted.

Higher Broughton, Manchester.

ERRATUM.

On Page 94, for *Textile Manufacturer*, read *Textile Recorder*.

CONTENTS.

"THE MANCHESTER REBELS."

2

BIBLIOGRAPHY.

" *Memoirs of the Rebellion in* 1745 *and* 1746." *By the Chevalier de Johnstone. London,* 1820.

" *March of the Highland Army in* 1745 *and* 1746," *being the Order Book of Captain James Stuart. (Miscellany of the Spalding Club, vol. i.) Aberdeen,* 1841.

"*Journal and Literary Remains of John Byrom." (Chetham Society, vols. xxxii., xxxiv., xl., xliv.)*

Tracts relating to the Rebellion. (In the Manchester Free Library.)

MS. Memorandum Book of one of the Rebel Soldiers. (In Chetham's Library, Manchester.)

" *History of the Rebellion." By James Ray. Manchester,* n.d.

" *History of the Rebellion of* 1745." *By John Home. Edinburgh,* 1802

The " *Manchester Rebels* " *first appeared in* " *The Shadow,*" *Nov.,* 1870.

"THE MANCHESTER REBELS."

"BONNIE PRINCE CHARLIE!" The words of endearment fall almost unconsciously from the lips in thinking of the unfortunate Stuart who made so gallant a struggle for the recovery of the crown of his ancestors. He is one of the heroes of childhood : the nurse dandled the babe on her knee, and rocked it to sleep, crooning quaint Jacobite laments for the "banished rose of snow ;" the youthful imagination is fed with the witchery of that wizard of the north who has cast such a halo of romance around the Young Chevalier. We followed his fortunes with breathless interest ; saw him land at Moidart with his seven companions, determined to overthrow the usurper who sat upon his father's throne ; saw his courage and audacity overcome the prudence of the Scottish chieftains ; watched the victorious progress of his Highland army ; shared the hesitations as to the descent into England ; mourned over the want of courage and want of faith of the southern Jacobites, who were willing enough to feed the false hopes of the Pretender, by hectoring as to what they would do when his standard was set up, but whose pot-house valour, like that of Bob Acres, oozed out at their finger-ends when the hour of trial came. We sympathised with the dejection of the young chevalier as day by day made more apparent the falsity of the promises of support on which he had relied. And when the fatal retreat from Derby was decided upon, and the rebel army retraced with flying steps their victorious march, closely pursued by the troops of the Duke of Cumberland, until the battle of Culloden ended the hopes of the Prince, we shared in the grief and despair of the vanquished party.   One parts with many illusions in life ; and the sober prose of free institutions and equal laws is worth all the poetical sentiment that has given such a false glitter to the later career of that Stuart race whose history, in England at least, is one of unbroken conspiracy against laws and liberties.   Of all our monarchs, George II., with his meanness, vindictive cruelty, illiterateness, and sordid sensuality, was, perhaps, the most detestable; and yet, had he been dethroned, and the Stuart King " enjoyed his own again," the tide of civilisation would have rolled back a century, and the freedom bought with such lavish expenditure of blood, the liberties for which Russell and Sydney died, would have been lost, and Britain again have sunk to the disgraceful position of a pensioned minion of France.

The check suffered by the prompt suppression of the Rebellion of 1715 had done very little to alter the relative state of parties.   The sanguinary vengeance which was wreaked on those who had taken part in that unfortunate rising had disgusted many otherwise well-disposed persons, whilst amongst the disaffected, instead of striking terror, it had given rise to a passionate desire for revenge.   The political atmosphere was in a vitiated state.   Many were " holding with the hare and running with the hounds," anxious to see James III. King of England, but determined not to break with the Elector of Hanover until his case was hopeless.   Many public men belonged to the congregation of the Vicar of Bray. There was, however, no great chance of the French King aiding the Jacobites. Louis was probably more anxious to have the means of annoying the English King than really desirous of restoring the Stuarts. Tired of waiting for the long-promised army of France, the Young Chevalier at last determined to appeal to the loyalty and military ardour of the Scotch Highlanders. He had also received the most liberal promises of assistance from his English adherents.

The Lancashire gentry were known to be in many cases disaffected. In Manchester he had the sympathies of the clergy, and of the non-juring sect who were disciples of Dr. Deacon. John Byrom, whose wit and piety made him a man of influence, was also a Jacobite. These, with Francis Townley, a Roman Catholic gentleman who had served with distinction in the French army, were leaders of the local Jacobites. Townley was a man of the world, of the free-speaking type so common in the last century. He was " full of strange oaths," and his profanity was a great source of distress to his fellow-conspirator, Dr. Byrom, in the friendly symposia which they held in the little inn at Jackson's Boat. Swearing is not now the fashionable vice it once was, but yet the doctor's polished reproof is not without value :—

> O, that the muse might call, without offence,
> The gallant soldier back to his good sense ;
> His temp'ral field so cautious not to lose,
> So careless quite of his eternal foes.
> Soldier ! so tender of thy Prince's fame,
> Why so profuse of a superior name ?
> For the King's sake, the brunt of battles bear,
> But, for the King of kings' sake, *do not swear.*

There they drank the health of the king over the water, and entered into a correspondence with the exiled family ; there is even a tradition that Prince Charles came in disguise to Manchester in the summer of 1744 to confer with them, but the legend will scarcely bear examination. The Stuarts, it has been said, never learnt anything by adversity. The disasters of 1715 might have taught Prince Charles how little he could depend upon these promises. Of all the great men who, whilst attending the levées of George II. and eagerly snatching at such patronage as they could secure, had pledged themselves to restore the exiled family, not one ventured to join the standard .of the Stuarts, not even when it had streamed triumphantly across the land until it was within a hundred miles of London town. Sad, indeed, for the Prince must have been even that victorious progress, for in all those English shires through which he passed, and where the affection for his family was reputed strongest, scarcely a single man of consideration had joined him. Of all the northern towns where aid might reasonably have been expected, the only one where the Jacobites did anything to redeem their pledges was Manchester. Leaving the main record of the rebellion for other hands, let us now occupy ourselves with the part played in it by the inhabitants of Manchester.

By the 26th of November, 1745, news reached the town that the rebels, who had mystified Marshal Wade, after beating Sir John Cope, were on the road for Manchester. The wildest stories were current about the wild Highlandmen. They were said to be cannibals, with a *penchant* for plump little children ; their hands were like the claws of a beast of prey; they would murder and ravish all who came within their clutches. They were thirty thousand strong, and would soon have all England under their feet. The Whigs were in fear and trembling, and removed out of harm's way all their goods and chattels. Very few persons of wealth and position remained in the place. Walley, the constable, summoned meetings of the inhabitants at the Angel, the Bull's Head, and the Old Coffee-house, to deliberate on what was to be done. They seem to have decided upon a plan of masterly inactivity, acted on the let-alone principle, and trusted to that chapter of accidents which has wisely been called the bible of fools. The bellman was sent round to forbid the removal of bedding from the town; militia were called out, and supplied with brand new cockades, no doubt calculated to strike terror into the hearts of the rebels. Why these valiant soldiers were disbanded on the 27th is not so clear. One does not like to cast any reflections upon their prowess, but the same curious incident occurred at Carlisle, where the fire-eaters were sent back just too soon for them to give battle to and annihilate the rebel force. The next day, about three o'clock in the afternoon, two soldiers in Highland costume rode into the town. One of these was Sergeant Dickson, who had been in the English army, and was as brave as a lion, and much more rash. Behind him, on the same horse, rode his lady-love, with a drum upon her knee. As soon as they dismounted, with beat of drum they invited all loyal gentlemen to enlist in the service of Prince Charles. Thousands of spectators watched this curious triumphal entry, the plaid costume and the sergeant's target attracting great attention. Dickson was under the immediate command of the Chevalier de Johnstone, and had, in disobedience to orders, determined to have a day

in advance of the other recruiting sergeants, making no doubt
that in Manchester, notoriously disaffected, he should be able
to find friends. When the loyal portion of the inhabitants
learned that these adventurous three were all alone, and did
not expect the Prince and his army until the evening, they
surrounded them in a riotous manner, and determined to
make them prisoners, dead or alive. Dickson's blunderbuss
kept them at bay until the Jacobites, who heard of the
affair, flew to arms and rescued him from the tender mercies
of the Whigs. He was soon at the head of a band of five or
six hundred sympathising friends, 180 of whom he induced
to enlist in the service of the king over the water. The Duke
of Perth is said to have observed of these men, " that if the
devil had come a-recruiting and proffered a shilling more than
his Prince, they would have preferred the former." If the
remark was ever made, it was unjustifiable, for Dickson's
expenses for the day did not exceed three guineas ; and
amongst those who this day joined were Bradshaw, Tom
Syddall (whose devotion to the Stuarts was inherited from his
father, executed for his share in the previous rebellion),
Thomas Deacon (the son of the non-juring bishop),
George Fletcher, and Thomas Chaddock, all of whom
proved faithful unto death. That same evening Lord
Pitsligo's company of horse marched into the quiet town,
the streets of which were all deserted, the silver moon-
beams showing only here and there a straggling Jacobite, such
as Dr. Byrom, his fair daughter, and others who were anxious
to "behave civilly " and yet " keep themselves out of any
scrape." On the 29th, parties of the rebels kept dropping
into the town until three o'clock, when the main body, with
the Prince, marched in, amidst the hurrahs of the mob and

the joyous ringing of the bells. The handsome face and
noble bearing of the Young Chevalier, as he marched along
in his picturesque Scottish costume, surrounded by a body of
the faithful clansmen, would gain him many a good wish
from the "Lancashire witches" who beheld him ; and the white
rose of the Stuarts, which he wore conspicuously upon his
blue bonnet, would be the favourite flower that day in Manchester.   Little did they think how soon those leaves of snow
were to be drowned in torrents of blood.   As he marched
along the streets of Salford, the Rev. John Clayton, the
chaplain of Collegiate Church, a staunch old Jacobite, fell
down upon his knees, and implored the blessing of heaven
upon the Prince.   His quarters were fixed at the house of
Mr. John Dickenson, in Market Street Lane, long afterwards
known as "The Palace." The house has now been "improved"
out of existence, but its situation is indicated by the name of
Palace Street.   The Jacobite sympathisers were now in high
glee, and the Presbyterians and Whigs correspondingly depressed.   Miss "Beppy" Byrom, and other fair rebels, we
find sitting up till two o'clock in the morning, making St.
Andrew's crosses for the Prince's army; and as the 30th was
St. Andrew's Day, the manufacture was resumed with great
spirit until twelve o'clock at noon, although the day was
Sunday.   The following extract from her diary will show the
enthusiasm which the "yellow-haired laddie" inspired : "Then
I dressed me up in my white gown and went up to my aunt
Brearcliffe's, and an officer called on us to see the Prince ; we
went to Mr. Fletcher's and saw him get a-horseback, and a
noble sight it is, I would not have missed it for a great deal of
money; his horse had stood an hour in the court without
stirring, and as soon as he got on he began a dancing and ·

capering as if he was proud of the burden, and when he
rid out of the court he was received with as much joy and
shouting almost as if he had been King without any dispute ;
indeed I think scarce anybody that saw him could dispute it."

The number of recruits now amounted to about 300, and
Francis Townley, Esq., was appointed colonel of the band,
which was called the " Manchester Regiment." The clergymen
at the Cathedral discreetly prayed for the King and the
Prince of Wales, and "named no names." Cappock, a
young clergyman who had been educated at the Grammar
School, and on joining the rebels had been appointed chaplain of the Manchester Regiment, is said to have preached
before the Prince from the words, " The Lord is King, the
earth may be glad thereof" (Psalm xcvii. 1). After service
the regiment was drawn up in the churchyard, for the inspec-
tion of the Young Pretender. The officers had on plaid
waistcoats, white cockades, a sword by the side, and a couple
of pistols thrust in the girdle. Their flag was flying, with
" Liberty and Property " inscribed on one side of it, and on
the other, " Church and Country." The Prince supped that
evening with Mr. Fletcher ; and Byrom and Deacon were
brought as prisoners to see the Prince—a transparent artifice
which their colleagues, Clayton and Cattell, had the courage
to dispense with. Charming " Beppy " Byrom, in her white
robe, decorated with a St. Andrew's cross, was also one of
the party, and seems to have been somewhat surprised at the
civility of the rebel officers, who almost made them
" fuddled " (to quote the fair one's phrase) in drinking the
health of the Prince, whose leisure they were waiting. At
length came Secretary Murray with word that the Prince was
ready to receive them ; and the party were ushered into the

presence of the Prince for whom they had longed for years. With these men devotion to the Stuarts was not so much a political principle as an article of their religion; and the prospect of success which lay before the Stuart army must have added an exultant feeling to the respectful homage with which they kissed the hand of him who was, to them, the representative of the Lord's anointed.

The troops were already leaving the town. The main body, with the Prince at their head, left Manchester about six o'clock in the morning of the 1st December. With flags flying and music playing, the Highland army quitted Manchester. The hussars led the way, followed by the Prince, surrounded by his life guard; then Appin, Lochiel, . Cluny, with the royal standard, and the rest of the clans, the rear being Pitsligo's company. The Prince had issued this brief proclamation :—

Manchester, November 30th, 1745.

His Royal Highness being informed that several bridges had been pulled down in this county, he has given orders to repair them forthwith, particularly that at Crossford, which is to be done this night by his own troops, though His Royal Highness does not propose to make use of it for his own army, but believes it will be of service to the country; and if any forces that were with General Wade be coming this road, they may have the benefit of it.

C. P. R.

This sneer at their enemies seems to have been considered a good joke, for we find in the order book of Captain James Stuart this same command respecting Crossford Bridge, with the remark that it is done for the benefit of the country, and that Marshal Wade's army may pass with greater diligence. The main body of the rebels marched along the highway to Stockport. The utmost terror and alarm preceded them;

valuables were hid and buried in the ground, and many
showed great alacrity in evading the route of the terrible
Highlanders, who, on their part, were under strict discipline,
and appear to have been guilty of very little of that plunder
and outrage which sometimes accompany the march of a
victorious army. Horses were seized for the use of the army;
but on Peter Fernhead, of Old Platt Hall, remonstrating
with the Prince—whom he followed to Macclesfield for that
special purpose—on the seizure of two horses belonging to
him, the Young Chevalier, whose complaisance to the
English was not relished by his followers, bade them "Give
the man his baists agane." Some of the rebels are said to
have halted at Grindlow Marsh, which, says an apocryphal
tradition, the officer in command observed was a long sight
or view to Manchester, and hence "Longsight," the modern
name of this place! Charles, at the head of one of the
divisions, forded the Mersey near Stockport, and, though
he was a tall man, the water was up to his waist. On
the farther bank were some few of the Cheshire gentry
to wish him God speed; and with them we are told was
a white-haired lady, who had witnessed as a child the
restoration of Charles II. She came of a gallant Cavalier
family, who, having spared nothing in the service of the
thankless Stuarts, had been rewarded with neglect and
injustice. Every year this loyal Jacobite had sent half
her yearly income to the court of St. Germains, and
now she had sold everything of value she had, and
brought the proceeds as an offering to her Prince to
"aid the good cause." And when her eyes—grown dim
with looking for the happy day—beheld the handsome
form of her unknown idol,—when she kissed his royal

hand, and beheld him at the head of his gallant army, with every prospect of restoring the fallen grandeur of his house, she felt rewarded for all the years of struggle and prayer through which she had passed, and cried with pious favour, "Lord, now lettest thou thy servant depart in peace." And when the news came of the fatal retreat from Derby, and she saw all her fond hopes blasted, the blow was too strong, and broke her faithful heart.   She was a type of her party.   The retreat was the deathblow of the Stuarts.   Had the bold counsels of Prince Charles prevailed, and the army marched on London with all speed possible, there is at least a possibility that they would have been successful.   The English Jacobites in the southern counties were it was said prepared for 'rising; Sir Watkin Wynne was ready to bring his fiery Welshmen to the standard of the Stuarts; the Whigs were thoroughly disheartened; even Newcastle, the Premier, is said to have been wavering in his allegiance; the royal yachts, loaded with valuables, were at the Tower, ready to sail at a moment's notice. It was one of those supreme crises when everything depends upon a single step.   The Highlanders were ardently desirous of giving battle to the Duke of Cumberland; they were confident of success; one decisive blow, and the kingdom was theirs. The Prince also saw that the hour was come,—that to advance meant possibly to succeed, whilst to retreat meant to perish.   His appeals at the council of war were unavailing, his arguments disregarded, and he was compelled to accede to the determination of the Scottish chiefs to fall back upon the Highlands.   From this moment he changed; rage and despair took possession of him.   He marched dejectedly and moodily—no longer at the head of his troops, but ever dila-

tory and in the rear. The rank and file of the Highlanders
were highly incensed at the decision of their chiefs, and it was
with very different feelings that they re-entered Manchester on
the 9th of December. The Hanoverians had rallied; indeed,
the day before the great fire-bell was rung, and at the bellman's summons a large number of persons had assembled
to spoil the roads and resist the further progress of the
Prince. The magistrates, seemingly afraid of the spirit they
had raised, again sent round the bellman to declare that,
" Whereas a tumultuous mob has been raised, &c., this is
to desire that all the country folks will go to their own
houses, and that everybody will lay down their arms and
be quiet." One of the English volunteers was murdered in
the neighbourhood; but when the assassins—a woman and
her son—were brought to the Prince, he, with a clemency
highly distasteful to his followers, pardoned them. Syddall,
who dashed into the town alone on Sunday evening, was near
being apprehended, and the first batch of Highlanders were
greeted with a shower of mud as they passed (ominous
name!) Hanging Ditch, and the attack only ceased when they
threatened to fire on the mob. The Prince resented this conduct, and by seven in the evening the constables summoned the
principal men of the town to meet at the Old Coffee-house,
and there showed a warrant from him, commanding the sum
of five thousand pounds to be raised by four o'clock the day
following, on pain of military execution. As the town had
voluntarily raised three thousand pounds for the rebels during
their previous stay, it was thought impossible to raise this sum;
nevertheless, the magistrates, accompanied by their townsmen
the officers of the Manchester Regiment, went round soliciting
the patriotic liberality of the inhabitants. The next day a

number of persons waited on the Prince, and he was induced to lower his demands to £2,500 ; but Mr. James Bayley, a noted Whig, was seized as security. He represented, and successfully, that he was over seventy years old, and incapable of travel, and so was allowed to depart, on giving his word that the required sum should be raised. He immediately repaired to his friends at the Old Coffee-house, and the amount was raised on the promissory notes of himself and Mr. John Dickenson, at whose house the Prince was staying; and so, to be exact, the black-mail of £2,504 13s. was paid to the rebels about two o'clock in the afternoon. As they marched through Salford, some wretch fired at the last man from a garret window, which so greatly enraged the men that they turned round again, and swore to fire the town, but were ultimately pacified. Five guineas reward was offered for his apprehension, and the constable of Salford and his deputy were taken into custody until the culprit should be produced— certainly an odd method of securing the culprit's capture.

The greatest precautions were observed in Manchester. A detachment of Appin's men mounted guard at the Town-house ; a detachment of Cluny's regiment were stationed at Scotland Bridge, in Long Millgate; another of Glenbucket's on Salford Bridge; whilst the Artillery Park, at Campfield, was jointly guarded by Glengarry and Perth's men. The prisoners were under care of the Town-house guard, with strict injunctions against allowing any of them to escape. All vigilance was enjoined, and every half-hour the guard patrolled at their post, and every quarter of an hour the sentries cried to each other that all went well. Some of Cluny's regiment were about a mile from town, on the Rochdale Road, on which the life guards were to patrol. This duty was performed by some of Kilmarnock's men on Stockport Road, whilst the town was kept in order by a detachment of Lord Pitsligo's horse. The first intention of the Young Chevalier had been to halt a day longer in Manchester, but Lord George Murray advised him to proceed at once, and the hurried retreat was resumed. William of Cumberland, who was hurrying after them, did not come up with their rearguard until they were at Clifton Moor, and then his forces received a check which prevented them from further annoyance of the retreating army, which entered Carlisle early on the morning of the 19th December. Lord George Murray advised that the town should be evacuated, the castle blown up, and the stores that could not be carried off all thrown into the river. Their own quick conquest of Carlisle was sufficient to show it could not stand a siege. In an evil hour it was determined to leave a garrison, who might hold it as the prey for a future and speedy descent upon England. It was but a gloomy prospect; yet Colonel Townley volunteered for the desperate post, and the defence of the city was entrusted to him, the Manchester Regiment, now reduced to about 120 men, being strengthened by a small party of Highlanders, four French officers, and a handful of privates of the same nation. The entire garrison would scarcely number more than 400 men. They were all drawn up to receive the parting address from the Prince, who thanked them for their past exertions, and promised to return to their relief before the enemy could reduce the town. The Highlanders had hardly departed before the duke reached Carlisle, which he immediately invested on all sides, styling it " an old hencoop, which he would speedily bring about their ears, when he should have got artillery." The beseiged had probably counted on the absence of artillery in the English army, but on the 27th six 18-pounders were brought from Whitehaven and placed in the batteries, whose erection the ineffectual fire of the rebels had not been able to prevent. All day on the 28th shot and shell were rained down upon the rebel garrison, battering down the earthworks which sheltered their chief defence, so that not a man could stand in the four-gun battery. In the night time they repaired this breach, and on the 29th recommenced their fire upon the English troops, whose ammunition was failing ; but about two o'clock a fresh, supply of ball having arrived, the bombardment was renewed with increased vigour. Meanwhile the situation of the rebels was becoming desperate ; they were short of provisions, hemmed in by the enemy, and the castle wall was already tottering. Hamilton, the governor of the castle, was for capitulating ; but Townley, more resolute, flew into a rage, and swore " It was better to die by the sword than fall into the hands of those damned Hanoverians." Hamilton, however, sent a messenger to the duke, offering to surrender the town if the besieged were allowed the honours of war. The reply to this was the pinioning of the envoy, who was committed to close custody. On Sunday evening more cannon arrived from Whitehaven, and a battery for their reception was completed in the night. When the garrison, at daybreak, beheld this new and formidable addition to the attacking powers, they felt that further opposition was useless, hung out the white flag, and intimated that they were ready to exchange hostages. The duke sent Colonel Conway and Lord Bury to inform them that he would make no exchanges with rebels, and with a further message to the French officers—who had complained previously of the employment of Dutch troops as an infraction of the treaty of Tournay—informing them "that there are no Dutch troops here, but enough of the King's to chastise the rebels and those who dare to give them any assistance." At the moment this veracious message was sent, a thousand Dutch troopers were at Stanwix Bank, from which position they had shelled the town! Hamilton now sent a messenger to ask what terms the duke would grant the garrison. Colonel Conway conveyed a written message that "all the terms his Royal Highness will or can grant to the rebel garrison of Carlisle are, that they shall not be put to the sword, but be reserved for the King's pleasure." The fate of their predecessors in the rising of 1715 might have taught them how hopeless was any expectation of mercy from the royal house of Brunswick. Townley's blunt expression was prophetically true—better for them to have died sword in hand than to linger long in doubt and suspense, and finish with a traitor's block at last. They agreed to the terms, recommending themselves to "his Royal Highness's clemency." Unfortunately, he never had any. Cumberland speedily returned to London; General Hewley was sent to pursue the Highlanders, and General Sir Charles Howard, on the 10th of January, 1746, assumed the command of Carlisle, where a large garrison was left. The rebels, who had been confined in the cathedral, of all places in the world, and had been very harshly treated, were now marched, with all circumstances of indignity, to York, Lancaster, and other places, to await their trials. On July 15, 1746, Colonel Townley was tried at Southwark by a special commission; George Fletcher, Thomas Chaddock, William Brettargh, on the 16th; Thomas Deacon, James Dawson, and John Berwick on the 17th; David Morgan on

the 18th. These men were all officers of the Manchester
Regiment, and there was no lack of evidence to establish the
fact that they had waged war against King George II. Their
several defences were necessarily of the weakest nature.
Townley urged that his commission as an officer of the
French army entitled him to be exchanged as a prisoner of
war. The doctrine of allegiance was too strong for this plea;
he was confessing an act of rebellion in addition to that with
which he was charged. Dawson, in his defence, said, "I had
a promise of mercy from His Royal Highness the Duke of
Cumberland upon the capitulation of Carlisle, and I hope
the court will consider my case." From the uniform testimony of the rebels, there would seem to have been some
promise of mercy given at the surrender of Carlisle, leading
them to expect a different treatment to that which they actually
experienced. Their view of the case is not borne out by
existing documents; but there is no strong reason for
supposing the duke incapable of giving and breaking such
a pledge. They were all found guilty and condemned
to undergo the full penalties of the law. They prepared for
death with courage and composure. On the 29th of July
came the death warrant; they were to die the day after. The
next morning, 30th July, 1746, they were roused about six o'clock,
"and unloosed from the floor, to which they had been chained
down ever since sentence of death was passed upon them."
After breakfast, their irons were struck off and their arms
pinioned. Outside were waiting the sledges, surrounded by
foot soldiers. In the first sledge rode Townley, Blood,
Berwick, and the executioner, with a shining scimitar in his
hand; Morgan, Syddall, and Deacon were in the second;
Dawson, Fletcher, and Chaddock in the third. So the

sorrowful procession marched to Kennington Common, where block, and gallows, and faggot-pile were awaiting them. No clergyman attended them, but Morgan read prayers from a book, and they all joined reverently in the devotions, which continued about half an hour. Then they threw printed papers to the populace, containing professions of loyalty to the exiled Stuarts, and diatribes against the usurpation of the Elector of Hanover. The white caps were drawn over their faces; another moment and nine bodies swung in mid-air. Then commenced the horrid butchery of a political execution. When they had hung three minutes, they were stripped of their clothing by the soldiers and the hangman. Townley's body, warm and palpitating, was then cut down and placed upon the block. The hangman, more tender than the law, whose officer he was, struck several heavy blows on the chest for life was not extinct. Finding his humane intention unsuccessful, he drew his sword across the victim's throat before he proceeded with his task. The heart, with hot blood streaming from it, was torn from Townley's breast and cast into the flames; the body was cut into four quarters, " to be at the King's disposal;" and the ghastly head was held up to the savage crowd as that of a traitor. Nine times did the hangman go through this cruel performance. Nine true men, whose crimes were such as " leaned to virtue's side," were done to death in this manner in the eighteenth century of Christian charity and forgiveness, and in free and happy England, by the orders of the most merciful of monarchs, George II., by the grace of God, King of England, Defender of the Faith. Did the court chaplains that day, as they drawled out the Lord's Prayer, emphasise that sublimest request that erring mortals can offer up to heaven, " Forgive us our trespasses, as we forgive them that trespass against us?" And he for whom they had risked life and limb—did Bonnie Prince Charlie, in his cruel wanderings as a fugitive, with a price upon his head, think of them that day?—of the grim tragedy that was being enacted amid the falling rain, beneath the leaden sky of London, in presence of a larger number of people than had ever gathered there "within the memory of man?" The courage of the victims, their youth and reverent bearing, tamed even the stony heart of the mob. When the hangman had finished his bloody work, and cast into the fire the heart of handsome Jemmy Dawson, he cried aloud, "God bless King George," and the great multitude gave an answering shout. Dawson was tenderly loved by a young lady, who determined to see the last of her darling upon earth. Accompanied by a male relation and a female friend, she followed the sledges in a hackney coach, and watched with blanched cheeks all the horrible details. When she saw her lover's lifeless form dismembered; the head that had rested on her bosom held up for scorn and execration; the faithful heart cast into the devouring flames, already glutted with blood, her own true heart broke beneath its heavy burden of sorrow, and with the words, "My dear, I follow thee! I follow thee! Sweet Jesus, receive both our souls together," she fell dead upon the neck of her friend.

COLOUR - NAMES AMONGST
ENGLISH GIPSIES.

BIBLIOGRAPHY.

" *Homeric Studies.*" *By W. E. Gladstone.* 1858.

" *Die Entwickelung des Farbensinnes.*" *Von Hugo Magnus.* 1858.

" *De geschichtlicke Entwickelung des Farbensinnes.*" *Von Hugo Magnus.* 1877.

" *The Colour Sense,*" *by W. E. Gladstone* ("*Nineteenth Century*" *for October,* 1877).

" *Colour Sense.*" *By Grant Allen.* 1879.

"*Contributions to History of Development of Human Race.*" *By L. Geiger.* 1880. (*First published in German, in* 1867.)

" *The Development of the Colour Sense.*" *By Dr. M. Lubbock* (*British Association Report, p.* 715).

" *Remarks on the Terms used to Denote Colour.*" *By Dr. Edward Schunck* ("*Memoirs of Manchester Literary and Philosophical Society,*" *Third Series, vol. viii.*).

" *The Colour Sense in the Edda.*" *By Arthur Lawrenson* ("*Transactions of the Royal Society of Literature,*" *vol. xii.*). 1881.

"*Colour Blindness and the Development of the Colour Sense.*" *By Paul von Seydowitz* ("*New Orleans Medical and Surgical Journal,*" *for August*).

" *The Colour Sense and Colour-Names.*" *By William E. A. Axon* ("*Proceedings of Manchester Literary and Philosophical Society,*" *vol. xxi.*). 1882.

" *The Dialect of the English Gipsies.*" *By H. T. Crofton and B. C. Smart.* 1875.

This paper was read at the Manchester meeting of the British Association, 1887.

COLOUR-NAMES AMONGST THE ENGLISH GIPSIES.

THE discussion which has been in progress for about thirty years as to the development of the colour-sense has attracted widespread interest. In 1858 Mr. Gladstone, in his " Homeric Studies," noticed the fewness and the inexactness of the colour-names used in the Iliad, and suggested as an explanation that the colour-perception had been then only partially developed amongst the Greeks. The theory was taken up by the late Professor Lazarus Geiger, who tells us that blue is not used as an epithet of the sky in the Rig-Veda, the Zend-Avesta, the Old Testament, the Homeric poems, nor in the Koran, and that Alkindi, writing in the ninth century, is the first to speak of the azure of the sky. Geiger also says that green is not named in the Rig-Veda; that Aristotle speaks of the rainbow as red, yellow, and green; that Xenophanes regarded it as purple, reddish, and yellow; and that Democritus regarded black, white, red, and yellow as the fundamental colours, and that these, with the addition of green, are now so regarded in China. The theory was further endorsed and developed by Professor Hugo Magnus. Mr. Gladstone returned to the subject in 1877, and then held that archaic man had a positive perception only of light and darkness, and that in Homer's time he had advanced to the imperfect discrimination of red or yellow, but no further; green of grass and foliage, or the blue of the sky, being never once referred to. The theory depends upon philological evidence, and it is argued that as the Rig-Veda, the Zend-Avesta, the Old Testament, and the Homeric poems contain no reference to the sky as blue, the peoples to whom these books belonged were incapable of discriminating the finer shades of colour. The weak part of such an argument is that it may possibly confuse mere poverty of nomenclature with defective perception. This in effect is the reply of Seydowitz and others who are not able to accept the theory propounded by Geiger. In the Kaffir language, although there are more than twenty-six distinct names for the colouring and coat of cattle, one term is used for both blue and green, although the people who use it are perfectly well able to tell the one from the other. If we take the savages of the present day, we see no reason to suppose that their appreciation of colour is inferior to that of civilised races. Mr. Grant Allen has made extensive inquiries on this point, and his researches lead him to the supposition "that the colour-sense is, as a whole, absolutely identical throughout all branches of the human race."

The reason why colour plays so subordinate a part in the older literature of various nations is chiefly the direct and simple manner in which the story is related. The ideas are concrete. The need of picturesque details does not occur to the writer or the singer. He is speaking often of familiar things, and feels no necessity to describe them. If he does enter upon description, the shining and glittering of spears and bucklers are more likely to arrest his attention than their precise colour. Mr. A. R. Wallace says that in the long epochs during which the colour-sense was being developed the visual organs would be mainly subjected to two groups of rays—the green from the vegetation, and the blue from the sky. This makes it all the more remarkable that blue should be so largely absent from early colour vocabularies. But much confusion has' resulted from the poverty of the colour vocabulary.   In quite recent literature we find the same objects described by the terms "blue" and "green."

Dr. Montague Lubbock has shown that even in the Stone Age there was a perception of colour.

The speculations of Geiger are by no means universally accepted, and less so now than when they were first broached. Dr. Krause, an earnest follower of Darwin, opposes them. The matter has also been investigated by Dr. Paul von Seydowitz, of New Orleans, who also rejects the theory that he ancients were colour-blind.   Mr. Grant Allen, whilst holding that the colour-sense has been developed from the partiality of man's frugivorous ancestors for bright-coloured fruit, is also a decided opponent of the idea that this has been done within the historic period.

The very basis of Geiger's theory is the exact conformity of colour-sense and colour-terminology.   This theory may be tested by the facts as to the colour-names used by the English gipsies.   Taking the learned monograph in *The Dialect of the English Gipsies*, by Mr. B. C. Smart and Mr. H. T. Crofton, it is an easy matter to collect the words forming the scanty colour vocabulary of the British Romanies. For Gray they use the word bal, balaw ; *hair, hairs*.   Thus the tribe-name of the Greys is the plural Balaws, and the same word is used for the Hernes, whose name is apparently connected with hair.   The tribe of the Herrings are similarly styled Balaw—matcho, *hair-fish*, apparently a punning translation of their English name.   Gray, it may be remarked, when used in the Bible, is used in the sense of hoary, and applied to hair.

To express Green the gipsies say Chor-diking, *grass-looking*. Sometimes they use greeno instead. Leland mentions also selno. The word for Black is Kaúlo. The word is applied also to common-heath, from the waste lands of the Black Country and of Birmingham. The Turkey is called Kauli-rauni, *black lady*. The word for Red is lálo or lólo. Cherries are lálo-koóvaw, *red things*. The Salmon is lolo-matcho, *red-fish*. Luller is to *blush*. The word for White is pórno, which is also used for *flour*. A Swan is pórni-rauni, *white-lady*. Porno-saster is tin, *white-iron*. When the words for sky, morning, &c., are examined, they are found not to have relation to colour. The Sky is dúvel, *God;* or miduvelesto-tem, *God's country;* or poodj, a *bridge*. Morning is saúla, the *dawn*. The Moon is miduvelesko-dood, *God's light;* or sikermengro, the *Showman*. Its common name is shoon, probably from the Sanscrit root, Tchadi, *to shine*. The Sun is kam, from the Sanscrit root, gharma, meaning *heat*. It is also called tam, probably a corruption of kam. Tamlo means both light and dark. Amongst the Turkish gipsies tam means *blind*, from the Sanscrit tama, *darkness*. The name of the *Orange*, pobomus, is derived from pobo, *Apple*. The Orange is sometimes called waver-temeski-lolo-pobo, *the-other-country-red-apple*.

The colour vocabulary of the English gipsies is thus limited to *green, black, red,* and *white*. We have, then, the notable fact that *blue*, on which so much stress has been laid in the discussion of the colour-sense, is entirely absent from the English gipsy vocabulary. This is emphasised by the fact that the gipsies sometimes use the word blue-asar, the suffix being that which is generally added in Romany to disguise a borrowed word. So their name for *toadstools* is

blue-leggi, because the *agaricus personata,* which they
regard as a delicacy, has blue stalks.   Clearly, if they had
now in Romany a word for blue they would not appropriate
that of gaújo.   And if any evidence were needed that the
Romanies are not colour-blind, it is afforded by their appropriation of the English word for *blue.*   It only remains to add
that yack and erescare are both given by Pott as gipsy
equivalents for blue.   If these words are genuine—which
may be open to doubt—it is apparently possible for a race
to possess and to lose a colour-name.   This brief investigation
of the English gipsy colour vocabulary will show the danger
of accepting the negative testimony of philology as conclusive.
The positive evidence of linguistics no one need doubt.
It is clear that there is no relation between the colour-
perception and the colour-nomenclature of the English
gipsies.

THE RELATION OF ARCHÆOLOGY TO ART.

The following is an Address, delivered before a meeting of the Manchester Academy of Fine Arts, 8th March, 1881.

THE RELATION OF ARCHÆOLOGY TO ART.

IN Ghirlandajo's famous picture of the "Birth of the Virgin" the painter has represented one of the Florentine beauties of the fifteenth century, who, clad in the rich costume of the period, is stepping forward as though on a visit of congratulation to the Jewish mother. In speaking of this and similar anomalies, Mrs. Jameson has evolved an ingenious but insufficient defence.

The idea of crowding these sacred and mystical subjects with portraits of real persons, and representations of familiar objects, may seem, on first view, shocking to the taste, ridiculous anachronisms, and destructive of all solemnity and unity of feeling. Such, however, is not the case, but the reverse. In the first place, the sacred and ideal personages are never portraits from nature, and are very loftily conceived to belong to all time, and to have no especial locality; and they have so much dignity in their aspects, the costumes are so picturesque, and the grouping is so fine and imaginative, that only the coldest and most pedantic critic could wish them absent.

This is probably as good an excuse as could be made for a practice essentially vicious. The inartistic quality of the dress of men of the nineteenth century will probably be a sufficient safeguard against the introduction of modern costumes into the historical paintings of to-day. The mural decorations in the Manchester Town Hall are not likely to include a procession even of blue-gowned councillors assisting at the "Expulsion of the Danes" from the city. But is it to be seriously supposed that only a "cold and pedantic critic"

4

would object to the figure of a Lancashire witch, her native beauty set off by an undeniably picturesque costume, being introduced as a spectator of the "Building of the Roman Fort of Mancunium?" The fact is that accuracy of detail in costume and accessories and truthfulness of local colour was not felt as an artistic necessity. The old artist could fully appreciate the permanent element in the story he endeavoured to transfer to canvas or to stone. Of the poet and the historian he might have said, "He was not for an age, but for all time." The artist, then, translated the past into the present, and the personages of history and of mythology were so vividly real to him that he thought of them as fellow-citizens of his own good town, whether that town were in Germany or in Italy. No rule is without exception, but from the new birth of pictorial art in Europe to the middle of the last century every school affords proof that historical accuracy was not deemed essential or important. Art was independent of archæology.

Archæology is the science of the past, and aims at reconstructing the life and thoughts of bygone centuries. Archæology is modern, because it is the scientific expression of a sense of historical consciousness that has only fully developed within the last hundred years. The disregard of local and historical accuracy was habitual. When Benozzo Gozzoli was engaged in painting the "Building of the Tower of Babel," he unhesitatingly introduced into the composition portraits of the great Cosmo de Medici and others of his contemporaries, all in the habit of their time; and when he painted the story of Joseph, the long perspective of Italian architecture ends in the Cathedral of Pisa. Late in the fourteenth century we find a mediæval artist giving his idea of the hierarchy of the angels.

The celestial dominations are represented as kings, and the principalities as mailed warriors, the only indication of supernatural character being their outspread wings. Lucas Cranach, in drawing the "Martyrdom of St. Matthew," shows us the towers of a German town in the distance, and a small crowd of Teutonic burghers occupies the foreground. The executioner wears a slashed doublet, and the instrument of death is that which was known as the maiden in Scotland and the Halifax gibbet in England. In Guercino's "Death of Dido" the costume of the queen and her attendants is as far from the classical as possible, and amongst the male spectators is a portrait of the artist in a rich dress of the seventeenth century.

From these ludicrous instances we may see that the most obvious function of archæology in relation to art is that of enabling the artist to give us the very form and pressure of the hour and the man he is celebrating. · Archæology seeks for truth in art, and protests alike against modern accessories ignorantly placed amidst the scenes of ancient days, and against the pedantry of classical tradition preserved amidst the incongruous scenes of modern times. English sculptors in the last century insisted upon representing the warriors and statesmen of England in the garb of ancient Rome. Roubiliac broke this rule, "more honoured in the breach than in the observance;" yet it survived his days, and led to the anachronisms in stone which crowd St. Paul's and Westminster Abbey. Witness the dreadful allegories perpetrated by Thomas Banks to the memory of Burgess and Westcott, two gallant English sailors, who are represented lying in a semi-nude state, whilst a portly and well-draped Victory approaches and crowns them with laurel. The incongruities

of this composition are sufficient to make it ridiculous. The
English sailor is not always particular as to dress, but
surely no one ever dreams of him fighting amidst showers of
shot and shell in a dress composed of a scarf and a pair of
sandals. Yet Banks, the author of this pretentious failure,
achieved a noble success when he trusted to nature. He is
the artist of that pathetic monument in Ashbourne Church to
the memory of the infant daughter of Sir Brooke Boothby.
Who does not remember this image of suffering innocence?
The child lies as though she had just fallen asleep after
feverish tossings to and fro; the anodyne of slumber has not
yet smoothed away all the air of pain, but the little fevered
hands are at rest, and by a transition so gentle as to be
imperceptible Sleep has given place to his brother Death,
who has come, not

> . . . pale as yonder waning moon,
> With lips of lurid blue;

but

> . . . rosy as the morn
> When, throned on ocean's wave,
> It blushes o'er the world.

This sculpture of Banks may remind the historical critic of
a still earlier artist who has immortalised a mother's sorrow.
Amongst the hundreds of monuments with which the venerable
Abbey of Westminster is crowded there are few which touch
the sympathies more deeply than the Cradle Tomb, at the
east end of the north aisle of Henry the Seventh's Chapel.
It is a monument to the memory of an infant child of James
I., and represents a babe asleep in its quaint hooded cradle;
the armorial decorations of the coverlet marking the royal
estate of the unconscious sleeper. At the head of the cradle

is this inscription: Sophia, Rosvla Regia, præpropero fato decerptæ, et Jacobo Magnæ Britanniæ Franciæ et Hiberniæ regi, Annæque Reginæ, parentibus erepta, vt in Christi Rosario Reflorescat, hic sita est. Junii xxiii., Regni, R.I. IIII. MDCVI.

It is the old woe, the cry of Rachel mourning for her children. How many sorrowing hearts have sought for consolation in the thought that the rosebud over whose broken stem they mourn blossoms fairer and brighter in the childgarden of another world. It is a touch of nature which makes the whole world kin.

Banks, in his pseudo-classical absurdities, merely followed the foolish fashion of his time. When Nollekins was engaged upon the bust of Dr. Johnson, he took great liberties with the aspect of the Colossus of literature, whose bald cranium was surmounted by a wig, which offended the artist's conventional rules. He suggested that natural hair should be substituted in the "animated stone," as this would make Johnson more like an ancient philosopher! The Doctor exhausted the subject, so far as argument is concerned, by saying, "A man, sir, should be portrayed as he appears in company." But as reason does not convince the conventional, the artist persisted, and an Irish beggar, with flowing locks, was called in as a model, and soon the world was the richer by a mongrel portrait representing, in unequal proportions, the author of *Rasselas* and an Hibernian mendicant. Bacon's statues of Johnson and Howard are in the same taste, and are said to have led to an amusing mistake on the part of a visitor from another country to St. Paul's Cathedral. They are arrayed in sham classical drapery; the lexicographer grasps a roll— perhaps "copy" for the printers of the dictionary—and the prison reformer holds a key in his hand. The intelligent foreigner saw at a glance from their costume that they were not Englishmen, and naturally concluded that they were those two twin stars of the infant Church, St. Peter and St. Paul!

This classical idea dominated monumental work, whether of canvas or stone. When Benjamin West painted the "Death of Wolfe," he had the good sense to portray the soldiers in the uniform of King George and the Indians in their war paint. The critical world was at once in arms. The King, who had been the constant friend and patron of the artist, refused to buy a picture in which the conventional canons of art were thus set at defiance. The Archbishop of York, a still older patron, to whose help West owed much of his worldly success, begged him to avoid such revolutionary notions. Sir Joshua Reynolds, in a friendly spirit, urged him not to sèt the public taste at defiance. West had a simple and straightforward answer to all this. The Greeks and Romans knew nothing of America, and their costume, however picturesque, was not the dress of the New World. A painter should paint truth, and not fiction. Reynolds was convinced, and prophesied that the picture would occasion a revolution in art.

If the true archæological spirit had done nothing more than relieve art from these chains of ignorance and convention, it would have been a mighty service. There is a wide tract of art in which the archæologist can be of no service to the painter or the sculptor. When, however, the artist leaves the ground of imitative art and essays a nobler flight; when he would place before us those memorable deeds that have transformed the destinies of nations; when he would illumine the present by imagery of the pathos, the heroism, and the endeavour of the past, then he must seek the aid of the archæologist. The most heroic and spiritual Joan of Arc that artist ever drew would be laughed at in the present day if represented as wearing the cap of the vivandière or the head-dress of a British drummer-boy.*

Archæology is the science or knowledge of the past, but

---

* Planché tells two anecdotes which are apropos to this subject :—

Sir David Wilkie did the writer of these lines the honour of consulting him respecting the elaborate picture of "John Knox Preaching the Reformation." He was desirous, he said, of being very correct in the costume he had introduced, and requested a candid opinion upon it, the picture being then finished, and ready for removal to the Royal Academy for the purpose of exhibition. On its being pointed out to him that he had introduced in the gallery of the church military personages wearing the barred helmets of the time of Charles I. in the reign of Mary Stuart, he replied that his reason for so doing was that these persons were to be supposed as having visited the church with a desire to be unknown ; and yet he had actually selected—more in the spirit of an Irishman than of a Scotchman—the open headpiece of the 12th century, through the bars of which the face was distinctly visible, in preference to the helmet of the 16th, the closed visor of which would have defied scrutiny ! The glaring absurdity of this anachronism was, notwithstanding, allowed by the great painter to remain, and to be disseminated by the burin of the engraver, although it might have been remedied in half an hour with as much advantage to the effect of the picture as to its historical accuracy.

This anecdote "reminds us," as an inveterate story-teller would say, of one more creditable to the taste and intelligence of another royal academician, Mr. A. Cooper's " Battle of Bosworth," by permission of the Earl of Durham, the walls of the gallery of modern artists in this exhibition (No. 195). While at work upon it the painter consulted Sir Samuel Meyrick, as to how King Richard III.'s horse should be caparisoned. "In silk housings, embroidered with the royal arms," was the answer, "covering the steed from his ears to his hoofs !" "Oh !" exclaimed the mortified artist, "that will never do for me ; my principal object is to paint White Surrey, and if I cover him from head to foot, as you describe, I may as well not paint him at all." "But," rejoined the antiquary, " you tell me the moment you have chosen is that in which Richard made his last desperate charge, and slew Sir John Cheney, Richmond's standard bearer. Now, as this was at the close of the battle, the caparisons of the horse would probably by that time have been cut and torn to shreds, and the colour and anatomy of the horse in that case might be rendered sufficiently visible for your purpose." The true artist jumped at the suggestion. Look, reader, at the result : the silken housings rent to ribbons, streaming in the wind, add action to the horse, tell a terrible tale of the fury of the fight, and completely satisfy the archæologist, while they display the peculiar genius of the painter, and give additional effect to the picture.—(Handbooks to the Art Treasures Exhibition. The Armoury, by J. R. Planché. London, 1857, p. 60.)

the past is that of man alone. There is an archæology of nature, but it has another name, and so far the feet of the artists have not wandered far into its tangled mazes. Even when thus restricted, the field it opens to the view is one of prodigious extent. Whatever can be learned of the past life of the human race—their religions, laws, literature, arts, and customs—belongs to the domain of archæology. Thus it fairly includes even such independent studies as philology and history. Sometimes it is used in a more popular sense as a synonym for the antiquities of a particular place or people. The modern archæologist is the antiquary " writ large ; " but the tendency of the present time is to value specimens of antiquities not as curiosities, but as documents helping us to recall the fashions and thoughts of our dead ancestors. The archæologist is now animated by a more scientific spirit, and his efforts are made in more varied directions. Whilst he takes note of the pyramids of Egypt and the temples of Mexico, he does not disdain the peasant's homely songs nor the traditional stories with which the nurse lulls her babes to sleep. The vast field of archæological research opening out to the student of folk-lore can have only the most incidental relation to art, and may therefore be passed over in silence. The connection between art and bibliography may be regarded as somewhat closer. Still stronger is the tie between art and palæography. It is not intended to be argued that a knowledge of diplomatics is an essential of artistic education, but anyone who will examine the magnificent work of M. J. B. Silvestre on Universal Palæography will see how closely related the two have been in the past. In passing we may recall the fact that the written languages of the world, the ideographs of China, the syllabaries of Assyria, and the alphabet which from Phœnicia has spread over the civilised world, all owe their origin to the exercise of man's capacity for pictorial design.

The closest connection between art and archæology is in that wide and varied field dealing with the monuments, whether mighty or minute, which attest the existence of former ages. There is the architecture of the past, including alike the rude form of Stonehenge and the classic beauty of Parthenon. The mines worked and abandoned before we were a nation, the forts and roads which mark the progress of victorious conquerors, the remains of engineering skill which dwarf our modern endeavours, the weapons of war, the implements of peace, the dress, the sculpture, the painting, the numismatics of past ages, all bring material to the science of archæology.

We have seen at how recent a period the artist began to think it necessary to acquire the learning of the archæologist. The study of archæology was centuries old before historical impossibilities in pictorial art offended the critical taste. With the burst of splendour that accompanied the new dawn of literature in Europe, when " Learning triumphed o'er her barbarous foes," the investigation of classical antiquity became a favourite object of study. That enthusiasm with which men applied themselves to the investigation of the literature and art of Greece and Rome is not yet exhausted, though it may not be so strong now as when the philosophers and poets of classical antiquity shook off their monkish cerements and re-formed the world. Raffaele, although he placed Italian towers on the shores of the lake of Gennesaret, had something of the archæological spirit, and took an active interest in the excavation of the Eternal City, so that it was said of him that he had discovered a new Rome. In the last century Herculaneum and Pompeii were brought to light after an entombment of eighteen centuries. The grave yielded up some of her secrets, and showed us not only Pompeii, with its love of art and pleasure and splendour, but the same gay city in its last agony, when the angry heavens rained down the liquid fire that overwhelmed it. The very site was forgotten, but the patient archæologist unearthed it, literally as well as metaphorically. He drew from the oven the loaves that had been baking for eighteen hundred years. He found that nameless hero who preferred death to the abandonment of duty, the sentry who refused to leave his post, who was entombed by the volcanic downfall, and remained through all those generations of darkness the dead guardian of a dead and buried city.

In the sixteenth and seventeenth century some archæologists escaped the prevailing spell of classical study, and devoted themselves to the elucidation of the life and thought of the middle ages. In our own country, Dugdale and Camden have never wanted for zealous disciples. The artist who seeks to illustrate the verses of him who sang the *Canterbury Tales* may find abundant help from the archæologist, for by the labour of many generations the varied aspects of the life of middle ages is now known to us with a completeness we could hardly have hoped for, and we can see again its coarseness, its quaintness, its arrogant ambition, its piety, self-sacrificing even when most mistaken, its struggles for liberty, and all the lights and shadows of its many-coloured existence.

The present century has witnessed an increasing zeal in archæological study. The mysterious hieroglyphics of

Egypt have yielded the secret they guarded for ages. Temple and tomb alike gave up their spoil. We know the fairy tale that Moses may have listened to when a babe. The archæologist speaks, and, "as at the touch of an enchanter's wand," we see the stately palaces of that ancient empire as they flourished in the dim morning land of history.

Not only Egypt, but Assyria has come forth from the sleep of ages. We know not only the wars and treaties of the kings, but the daily life of the people stand revealed. In those buried cities how many gorgeous "chambers of imagery" there are to waken alike the enthusiasm of the artist and of the archæologist !

In the Indian empire the archæological interest, awakened towards the end of the last century, has never since been dormant. We are slowly garnering a rich harvest that may hereafter greatly modify some of our artistic traditions. The rock-cut temples of India, the stupendous memorials of the faith of Sakyamuni, with their exuberant wealth of artistic ornamentation, open out a new and entrancing volume on the history of art of which we have yet scarcely turned a page.

The archæologist is not bounded by the broad seas which separate the new from the old world. For three centuries America has been known to Europeans, but it is only in the present age that any serious attempt has been made to investigate its antiquities. The stately monuments of Mexico and Yucatan point to a civilisation and art once full of life and vigour, and still awful in decay. The relics of the aborigines of North America, though scantier, are full of interest. From these we know that the mound builders possessed no small amount of artistic taste and skill. This shows the great antiquity of art. The Old World curiously

confirms the New in this respect, for the Cave men of Europe
have left behind them convincing proofs of skill in that
department of art which Landseer has made his own.

We have thus seen that archæology aids art by enabling
the artist to attain reasonable certitude in his historical
studies. We have also seen how grand and diversified are
the fields in which it invites him to labour. Wordsworth
says :

> While poring antiquarians search the ground
> Upturned with curious pains, the bard, a seer,
> Takes fire—the men that have been reappear ;
> Romans for travel girt, for business gowned :
> And some recline on couches, myrtle-crowned,
> In festal glee.

The artist, also, is a seer, and the archæologist can feed
his faculty divine. He can conjure up the men that have
been and the glories of the empires that have passed away, and
bring before the mind's eye the kings and priests of Egypt
and Assyria, the artists who gave beauty and the philosophers
who gave wisdom to Greece, the soldiers and sages who buiit
up the mightly empire of Rome, the turbulent chieftains, the
peaceful burghers, the proud prelates of mediæval Europe, the
mighty warriors and mightier saints of Hindostan, and the
dim figures of those who in the New World reared a great
civilisation in ages beyond human ken. To such themes
does archæology invite her artistic students. Archæology
aims at truth, and strives to know the message of the past,
and to teach its lesson to the· present. The archæologist is
like Shelley's Alastor, for—

> His wandering step,
> Obedient to high thoughts, has visited
> The awful ruins of the days of old ;
> Athens, and Tyre, and Balbec, and the waste

Where stood Jerusalem, the fallen towers
Of Babylon, the eternal pyramids,
Memphis and Thebes, and whatsoe'er of strange
Sculptured on alabaster obelisk,
Or jaspar tomb, or mutilated sphinx,
Dark Ethiopia on her desert hills
Conceals. Among the ruined temples there
Stupendous columns, and wild images
Of more than men, where marble demons watch
The zodiac's brazen mystery, and dead men
Hang their mute thoughts on the mute wall around.
He lingered, poring on memorials
Of the world's youth through the long burning day;
Gazed on those speechless shapes, nor, when the moon
Filled the mysterious halls with floating shades,
Suspended he the task—but ever gazed
And gazed, till meaning on his vacant mind
Flashed like strong inspiration, and he saw
The thrilling secrets of the birth of time.

BYRON'S INFLUENCE
ON EUROPEAN LITERATURE.

BIBLIOGRAPHY.

Lord Byron's Einfluss auf die europäischen Litteraturen der Neuzeit von Dr. F. H. Otto Weddigen. Hanover, Arnold Weichelt, 1884.

General Catalogue of the Library of the British Museum : article, Byron.

This paper was read before the Manchester Literary Club, and appeared in the Manchester Quarterly for October, 1884.

BYRON'S INFLUENCE ON EUROPEAN LITERATURE.

THERE has been something of a change in the estimate of Byron, who " awoke one morning and found himself famous." He was the idol of a past generation, but we are now assured by Mr. J. A. Symonds that "at the present day it is common to hear people say that Byron was not a true poet." The same critic very rightly observes that the sudden burst of his glory and the indiscriminate enthusiasm of his followers have stirred the critical mind to a reaction. Further, "men nursed on the idyllic or analytic kinds of poetry can hardly do him justice ; not because he is exactly greater, or they indisputably less, but because he makes his best points in a region which is alien to their sympathy." There is danger that less than justice may now be rendered to the mighty genius of Byron. It may not be unimportant to note what his influence has been upon foreign literature. Some materials for such an inquiry have been brought together by Dr. F. H. Otto Weddigen ; but it is proper to add that the present writer has not been dependent entirely upon this source for his bibliographical material, as the British Museum contains a remarkable series of the translations of the great English poet, many of which are quite unknown to Dr. Weddigen.

Byron's popularity is shown by the many editions of his writings which have appeared, not only in his own country,

5

but in other lands.   His complete works are included in the Tauchnitz Series, and not less than five distinct editions were printed in Paris.   His poems were reissued in the United States in his lifetime, and the " English Bards " could be bought in Boston even when it was suppressed in London. Several independent editions of his works, one under the care of Fitz-Greene Halleck, have appeared.   If we apply the truest test of influence—that is, translation and imitation, it will be evident, apart from English literature, how much light would depart from modern literature if Byron's name were blotted from the record.   He had the admiration of Goethe, who translated the opening of " Manfred."   Wilhelm Müller wrote his " Todtenlied."   Platen, Chamisso, Immermann, Grabbe, who wrote " Don Juan und Faust," Waiblinger, Gustav Pfizer, are all influenced by Byron.   His glowing pictures of oriental life introduced a new element by which Bodenstedt and others have prospered.   The scepticism of Börne and the cynical wit of Heine owe not a little to Byron.   Could Anastasius Grün have written " Der Thurm am Strande " if the " Prisoner of Chillon " had not appeared ?   Lenau's " Don Juan " is not his only witness to Byron.   Beck, Moritz Hartmann, who wrote "Der Gefangene von Chillon," and Alfred Meissner, may also be named. The revolutionary muse of Byron found an echoing voice in Herwegh, Hoffmann von Fallersleben, and Freiligrath, who translated " Mazeppa " and other pieces.   Nor would it be wrong to say that Byron has influenced Gutzkow, Laube, and other German novelists.   Ernst Willkomm wrote " Lord Byron, ein Dichterleben."   Adolf Böttger, who translated Byron, wrote, amongst other poems, a continuation of the "Heaven and Earth."   Rudolph von Gottschall is the author of a drama on Byron's life in Italy. Salomon Mosenthal's drama of " Parisina" is identical in subject with the work of the English poet. Albert Linder and Heinrich Krause are each the author of a " Marino Faliero." The writings of Adolf Friedrich von Schack are modelled on those of Byron. Four translations at least of Byron's complete works have appeared in Germany, and of various poems there are versions by Freiligrath, Heyse, Döring, and others. A new translation of Byron, by W. Kirchbach, is announced. Many German scholars have turned their attention to Byron, and in treatises like that of Schaffner, on " Byron's Cain und seine Quellen," have sought to elucidate his writings. We may safely say with Dr. Weddigen that Byron has had a share in modifying the literary, theological, political, and philosophical thought of Germany. In the Netherlands the admirers and translators of Byron have included Bilderdyk, J. da Kosta, Ten Kate, Anna Toussaint, J. van Lénnep, J. J. Abbink, and N. Beets, who is the chief of the Dutch Byronists.

Further north we have the Danish Paludan--Müller as imitator ; and, as translators, Adolf Hansen, Thaarup, Schou, Lembcke, and Drachmann. In Norway, Ibsen, Wergeland, and Björnson are cited by Dr. Weddigen ; and, in Sweden, Vitalis and Tègner. There are translations in some cases of more than one of Byron's most important works. " Childe Harold" was translated by A. F. Skjöldebrand in 1832. The " Prisoner of Chillon " has been translated into Icelandic by Thorsteinson.

If we turn to the literature of the Latin races, the record is even more striking. Lamartine wrote the " Le dernier chant du pelerinage du Childe Harold" in 1825, and many of his works show how deeply the words of the English poet

had sank into his mind.   Some of the early verse of Victor
Hugo shows Byron's influence, as also do the writings of
Nodier.   We must include Alfred de Musset, notwithstanding
his disclaimer—

> On m'a dit l'an passé que j'imitais Byron ;
> Vous qui me connaissez, vous savez bien que non.
> Je hais comme la mort l'état de plagiaire ;
> Mon verre n'est pas grand, mais je bois dans mon verre.

It would be as mistaken to deny Byron's influence as to
accuse de Musset of plagiarism because of it.   But it would
be difficult to name any of the French romantic school who
have not been more or less under the spell of Byron's
witchery.   Even in the patois literature this influence has
been felt, and may be traced in Reboul, if not in Jasmin.
There are several French translations.   Those of Larroche,
Barne, Hunter et Rame, Paris, are not so well known as that
of Amédée Pichot.   The publishers of that remarkable
series of cheap books—La Bibliothèque Nationale—have
included the "Corsair," "Lara," and the "Siege of Corinth"
in that collection intended for the French working class.
What French author would an insular publisher include in a
similar publication addressed to English workmen ?   In
Italian literature it has been said that there is some resemblance between Byron and Foscolo.   No one can doubt
that Prati owed much to the author of "Childe Harold," and
the same may be said of Stecchetti and of his greater
countrymen, Manzoni and Leopardi and Silvio Pellico.   It is
not without significance that Zendrini translated into Italian
Heine's poem on the dead poet.   Many of Byron's works
have been translated by Andrea Maffei ; the "Hebrew
Melodies " by P. Parzanese ; " Childe Harold " by Leoni,

by Carlo Faccioli, by Giovo, and by Francesco Armenio ;
and the " Giaour " by the deputy Carmine Modestino.
Some of the poems were translated by Isola and by
Niccolini. There are two complete collections, by several
translators, one with a preface by Cesare Cantù. There
are, in addition, other versions of " Don Juan " by
Batteloni, by E. Casali, and Antoinetta Sacchi. There are
many other indications of admiration of which we need only
name the " Ore d'Ozio " of A. Dalmedico. Spain has had
its worshippers of Byron. Saavedra Rivas, who had been in
exile in England, Mariano de Lara, the Count Campo Alange,
and especially Espronceda, may be named. In our own days
Castelar has written his life. In the New Spain of South
America there are the translations of Antonio Sellen, nor
could any one doubt as to whence Andres Bello, Heraclio
de la Guardia, and Gertruda Avellaneda derive some of their
inspiration. F. Villalva translated " Don Juan," and of
" Manfred " there are two versions, one by Chaves and one
by Alcalá Galiano. " The Prophecy of Dante " was translated
by A. M. Vizcayano, and published in Mexico in 1850.
There is a translation of Byron's poems by Ricardo Canales.
In Portuguese there is but little trace of Byron, but " La
muerte de Don Juan," by Guerra Jungueira, is noteworthy in
this connection. " Childe Harold " and " Sardanapalus "
were translated by Pinheiro Guimarães. Amongst the authors
who have been influenced by Byron we must name the
accomplished Queen of Roumania, who has conquered a
place in literature as " Carmen Sylva." There are prose
translations in Roumanian of " Don Juan," " The Corsair,"
" The Prisoner of Chillon," " Beppo," the " Lament of
Tasso," and " Lara." Of the last named there is a metrical

version by Macedonski. "Manfred" has been translated in the original metre by Constantine Rossetti. Two other Roumanian poets, Grandea and Eliade, are named by Weddigen for their love of Byron.

Sclavonic literature is now attracting attention. Mickiewicz has said that it is Byron who links the poetry of the Slavs to the literature of the West. His influence on Poland has been styled electric, and undoubtedly his passionate songs of freedom would find an echo in the fiery heart of the Polish race, crushed as it was by tyranny. Mickiewicz was no servile imitator; but he, no less than Zaleski, Goszczynski, Slowacki, and Krasinski, felt the spell. In 1857 there appeared at St. Petersburg the first part of a Polish translation of Byron's poems. The "Corsair," "Mazeppa," and the "Bride of Abydos" are translated by Odyniec. "Cain" was translated by A. Pajgert and "Childe Harold" by Baworowa. In Russian there are various traces. Kostomarov translated the "Hebrew Melodies" into Little Russian. Shukoffski's version of the "Prisoner of Chillon" is said to be remarkable for its strength and beauty. Batjusschkow translated part of the fourth canto of "Childe Harold." Not only Kosloff but the greater Puschkin felt this influence, for "Eugen Onagin" has been styled a mixture of "Don Juan" and "Childe Harold." The impulse given to Russian literature by Puschkin led to an array of Byronic writers, of whom the greatest were Herzen, Ogarew, and Lermontoff. The last named, an extraordinary youth, slain in a duel at the age of twenty-six, incessantly quoted Lamartine and Byron. His "Demon" recalls at once the Faust of Goethe and the Lucifer of Byron's "Cain." Nor should we be far wrong in attributing a share of the revolutionary spirit and bitter melancholy of Turgenieff to our English singer.   A Russian edition of Byron appeared in five volumes published between 1864 and 1866.   There is a Servian version of "Lara."   There are translations of various of his poems in Bulgarian.   The "Bride of Abydos" was translated into Bohemian by J. A. Frick, and "Cain" by Durdik.   The political circumstances of Hungary were not favourable to poetic influences, but Arany may be said to have written with Byron's verse open before him.   Johann Bulla has written a new "Don Juan."   The translators are Lázár, Lukács, Eotvos, Radó, Kludik, and others.

It is the irony of fate that Greece, beloved by Byron, has in its literature fewer traces of his influence than any land. Dr. Weddigen can only name a translation of the "Giaour" by Madame Dosios and a version by Spiridion Tricoupis of "'Tis time this heart should be unmoved"—the noble verses written by Byron at Missolonghi on his thirty-sixth birthday. To this may be added a version of "Manfred," published in 1864, and Parmedion's translation of "Sardanapalus."

Byron's poetry lends itself more readily to effective translation than would be the case with some of his successors in English poetry, whose high-wrought verse and delicate art must necessarily suffer in such an interpretation.   Byron had a matchless command of the mother-tongue, but he was sometimes even culpably careless.   With him the matter was greater than the manner, and whatever the purely literary critic may object, this must be so with one who is to move the world.   Byron is the Spirit of Revolt that turned to rend that which was pure and lovely in the past as well as that which was tyrannical and hateful.   But even the shadows that lay upon his private life made him the fuller and completer representative of the new forces, not wholly, though mainly, beneficent, that were to transform Europe. We have seen that his words have gone throughout the length and breadth of the civilised world, and everywhere have been as a sharp sword penetrating to the very marrow of hypocrisy and despotism. Even this rapid and imperfect bird's-eye view of the subject will vindicate the truth of Mazzini's emphatic utterance that Byron "led the genius of Britain on a pilgrimage throughout all Europe." No English writer, since Shakspere, has had so marked an influence upon the literature of the world.

THE INVENTION OF PAPER MONEY.

BIBLIOGRAPHY.

' Origin of Paper Money." By J. Klaproth. London, 1823.

" Book of Ser Marco Polo." Edited by Colonel Henry Yule. London, 1871 (see in particular the references given at page 385, vol. 1).

" On Money and Currency" (with an Appendix on the Paper Money of the Chinese). By Travers Twiss. Oxford, 1843.

" Coins of the Ta-Tsing." By A. Wylie. Shanghai, 1857.

" On Chinese Currency: Coin and Paper Money." By Dr. Willem Vissering. Leiden: E. J. Brill, 1877. The main part of the book consists of extracts from the treatise on currency written by Ma-twan-lin about the year 1321, as part of his great cyclopædia. On this book Dr. W. Stanley Jevons, in the " Manchester Guardian," 13th June, 1882, said: " As regards coinage, our bi-metallic friends will be interested to learn from Dr. Vissering (p. 136) that the Chinese, in attempting to make use of two metals as concurrent money, got into greater difficulties than any European Government has ever done. It was not a question with them of gold and silver, but of copper and iron. The intensity of the difficulty, however, may be judged from the fact that the premium to be gained varied from 100 to 200 per cent. ' It is remarkable,' says Dr. Vissering (p. 137), ' that in order to remove the difficulties of a double standard the Chinese financiers at length took the very same measures as afterwards were taken in Europe; they instituted again the single standard under the flag of the bi-metallic system.' "

This paper was read before the Numismatic and Antiquarian Society of Philadelphia, Oct., 1886.

THE INVENTION OF PAPER MONEY.

READERS of the travels of Marco Polo will remember his quaint account of the financial operations of the great Khan of the Mongols, the masters of China. "The Emperor's Mint," says that famous explorer, "is in this city of Cambalue, and the way it is wrought is such that you might say he hath the secret of alchemy in perfection, and you would be right." He then details the process by which "the great Khan caused the bark of trees, made into something like paper, to pass for money over all his country." These notes were legal tender wherever the Emperor had dominion. Marco Polo describes those bank notes as something resembling sheets of paper, but black, and of different sizes. He says they are made from the bark of the mulberry tree. Some four centuries after the time of the Venetian Magaillans denied that such a paper currency had ever existed, although there was corroboration of the accuracy of Marco Polo's statement in the testimony of Rubruquis and many others. There can be no doubt, however, that the Chinese had a paper currency, and had invented it before the advent of their Mongolian conquerors. Klaproth says that under the great Han dynasty, a century before the Christian era, there was what was known as *phe-pe*, or values of skin. These were pieces of leather made from the skin of white stags fed in the palace park, and were sold to the grandees as tickets for admission to the ceremonies of the court. In one sense this affords some analogy to a forced currency, but these leather tablets do not appear to have circulated as money. In the seventh century of the Christian era it is stated that iron, rags of cloth, and pasteboard were used as money. Early in the ninth century the increased manufacture of images of Buddha caused a scarcity of copper, and a paper currency known as flying money was introduced, but its use was soon prohibited in the capital. These notes were, or were supposed to be, bonds for coin actually deposited as a forced loan in the imperial coffers. Under the Sung dynasty the quantity floating was in 997 held to represent 1,700,000 ounces of silver.

Klaproth thinks the true paper money was first introduced into the province of Sze-Chuen by one Chang-Yung, who brought it into circulation in order to supply the place of the ponderous iron money. These assignats were issued by private firms, but a series of bankruptcies were followed by an edict which made the issue of paper money one of the prerogatives of the crown. In 1068 forgery prevailed extensively. Colonel Yule, more cautious than Klaproth, is content to say that paper notes are "at least as old as the beginning of the ninth century." By 1160 the system had been so recklessly used that a nominal value equivalent to 43,600,000 ounces of silver was issued in six years. The "Golden" dynasty (Kin) issued notes that were current for seven years, when fresh ones were issued to the holders at a deduction of 15 per cent. The Mongols began to issue notes in 1236. Kublai Khan issued them from the first year of his reign. His total emission of paper money was in nominal value equal to £124,827,144. The Ming dynasty paid in notes, but insisted upon being paid in metal. The paper currency became more and more depreciated, and appears to have been abandoned during the second half of the fifteenth century, when it is last mentioned by the Chinese annalists. But in spite of the disappearance of the government notes there has been a considerable use of private and local promissory notes for currency purposes, and in 1858, if not earlier, there was an imperial issue. The Regent Sushun issued vast quantities of his own, which he failed to redeem, and his execution in 1861 was witnessed by a large number of his deluded creditors.

The Japanese had a paper currency in the fourteenth century. An attempt to imitate the policy of Kublai was made in Persia in 1294, and the description of the preparation of the notes shows that block printing was in use at Tabreez at the end of the thirteenth century. The Persians resented the innovation; the projector of the scheme was murdered, and the innovation abandoned. A few years before the birth of Marco Polo, the Emperor Frederick II., whilst at the siege of Faenza, made an issue of leather money. The pieces were marked with the golden fleece, and afterwards duly honoured at his treasury. Colonel Yule says: "I have never heard of the preservation of any note of the Mongols; but some of the Ming dynasty survive, and are highly valued as curiosities in China. The late Sir George Staunton appears to have possessed one; Dr. Lockhart formerly had two, of which he gave one to Sir Harry Parkes, and retains the other. The paper is so dark as to explain Marco's description of it as black." At the meeting of the Asiatic Society of Bengal on the 5th of April, 1881, Sir John Pope Hennessy exhibited a very rare Chinese bank note of the Ming dynasty, dated 1368. On comparing the original with the facsimile given by Colonel Yule in his edition of Marco Polo, it was seen to be twice the length and breadth of the latter, of a darker shade, and with some variation in the conventional ornamentation. The upper line of Chinese characters on the bank note exhibited show that it was printed in the Hung period of the Ta Ming dynasty (A.D. 1368), so that it is about five hundred years old. It bore the seals of the revenue officials, and appeared to be of imperial currency, as distinguished from the local or provincial paper money now used in some parts of China. The inscription on it declared that anyone convicted of forging the note would be punished by decapitation, and any informer would receive a reward. The note appeared to be printed from a block. The seal, of which a slight vermilion impression was visible, is similar to those now in use in official documents. Facsimiles of these notes are given by Du Halde, Yule, Vissering, and Hennessy.

THE OLD ENGLISH GUILDS.

BIBLIOGRAPHY.

" *Die Arbeitergilden der Gegenwart, von Dr. Lujo Brentano.*" *Leipzig,* 1871.

" *Diplomatarium Anglicum Ævi Saxonicum.*" *By Benjamin Thorpe. London,* 1865.

" *English Guilds.*" *The original ordinances of more than* 100 *Early English Guilds. Edited, with Notes, by the late Toulmin Smith. With an Introduction and Glossary, &c., by his daughter, Lucy Toulmin Smith. And a preliminary Essay on the History and Development of Guilds, by Lujo Brentano. London,* 1870. *Printed by the Early English Text Society.*

This article appeared in the Companion to the British Almanack for 1878.

THE OLD ENGLISH GUILDS.

THE middle ages offer few phenomena to the consideration of the antiquary more striking and noteworthy than the associations known as guilds. If he is investigating the civic history of some ancient borough, he finds how potent was the influence of the guild upon its internal economy; if he is looking through the records of a church, he will probably find that it owed some of its adornments to the action of a guild. If he inquire into the slow steps by which our commerce has been developed, he finds himself once more in face of the operation of the guild. If he seeks to read the faded chronicle of industrial life in past centuries, he will again have to appreciate the action and services rendered to the crafts and craftsmen by their guilds. In what manner these associations commenced is a matter of doubt. Dr Brentano does not think that they originated in the family feasts, by which the German tribes celebrated births, deaths, marriages, and other important events. These gatherings had in them something of a religious nature. They were held on great sacrificial occasions, they formed also opportunities at which questions of policy and of future action were discussed. These assemblies were called guilds, because each freeman brought to them his own contribution of food and drink. The primary meaning of the word appears to be that of " a sacrificial meal made up of common contributions; then a sacrificial banquet in general; and lastly a society." Brentano,

6

in common with Wilda and Hartwig, from the absence of any trace of the element of self-help and brotherhood in these ancient assemblies, does not regard them as the forerunners of the guilds, such as we know them at a later period. This does not detract, however, from the probability of the theory that the guild was developed from the earlier Teutonic family relations, and that the festal element was naturally transferred to the new institution. One of the striking points in the description which Tacitus has given of the Germanic tribes is that respecting the system by which the land was held, not by individuals, but by families or *cognationes.* The members of these confraternities were bound alike by the friendships and antagonisms of the bond at large. The family exercised full powers over its members, and was in like manner responsible for all their misdeeds. It controlled the actions, paid the taxes, and made amends for all. This, though an effective system, and one that, with some modifications, still survives in many parts of the world, is one that contains the seeds of dissolution, and the influence of these discordant elements would be active in proportion to the energy and enterprise of the tribe. Gradually the time must come when by the action of war, death, emigration, and marriage, neighbours are no longer kinsmen forming a compact *maegd.* The next step is an organisation differing indeed from the old, but clearly based upon it, and preserving its features so far as altered circumstances will allow. This is the mark. Neighbours band themselves into small confederations for the same purposes of mutual help and protection that the families had previously done. The members of the ancient mark were divided into tithings (tens) and hundreds, each having presiding officers. These associations were styled guilds.

Another derivation of the word makes it to mean sharing, either in payments or in worship, probably the former. Tithing and hundred, though now only territorial divisions, originally indicated the relations of individuals. In some parts the word ten-man-tale was used as an alternative term. The London frithguilds were associations of ten men united for the preservation of the common peace. Ten of these guilds formed the hundred. The object was, says Kemble, "that each man should be in pledge or surety *(borh)* as well to the State, for the maintenance of the public peace; that he should enjoy protection for life, honour, and property himself, and be compelled to respect the life, honour, and property of others; that he should have a fixed and settled dwelling, where he could be found when required, where the public duties could be levied, and the public services demanded of him; lastly, that if guilty of actions that compromised the public weal, or trenched upon the rights and well-being of others, there might be persons especially appointed to bring him to justice; and if injured by others, supporters to pursue his claim and exact compensation for his wrongs. All these points seem to have been very well secured by the establishment of the tithings, to whom the community looked as responsible for the conduct of every individual comprised within them; and, coupled with the family obligations which still remained in force in particular cases, they amply answered the purpose of a mutual guarantee between all classes of men." In addition to these high duties, the guilds also served as arbitration courts for their own members, matters of small importance being thus adjusted without the delay, expense, uncertainty, and it may be occasional injustice of the regular tribunals. They took part in the funerals of

deceased members, and in some cases were bound to distri-
bute alms and have religious services performed for the
dead brother. The responsibilities which could not be fixed
upon the tithing association were borne by the hundred.
Later in our own history, the hundreds were consolidated
for judicial purposes.. The London frithguilds returned to
the brethren who had suffered theft of cattle the value of their
loss, according to a fixed tariff. For the better knowledge of
each other, they met together at a common banqueting table.
These *geborscipe* or beer-drinkings may have been, and
probably were, a survival of the family festivals of an earlier
period.

The laws of Alfred declare that when one man has killed
another, a third of the fine of blood shall be paid by the
paternal relatives, or in default by the mother's side, another
third by the *gegildan*, and the remainder by the man himself.
If the murderer were without relatives, the *gegildan* were to
pay half, and for the other half, "let him flee." In the
converse case, the *gegildan* received half of the fine of blood,
and the King the remainder. There is strong reason here to
suppose that guild-members are intended.

The comprehensive nature of the objects sought by the
guilds is most interesting. They were municipal institutions,
friendly societies, burial clubs, and charitable associations, all
combined. They were also stock insurance companies.
They had to keep the brother out of crime, or be responsible
for his evil-doing; they had to pay the taxes, and render the
service due to their lord; they had to help the members when
sick, bury them when dead, and offer up masses for the repose
of their souls; they had also to teach the necessity of kindly
courtesy, and to punish any breach of it by suitable fines and

penalties.   In addition to this, there were certain festal
observances with which they were closely identified.   The
character of the Anglo-Saxon guilds may be exemplified by
the foundation agreement of a Social Guild at Exeter.   "This
assembly was collected in Exeter for the love of God and for
our souls' need, both in regard to our health of life here, and
to the after days, which we desire for ourselves by God's
doom.   Now we have agreed that our meeting shall be thrice
in the twelve months ; once at St. Michael's Mass, the second
time at St. Mary's Mass, after midwinter, and the third time
on All Hallows Massday, after Easter.   And let each guild-
brother have two sesters of malt, and each young man one
sester and a sceat of money.   And let the mass-priest at each
of our meetings sing two masses, one for the living friends, the
other for the departed ; and each brother of common condition two psalters of psalms, one for the living, and one for the
dead.   And at the death of a brother, each man six masses
or six psalters of psalms ; and at a death, each man five
pence.   And at a houseburning, each man one penny.   And
if any neglect the day for the first time three masses, for the
second five, and at a third, let him have no favour unless his
neglect arose from sickness, or at his or his lord's need.   And
if any neglect his contribution at the proper day, let him pay
two-fold.   And if any of this brotherhood misgreet another,
let him make boot with thirty pence.   Now we pray for the
love of God, that every man hold this meeting rightly, as we
rightly have agreed upon it, God help us thereunto."

In Edgar's reign there is said to have been a Cnighten-
guild instituted, of which there are contradictory accounts.
Stow narrates that thirteen knights, in recognition of services
to the State, requested and obtained a grant of a desolate

plot of land from the King, with liberty for a guild for ever. The name of Portsoken Ward Stow connects with this guild, and supposes it to imply a franchise at the gate. There was no written charter till the reign of Edward the Confessor. This grant was confirmed by William Rufus, who maintained them in their rights of fraternity, soke, and guild. But it seems more probable that the word Cnighten does not, in this case, refer to members of an order of knighthood at all, but, as Madox suggests, simply implies a guild of the young men who had not yet attained the full dignities of citizenship. The wards of London were anciently called guilds, and this may be the origin of the name of Portsoken Ward. The Cnighten-guild conveyed its lands and privileges to the canons of Holy Trinity, London, and the transfer was confirmed by the Conqueror and his successors. The Prior of Holy Trinity, probably by virtue of this concession, was alderman of the Ward of Portsoken, and, according to tradition, sat in the assemblies, and took his place in the processions, his purple robes distinguishing him from the scarlet gowns of other aldermen.

The earliest of the London trade-guilds was that of the Easterlings, or Merchants of the Steelyard. This "Gilda Theutonicorum" is supposed to have given rise to the famous Hanseatic League, formed to protect the Baltic trade from the Northmen pirates of the eighth century. They are, with good reason, regarded as our "masters in the art of commerce." As early as 967, King Ethelred ordains that the Easterlings coming to Billingsgate with their ships shall be considered law-worthy, and be admitted to trade freely. This was on condition that they did not forestall the markets from the citizens of London, and paid toll at Christmas and

Easter of two gray cloths and one brown one, with 10 lbs. of pepper, five pairs of gloves, and two vessels of vinegar. They lived together in a common building, the Gilhalda Theutonicorum, which stood in Thames Streeet, where they had spacious quays. Increase of trade led to the enlargement of their factory, and to sundry additions to it from time to time. It was in this way they became owners of the Steelyard, by which name the guild came to be known. These possessions were guaranteed to them by the treaty of Utrecht in 1478. They lived in monastic fashion, each man having a separate cell, but meeting at a common table. Any brother who was unable to resist the charms of the fair ladies of London, and became married to an Englishwoman, was *ipso facto* disfranchised. The guild, being large, was divided into companies, each with its own master. There was an alderman, who, with two deputies and nine councilmen, managed the business of the association. The men from Cologne, Guildern, and the trans-Rhenish provinces formed one apartment, those from Westphalia, Berg, the Netherlands, the Lower Rhine, the Saxons, and the Wends formed another, and those from Prussia, Lithuania, and Scandinavia, a third. Each of these rooms elected yearly four men from another apartment to serve on the council. The alderman was elected by ballot. The officers were bound by an oath to maintain the rights and privileges of the merchants in England, and to deal justly towards every one, " be he rich or poor." After taking this oath the new alderman received from his predecessor the key, which was the symbol of his power and functions. In a fortnight after the election a grand meeting of the guild was held, at which the privileges of the merchants, and the laws to which they were subject, were read over. Whether the brethren of the Steelyard did always act up to their oath we know not, but it is certain that they became obnoxious alike to the merchants and to the mob of London. Under Tyler's rebellion a number of the Flemings were seized in the churches, and the shibboleth of "bread and cheese" propounded to them. Those whose foreign tongues pronounced the words *brot* and *cawse* were instantly put to death. Stow narrates a curious controversy which arose in 1282 between the Lord Mayor and the merchants of the Steelyard. One of the conditions by which they held their privileges was that of keeping in repair the Bishopgate. When this was likely to fall, the "Teutonics" declined to be at the cost of making it safe, and an action in the Exchequer was requisite to bring them to terms, when they had to make a grant of 210 marks for the repair of the gate, and further to undertake its maintenance and give a promise to bear a third part of the cost in money, and men to defend it if need were. In consideration of this they were to be confirmed in their ancient privileges, and allowed to keep corn in their garners for forty days before selling it, unless they were forbidden to do so by the Lord Mayor by reason of a dearth in the city. The "Gilda Theutonicorum," which at one time had exported 40,000 pieces of woollen, where all the English merchants only exported 11,000, fell upon evil days, and died from decay of nature in 1552.

There are but very faint indications of the guilds in Domesday Book. The guild-house in Dover may have been the hall in which the customs were paid to the King. Thurstan, Archbishop of York, granted to his burgesses of Beverley to have their "hanshus" or guildhall, and the same privilege as the guild of York. King Henry I. gave them a guild-merchant. This King gave charters to many guilds. In 1103, the Countess of Gloucester granted to Petersfield the same liberties as those enjoyed by the men of Winchester, " who are in guild-merchant." This was a confirmation of a previous charter. Stephen granted to the burgesses of Chichester to have the customs of their borough and merchant guild as they had in the time of King William, his grandfather.

In the reign of Henry II. the guilds are spoken of as common institutions, so popular, indeed, that it was thought wise to preserve for the Crown as tight a hold upon them as was possible. Eighteen of them were fined for having come into existence without the royal licence.

John gave a charter to Ipswich, freeing them from toll, and giving them a merchant guild. The Earl of Norfolk became a burgess of the town, and gave to the guild-merchant one ox, one bull, two quarters of wheat, and two quarters of malt, that he and his villeins should be free of toll in the town. Others of the nobility followed his example. King John also formed several *gildæ mercatoriæ* in London, York, and elsewhere. It was in the reign of this impecunious monarch that the Weavers' Guild had its rent raised from 18 to 20 marks. Henry III. made numerous grants; one of these was to Liverpool. In creating it a free borough he conferred upon it likewise a merchant guild. The guilds shared the .imperfections which are inevitable to all human institutions. Founded for honest industry and trade, for mutual help and the advancement of social courtesy and kindliness, they were not without their brawls and quarrels. In 1226 there was a serious difference between the goldsmiths and the tailors. What was the cause of the dispute does not appear ; perhaps the goldsmiths had made some unpleasant jokes about the

fractional humanity of the tailors, or the knights of the shears
had declared that the goldsmiths' glitter was not all gold. At
all events they decided to refer the matter to the arbitrament
of blows, and on an appointed night five hundred of them met
fully armed, and a bloody fray ensued.   It needed all the force
of the Sheriffs to put an end to the battle, and to secure the
ringleaders of the riot.   Thirteen of these were executed.
Henry III. confirmed the charters of the provincial guilds
created by his father, and erected into corporations the
cappers and parish clerks of London.   The history of the
guild of Reading shows a curious struggle for power. Richard
I. had granted the town and tolls to the abbey, and for a
time the ecclesiastics retained full power over the place.   In
the reign of Henry III. the burgesses strove to regain some
of their lost freedom, and obtained from Henry III., in 1242,
exemption from shires and hundreds, and all pleas and tolls,
and passage and coinage, that they might be free to buy and
sell wherever they would in England, and that none should
disturb the mupon forfeit of £10. Notwithstanding this,
the abbot did not give up his claims, and in 1254 the matter
was tried in the Court of King's Bench.   The burgesses
complained that they were forced to plead in other courts
than their own common guild, that the abbot had removed
the old market, and striven to enforce customs and services
not previously claimed.   It resulted in a compromise by
which the market was restored, and the abbot acquired the
power of nominating one of the members to be warden of the
guild.   The conflict occasionally broke out again, until the
dissolution, when the execution of the abbot left the Reading
guild free of its ancient danger.

Edward I. gave charters to the fishmongers and linen-armourers of London, and confirmed those of the weavers. The commerce of the period was very slight and inconsiderable, when measured by a modern standard. In 1298 we read of disputes between the weavers and barillers, which were referred to the arbitration of a court composed of deputies from each of the disputant bodies. Two years later, another dispute resulted in the regulation that no cloth should be allowed composed partly of Spanish and partly of English wool. The Guild of Bakers were allowed to have four hall motes or meetings in the year to determine the offences committed by members of the trade. They were only allowed to sell their ware in the market which was then held where Bread Street now stands. It is in the reign of Edward II. that the commercial basis of the civic constitution of London becomes clearly visible. In the charter granted by that King it is ordained that no person, whether inhabitant or not, shall be admitted to the freedom of the city unless he were already a member of one of the trades or mysteries, or unless the full consent of the whole community were obtained, only that apprentices might still be admitted. This reign may be regarded as the golden era of the London guilds. The old name of guild became generally exchanged for that of craft and mystery, and the assumption of a distinctive costume led to their being known as "livery companies." The King, anxious to promote the woollen cloth manufacture, which he foresaw as a mighty scource of wealth and prosperity to the kingdom, resolved to throw the patronage of royalty over the associations which were then the chief instruments of the commerce of the country. The "linen-armourers," now enlarged as the "Merchant Taylors' Company," was the first to have among its brethren a member of the royal house. In the reign of Richard II. this company counted four dukes, ten earls, ten barons, and five bishops on the roll. The Skinners could show an almost equally aristocratic list. The influence of the royal patronage of Edward III. and Richard II. had the natural effect of calling forth imitation from the nobles and knights of the court. The prosperity of the Grocers' Company excited the envy of certain persons, who forwarded a petition to Parliament, in which they set forth "that great mischiefs" had arisen from these wholesale merchants "who engrossed all manner of merchandise vendable," and ruled prices as they thought best for their own pleasure and profit. In consequence there was passed the statute 37 Edward III, cap. 5, which orders all artificers and people of mysteries to choose a trade before Candlemas, and to use no other. The unlucky Jack of all trades was to be punished by six months' imprisonment or other penalty. From this sweeping regulation the women who then followed the occupations of brewers, bakers, braceresses, textoresses, weavers, &c., are exempted. This regulation was strictly enforced, and several freemen were disfranchised for contraventions of it, but, so far as the merchants were concerned, it was repealed the next year. In 1355 many of the companies gave money to the King as contributions to the expenses of the French war. The highest sum given was by the Mercers, £41 ; the Skinners, Drapers, and Fishmongers, gave each £40 ; the Vintners, £33 ; the Grossers, £26 ; the Grossers in Ropery, £5 ; the Tailors, £20 ; and others smaller sums, the lowest being that sent by the two companies of Cappers, and amounting only to 13s 4d. The total amount of this royal benevolence was £428 9s. 4d. Some of the companies sent smaller donations next year. In 1375 a very important change was effected in the government of London, for in that year the commonalty of the city passed an enactment which transferred the election of all the civic dignitaries, including members of Parliament, from the representatives of the wards to the trading companies. The masters or wardens of the companies were to send a few of their members to the Guildhall for election purposes. Subsequently this meeting was thrown open to all members of the livery. The trade-guilds do not appear to be an integral part of our municipal institutions, but on account of their growing wealth and importance to have been admitted into the corporations already existing. Thus we find that places like Manchester, which do not appear to have had any mediæval trading guilds, possessed, in a rudimentary form at east, those powers of self-government now exercised by municipal corporations. In 1376 the companies sent representatives to the common council as under :—

Grossers, 6.	Ioigno's, 2.
Mercers, 6.	Chaundels, 4.
Drap⁵, 6.	Fullo'r, 4.
Pesson's [Fishmongers], 6.	Curreo's, 2.
Orfev's [Goldsmiths], 6.	Freemasons, 2.
Vynt's, 6.	Brac's [Brewers], 5.
Taillo's, 6.	Fleechs, 2.
Sellar' [Saddlers], 4.	Bakers, 2.
Webbe's, 4.	Pell's [Skinners], 6.
Tapicers[TapestryWeavers], 4.	Zona'rs [Girdlers], 4
Leathersells, 2.	Tinctores [Stainers], 4.
Foundo's, 2.	Burillo⁵ [Clothmeasurers], 2.
Hab'rdash', 2.	Armurery, 2.
Brasiers, 2.	Bochr's, 4.
Salt's, 4.	Cultella [Cutlers], 2.

Capellar [Cappers], 2.

Peutr's [Pewterers], 2.

Brewers (ales), 2.

Hur's [Hatters], 2.

Tab'm [Smiths], 6.

Horn's, 2.

Masons, 4.

Ir'mong's, 4.

Allucar [Leatherdressers], 4.

Sporiers [Spurriers], 2.

Plom's, 2.

Wax Chaundel's, 2

Tonsores [Barbers], 2.

Tann's, 2.

Pouche Makers, 2.

Wodmay', 2.

Pynn's, 2.

Towards the close of the reign of Edward III. the twelve companies come into greater prominence, and are styled the principal crafts, the chief mysteries, &c. From them for centuries the Lord Mayor was chosen, and they took precedence in matters of civic state. The twelve livery companies were not always of this importance, but had surpassed in wealth their ancient comrades, the Weavers and Saddlers, the Brewers and the Leather-sellers, who could boast of greater antiquity. In 1385 the companies were anxious to secure the re-election of Sir Nicholas Brembre, a member of the Grocers' Company, who was opposed by the entire body of the freemen. "Also this year," says the Chronicle of London, "Sir Nicholas Brembre was chosen Mayor again, by the said crafts and by men of the county at Harrow, and the county thereabout, and not by the free election of the city of London, as it ought to be; and the old hall was stuffed with men of arms over even by ordinance and assent of Sir Nicholas Brembre, for to choose him Mayor on the morrow, and so he was." This led to certain restrictions on the voting power of the companies.

The charters granted by Edward III. and his successors show that these guilds were originally trading companies following the industry by which the association was known, and working on a co-operative principle of participation in the benefits. All in necessity could claim to be relieved, and the funerals of the poor members were to be as greatly honoured as those of the rich. The privileges granted by the charters were commercial monopolies. The motive assigned for the exclusion of strangers from the city is, of course, the good of the people, so that they may not be victimised by cheap and nasty wares. How much of this was honestly meant we need not too curiously inquire.

The word mystery in relation to the guilds does not refer to any supposed occult knowledge or even trade secrets, but is simply our English adaptation of the French word mestiere (*métier*).

The Grocers' Company was founded by 22 persons, pepperers of Sopers Lane, who met together 12th June, 1345, at the Abbot of Bury's, in St. Mary Axe, and, having dined together, elected two wardens and a priest or chaplain. Each person had to pay 12d. towards the cost of the feast, and the wardens had afterwards to pay 23d. more. It was resolved to have a common livery, and that the priest should commence his functions on Midsummer Day, each member paying for his maintenance one penny per week. The Grocers' officers had the assay of drugs, as the Goldsmiths that of metals, and the Fishmongers the oversight of the fish brought up for the food of London. The Tailors, with their silver yard measure, had the right to test the length of the goods to be found in Cloth Fair. By way of providing for the poor and distressed members, many of the companies built almshouses for decayed companions of the guild. The Governor of the Taylors' Company was styled Pilgrim, because he travelled on behalf of the craft. The crafts were always of a semi-religious character, and usually placed themselves under the invocation of some particular saint. The Grocers were styled "the fraternity of St. Anthony," because they had an altar in the church of that name. The Fishmongers chose St. Peter, and met at St. Peter's. The history of the great companies of London lies outside the scope of the present paper, and they are only referred to here in their earlier stage when they were still clearly craft and trading guilds. Their varied history, and the records of their charities, must be sought in the pages of Herbert.

There were travelling guilds, chiefly of those engaged in the building trades, who went from place to place. These are named by Gervase, of Canterbury, at the commencement of the 13th century. Very few particulars remain to us of the internal regulation of the earliest trade guilds. There appears to have been usually a president or alderman, and a council, to govern the conduct and affairs of the associate members. A favourite number of the council was thirteen, in allusion to Christ and the company of the Apostles. Du Cange mentions one in which there were twelve men and one woman, the allusion in this case being to the Virgin Mary. This was probably a religious body. In the reign of Edward III. it was established in the law courts that the King alone can create guilds.

Much valuable information respecting the objects and working of the old English guilds is furnished by the returns made to a mandate of Richard III., who, in 1388, directed the Sheriffs to make proclamation, calling upon all the masters and wardens of "guilds and all brotherhoods" to send statements as to the foundation, statutes, and property of their associations. The returns so made were discovered by the late Mr. Toulmin Smith at the Record Office, and published by the Early English Text Society. From these we shall give examples. The Guild of Garlekith, in London, was begun in 1375, for the amendment of life and the nourishing of love. Each brother and sister took oath to obey the precepts of the order, each one was to be of good repute, and to pay 6s. 8d. to the common box on joining the fraternity. The wardens were to gather the subscriptions, and to give an account of their stewardship yearly. The members were all to be "clothed in suyt," which was to last for a year. There was an annual feast (to "norishe more knowlech and love"), costing xx*d.* a-head. The annual subscription of 4s. might be paid in quarterly instalments. Four business meetings were held each year. Members were encouraged to make free gifts to the guild, and those misbehaving themselves were excluded. The members were bound to attend the funeral of any brother or sister of the order under penalty. Quarrels were to be referred to the wardens, and those disobeying their award were excluded. Those who had been members seven years, and had become old and sick, were to have xiiii*d.* weekly from the common box. The same allowance was to be made any member falsely imprisoned by his enemy. The person chosen warden must serve, or pay a fine of 40s. The Guild of St. Katherine, Aldersgate, received new members with a kiss of charity and peace; it gave help in old age, and relieved loss by fire and water. The election followed an assembly, on St. Katherine's Day, at Botolph's Church. They made loans on security from the common box to the poor members. They kept candles burning on festivals in honours of St. Katherine, and

7

paid the friar minors to say masses for the dead brethren. Another of the Aldersgate guilds helped the young to obtain work. The Guild of St. Katherine, of Norwich, undertook to bring back for burial any member who died within eight miles of the town. The brotherhood of barbers of Norwich was instituted simply for the purpose of offering candles and "torches of wax" in the church on Midsummer Day. The Poor Men's Guild of the same city found a light in honour of "Seynt Austyn." The object of the Guild of the Young Scholars of Lynn was to keep an image of St. William, with six tapers burning before it, in the Church of Saint Margaret, and to pay for the funeral services of the members. They had spent all the good of the guild, but were hoping for more gifts. The Shipman's Guild has a provision against the entry of the ale-chamber, but on the feast days the alderman might drink two gallons of ale. In many of the guilds there is a rule that no one is to remain in the guild-house longer than the alderman. The officers were not always chosen by the general assembly, but in some—for instance, in the Guild of the Nativity of St. John the Baptist, at Lynn—the outgoing alderman nominated four members to elect his successor. Another guild provides that whoso "be rebel of his tongue" against the alderman at the "mornspeche" or meeting shall be fined a pound of wax. Members were not to come to the feast in a tabard or cloak, "ne barelegs, ne barefote." If a brother is noisy, and will not be silent, he shall hold a rod, or pay a fine. None at the feast to sleep nor keep the ale-cup to himself! Those who come not to the meeting are fined, and if they grumble at the infliction they incur a second fine. In several there are rules against any member going to law without having first obtained the consent of the alderman and council, who are to do their best to compose the difference. It appears from the ordinances of the Guild of St. John Baptist, West Lynn, that the offerings at the dirge were spent in buying bread for the poor. The Guild of the Holy Trinity of Wyngale, Norfolk, besides undertaking the burial of poor brethren, engaged that if one were drowned, he should be sought for six miles round. At York there was the Guild of the Lord's Prayer, originating from the circumstance that "once on a time, a play, setting forth the goodness of the Lord's Prayer, was played in the city of York, in which play all manner of vices and sins were held up to scorn, and the virtues were held up to praise." This had met with so much favour that a guild was instituted to perpetuate its performance. The guild also performed other duties. When the play was being acted the members rode through the streets in its livery, and preserved order. Another of the York guilds was for the procession of Corpus Christi. This appears to have been a clerical guild, and the laymen, although allowed to contribute, were not to have any share in the management. There were over 14,000 recorded members who took part in this solemnity. The Guild of St. Elene, of Beverley, had a yearly procession, in which a "fair youth" was dressed up to represent St. Helena, and was preceded by an old man bearing a cross and shovel, in sign of the finding of the cross. They maintained three or four bedridden people, kept lights burning, and had service for the dead. The Guild of St. Mary had a pageant representing the presentation of Jesus in the Temple.

Belonging to the class of craft-guilds, there is a return from the great Guild of St. John, of Beverley, of the Hans House. It recites the charter made by Thurstan, Archbishop of York, by the authority of Henry I., that the men of Beverley shall have the same privileges as those of York. He grants them a hanse and right of toll, save on three feast days, which are to be toll free.   Then follows the charter of Archbishop William, granting them a guild-merchant, and its confirmation by the Pope Lucius II. The Guild of the Fullers of Lincoln contains some curious particulars.   None of the craft were to work at fulling with a woman, unless it were the wife or handmaid of his master. Strangers coming to the city might work in the trade on making a small payment.   If one of the members started on a pilgrimage to Rome upon a holiday, the guild was to accompany him out of the town, each member giving him a halfpenny; on his return he was met with rejoicings.   The Guild of Kyllyngholm, in Lincolnshire, had a rule that if a poor member had a guest, for whom he could not buy ale, he should have a gallon of the best of the guild's brewing; but if it had been obtained by trickery, then he should "be in the gildwyt of half a bushel of barley."   At Stamford the guild owned a bull, which was hunted—not baited—then sold, and the proceeds spent in a guild feast.   The Guild of the Palmers of Ludlow provided for help in theft, fire, shipwreck, and other trouble, relieved its members unjustly in prison, gave aid in sickness, and to those incurably afflicted with a liberal hand, helped girls to marriage dowries, or to entrance into a nunnery.   Then follow some very curious particulars as to services for the dead.   No woman, except of the household of the dead, is allowed to keep a nightwatch; and a man only on pledging himself not to make a mockery of the corpse, *nor call up ghosts!*

The Guild Merchant of Coventry was ratified by letters

patent of Edward III. (1340), which were subsequently confirmed. The ordinances set forth that chaplains shall be
appointed after the poor of the guild have been provided for
and its other duties performed. Any man or woman of the
guild who has fallen into poverty shall have a free loan to
trade with; those who are old or sick shall be maintained as
befits their need. Criminals were to be excluded. There
was to be an annual business meeting, and a quarterly
meeting for prayers; quarrelling was "strictly prohibited;" the
dead member was to be chaunted for by his name and sur-
name of baptism; those dying outside the city were to have
the same services. The guild had tankards of pewter and
brass, and "napery," valued at xx*l.*; also chalices, vestments,
and so on for the chaplains; and it had £37 yearly rental
from lands, houses, and rent-charges, held for its benefit by
well-wishers until it obtain licence of mortmain from the King
and middle lords. From this rental the chaplains were paid;
they also maintained thirty-one men and women who were
unable to work or to gain their own living. They also kept a
lodging-house with thirteen beds for poor folks on pilgrimage.
"And there is a governor of this house, and a woman to
wash their feet, and whatever else is needed." On the feast-
day the brethren and sisters of the guild were clad in its livery,
some in suits at their own cost, others in hoods at the cost
of the guild. The almsmen were clad in gowns and hoods at
the expense of the fraternity. The Guild of Holy Trinity, of
Cambridge, had a special ordinance against the interference
of any ecclesiastical member in the government of the
fraternity. Its affairs were to be managed wholly by laymen.
The Guild of the Fullers of Bristol, in 1406, laid before the
Mayor of that city certain regulations for the trade, founded

upon older but less stringent rules. They ask that four persons be chosen to see that the work be well done and that the fullers do not have more wages than elsewhere, and that those who have their clothes fulled outside the town shall not have them finished in the city. If these officers failed in their duty, they were to be fined. The Guild of the Kalendars of Bristol, whose objects were to keep the ancient records and muniments of the town, is said to have been founded before the Conquest. Some of the guilds were musical. There was a guild of ringers at Bristol, and another at Westminster, and of minstrels and players at Lincoln. There was a long quarrel between the Town Council of Exeter and the Guild of Tailors of that place, which was only settled by an Act of Parliament. How real was the control exercised by the guilds is shown by some cases. A customer complained that the cloth given to one of the tailors had not all been worked up, but it was shown by "patrons of blacke paper in our comen Kofer of record," that there had been no stealing. In another case the craftsman is condemned to pay for the cloth, and to keep a gown which he has spoiled in making. The customer of a tailor failed to obtain redress because the "sayde John was neuer amytted for a fre sower," and so the injury done could only be remedied at common law. A master, having chastised his servant somewhat unmercifully, was ordered to pay the doctor's bill and the servant's board for a month, give him 15s., and a fine to the guild of 20 pence for "mysbehauing aynst the craift." A recalcitrant member was put in the stocks for a day and a night, and only released on sureties for his better behaviour in the future. This guild had a confirmatory charter as late as the reign of James II. Sometimes the guilds would unite and form one general town guild; of this we have an example in Berwick-upon-Tweed. The ordinances would, therefore, probably exhibit something of the characteristics of each of the bodies in union. There was to be only one guild, with a common stock. Brethren were expected to make bequests, and non-members could have the benefits of the guild by the same process. Unmannerly words were punished by fine, and still heavier amercements attended the infliction of bodily injuries. No weapons were allowed at the meetings. Other offences against decency were to be punished. New comers had to pay an entrance fee. The guild relieved sickness, furnished dowries, buried the poor brethren, helped those charged with wrong-doing beyond the city for two days. Those who disdain the guild shall be denied its benefits. The meetings were commenced by the sound of a trumpet. No lepers were allowed in the town, there being a place for them outside. No dust-heaps were to be placed on the Tweed. There was to be silence maintained in the court whilst causes were being tried. Every burgess worth forty pounds must keep a horse. No hand-mills were to be used, but the miller allowed his share. None but the brethren of the guild to trade in wool or hides. This did not apply to stranger merchants. Brethren sharing profits with strangers to be punished. Forestalling was not allowed in the market. Goods that are fair at the top and bad below are to be made amends for. The price of mutton is laid down by another ordinance. Butchers shall not be allowed to buy wool or hides. The ale-wives were fixed to a certain charge, varying within the two halves of the year, but not exceeding two pence a gallon. Brokers were to be chosen by the commonalty, and were to give a cask of wine to the town. The hucksters were not to buy up goods before the bell had rung. Wool and hides were not to be engrossed by a few buyers. "No burgesss to get an outsider to plead for him against a neighbour, under penalty of a cask of wine." Whoever tries to break up the guild shall pay a cask of wine. The affairs of the town shall be managed by twenty-four discreet men of the town, chosen thereto, together with the Mayor and four Provosts. These were to be chosen by the commonalty. Bewrayers of the guild to be heavily punished. No glover nor skinner to cut wool during the summer months. Buyers of herrings to share and share alike. The carriage of wine casks was regulated by ordinance. No woman to buy more than a chaldron of oats for making beer. Butchers not to forestall the market. Leather tanned by outsiders to be sold in the open market. No one was to have more than two pairs of mill-stones. No brother of the guild ought to go shares with another in less than a half a quarter of skins, half a dicker of hides, and two stones of wool. Sea-borne goods to be bought "at the Bray," and to be carried away between sunrise and sunset, under penalty of a cask of wine. Payments of dues by foreign merchants were to go to the stock of the guild and the borough fund, "save what is due to the Crown." Out-dwelling brethren of the guild must deal in town on market days. These ordinances were settled after five days' consideration in 1283 and 1284.

. The social or religious guilds are those in which perhaps the grand motives underlying the old guilds are most noticeable. The trade guilds and the guilds-merchant may appear to modern eyes simply the commercial or industrial enterprises, regulating not always wisely the business of the craft, and grasping sometimes at unjust monopolies. The guilds, in point of fact, embraced the entire of the common life of the middle ages, and bound it together in a circle of charity and brotherhood. Commerce, handicraft, social meetings, almsgiving, religious worship, funeral provision and prayers for the dead, were all cared for by the guilds. They mingled the functions of religion with the work of trade or charity, and up to their lights were in many instances noble exponents of the brotherhood of man. The moral basis of the guild is, then, most clearly seen in the case of charitable or non-trading bodies. There was, at one time, at least one guild in every church in the city of London. At Oxburgh, in Norfolk, the guild had a house where poor strangers were entertained out of charity, and pensions provided for poor persons. The books of a charitable guild at York, which numbered many persons of wealth and position in the twelfth century, are still preserved in the British Museum. A guild at Wolviston, Durham, in the fifteenth century, had for its object the relief of the sick and the burial of the dead. It had flocks of sheep and lambs, which grazed upon the common lands, and from the sales of which the necessary funds were obtained.

The Guild of St. George, of Bristol, had from Henry V. a charter constituting them a body corporate, capable of holding lands in succession. This is said to be the first distinct grant of the power of succession given to an eleemosynary brotherhood.

A curious anticipation of the charitable guilds was in existence at Alexandria in the third century. It was a fraternity having for its object the nursing of the sick, but in the course of its history became powerful in other matters, and a decree of Theodosius was issued in 416 to restrain it from interfering with non-religious matters.

The purely clerical guilds were often styled the Guilds of
the Kalendars, because the meetings were held on the kalends
of each month. Sometimes the clergy of a particular church
were erected into a religious guild. Of this we have an
example at Manchester. To provide a remedy for the evil
of non-residence, the rector of the place, who was also Lord
of the Manor, gave land and a hall for the maintenance of a
resident clergy, who were to perform the services of the parish
church, and were styled the " Guild or Company of the
Blessed Virgin at Manchester." Their lands were estimated
at 250 marks yearly.

There is a strong resemblance between the social guilds
and the modern friendly societies. This similarity has often
been remarked. In many Roman Catholic countries, alike
in the old and the new world, the work which is done in
England by burial clubs and friendly societies is still performed by guilds and confraternities, usually under the invocation of saints.

The particulars already given will enable the reader to
form some idea of what is known respecting the origin and
internal regulation of the guilds. He has seen, notwithstanding their varying action and regulations, that they were in the
main animated by that spirit of self-help and self-government
which forms so important a feature in the national character.
The abuses to which they were liable are not less easy to
perceive. As respects the social and charitable guilds, they
were involved in the destruction which attended the religious
foundations at the Reformation. Whatever enormities may
have disgraced the religious houses, the guilds, so far as can
now be discerned, were occupied in holy works of charity,
and not likely to be mixed up in theological strife. They

were undoubtedly devoted to "superstitious uses," for a portion of their money went in burning candles at the images of the saints and in masses for the repose of the dead. They were therefore included in the wholesale plunder of the Reformation. The alms intended for the relief of the poor and sick, for the succour of the wayfarer, for the dowering of portionless girls, were swept away to fill the coffers of king and courtiers. The history of the trade guilds was different. Membership conferred the right to exercise a certain trade, and the right could be acquired in no other way. They were thus trades unions with great powers, and even when tolerating the presence of the non-freeman, could bind him by their regulations. But industrial enterprise cannot be bound by such ties. The desire to make things too comfortable for the members, to crush competition, and to look to the narrow interests of the guild rather than the broader interests of the public, could not hold its own against the innovations of the modern manufacturing system. The encroachments by which guilds gradually absorbed all trade into their own monopoly received a check by a statute passed in 1496, wherein, after mentioning the regulations by which the mercers and other companies forbade persons to sell without having obtained their consent, it proceeded to enact that *all should freely sell without any exaction for their liberty to buy and sell.*

The guilds were essentially fitted only to deal with a system of small craftsmen. They could not have coped with the factory system, or with that congregated labour which is now the rule. In some cases the ancient trade of the place became extinct, in others it adopted itself to the changed conditions. In very few cases do the guilds retain any of their ancient powers. From their earliest existence the guilds appear occasionally to have had members who were not of the craft. As in process of time municipal and other privileges became attached to membership, admission was sought, and in some cases paid for at a high rate, and for reasons that would have been incomprehensible to the founders of the guild. It was not until the Reform Act that the election of members of Parliament was taken from the freemen of the trades and restored to the inhabitants at large.

With a plentiful admixture of errors in political economy, with an amount of superstitious observance that may be displeasing to some, and with a sometimes superfluous quantity of feasting and frippery, there is yet much that is good and worthy of admiration in them. They show us in what manner our forefathers organised trade and industry, how they punished the dishonest workman and the unjust merchant, how they gave gladness and colour by festivals and processions to the dull routine of labour, how they helped the lad to a trade and the lass to a husband, how they aided each other when broken down by misfortune, or made helpless by sickness and old age, and, when the curtain dropt upon the last scene of all, how they went as mourners in the streets, and placed their ancient comrade to rest in his long home.

VIRGIL AND COTTON.

This paper appeared in the " Textile Manufacturer," 1885.

VIRGIL AND COTTON.

THE year 1885 witnessed the celebration of the Cotton Centennial at New Orleans, and the erection, nearly two thousand years after his death, by his countrymen of a national monument to Virgil. The connection between the two events may seem remote, and yet it is a fact that before the birth of Christ Virgil is the only Latin author who mentions cotton.

The words occur in the "Second Georgic," in a passage beginning—

> Divisæ arboribus patriæ: sola India nigrum
> Fert ebenum : solis est thurea virga Sabæis.
> Quid tibi odorato referam sudantia ligno
> Balsamaque, et baccas semper frondentis acanthi ?
> *Quid nemora Æthiopium molli canentia lanâ ?*
> *Velleraque ut foliis depectant tenua Seres ?*

(You will find that countries are divided by their trees : India alone bears the black ebony: the Sabeans alone enjoy the bough of frankincense. Why should I mention the balsam which sweats out of the fragrant wood, and the berries of the evergreen acanthus ? *Why should I speak of the forests of the Ethiopians, hoary with soft wool ? And how the Seres comb the fine fleeces from the leaves of trees ?*)

Let us see how this passage has been rendered by translators of various nations. The Spanish version of Juan de Guzman reads—

> Ó para qué diré de aquellas selvas
> De la region, que cae en Etiópia,
> Que blancas siempre están con blanca lana
> Y de la suerte como de los hojas
> Peynan los Seres copos delicados !

Voss refers to

> Äthiopia's Haine, mit weicher Wolle beschimmert.

Soave speaks of

> . . . . gli Etiopi boschi
> Ognor bianchi di molle, e sottil lana.

Jacques Delille, in company with other commentators, interprets the leafy fleece of the Seres to be silk, and says—

> Là d'un tendre duvet les arbres sont blanchis,
> Ici d'un fil doré les bois sont enrichis.

We may now turn to the English translators, and first take Dryden, whose "mighty verse" cannot be said to be too literal :—

> The green Egyptian Thorn, for Med'cine good ;
> With Ethiop's hoary Trees and woolly Wood,
> Let others tell : and how the Seres spin
> Their fleecy Forests in a slender Twine.

It is scarcely a slander to think that the passage did not present any very clear idea to "glorious John," and that he has rendered the words without stopping to think if they had any meaning. Robert Andrews, whose "Works of Virgil Englished" was printed by Baskerville in 1766, has these lines :—

> What fine Wool whitens th' Æthiopian groves ;
> From China's leaves how draws the Silken Fleece ?

William Sotheby translates the passage—

> Soft wool from downy groves the Æthiop weaves,
> The Seres comb their fleece from silken leaves.

That accomplished scholar, Professor John Connington, renders it, " Why speak of the woods of the Ethiopians, with their hoary locks of soft wool, or how the Seres comb silky fleeces from the lambs?" The version of Lonsdale and Lee is as follows : " Why should I tell you of the balm that exudes from the fragrant stem and the berries of the evergreen acanthus? Why of the woods of Æthiopia, white over with downy wool, and how the Seres comb off from the leaves the delicate fleeces ?"

We may next quote the remarkable translation of the Rev. Joseph Warton, who asks—

> And shall I sing how teeming trees dispense
> Rich fragrant balms in many a trickling tear,
> With soft Acanthus' berries, never fear ?
> From Æthiop woods where woolly leaves increase,
> How Syrians comb the vegetable fleece ?

The reader of Warton might well apply to Virgil the words addressed to Bottom, the weaver, " How art thou translated." Dr. Ure holds up his hands in dismay and exclaims, " Woolly leaves and the Syrians combing the woods of Æthiopia ! What a pity he had not gone to school with Mrs. Malaprop and become acquainted with the *contagious* places. It was the Seres of whom Virgil speaks, an Indian people far enough from Syria, who were famous then, as they are now, for the growth and manufacture of cotton." This is not universally accepted. Lonsdale and Lee, whilst pointing out that the allusion in line 120 is to cotton, remark that " the Seres are supposed to be the Chinese."

8

Last we may quote the translation of John Ogilby, who, besides being the compiler of many ponderous folios of geography, was "His Majesty's Master of the Revels in Ireland." His version was first published in 1649, but we quote from the edition of 1668—

> Of trees in Ethiopia white with Wool,
> Where from the Leavs, the Seres fleeces cull.

In a note he gives, in a compact form, the opinions of the older commentators, and it may therefore be reproduced at length : "He seems to intimate that soft and light silken Wooll, by the Latins call'd Gossipium, growing from a shrub so call'd in the upper part of Ægypt towards Arabia. The Seres, Stephanus makes a people of India, others of Scythia, extra Imaum, of whom thus Pliny, The Seres are famous for Lanificious Groves, who comb from the Leavs of Trees besprinkled with water, a silken down ; This the Latins call'd Sericum, and the Garments made thereof *Sericas Vestes ;* heretofore (as Ammianus Marcellinus reports) onely worn by Nobles, afterwards (as the Roman luxury increast) by the Plebeians. See Scaliger Exercit. 158. Sect 9. Where he affirms this kind of silk to be made after the same manner in Calabria. Salmasius (on Solinus p. 300) reckons up from the Authorities of the Antients three several kinds of this *Sericum* one collected from the leaves, another from the Barks of Trees, and a·third from the threds of Silkworms. Lipsius (in Comment. ad. 2 Annal. Tacit.) and Delrius upon Seneca's Hippolytus, distinguish'd between *Sericum, Byssum,* and *Bombicinum ;* the first taken from the Leaves of Trees, the second growing out of the ground like Line or Hemp, and the third the work of Silkworms. So Beroaldus likewise in Annot. ad Servii Comment, and Bernactius in Sylv. Statii."

In the notes to Heyne's great edition of Virgil he refers to this passage in Pliny, descriptive of the cotton plant, which is noteworthy, The Seres, he says, steep the wool gathered in their forests, in water, and then comb off a white down that adheres to the leaves, and then give to the women of the western world the task of unravelling the textures and weaving the threads afresh. In speaking of the islands of the Persian Seas, he mentions a wool-bearing tree differing from that of the Seres. This description of the *Gossypium* closely agrees with that of Theophrastus. Some of the robes of the Egyptian priests are said to have been made of cotton. Quaint old Philemon Holland at once identifies Pliny's *Gossypium* with "Linsey-wolsey, or our own Fustians rather." Arrian also mentions that the Indians used dresses made from a substance growing upon trees. As to the Seres, Heyne mentions that it was the common opinion, until the time of Justinian, that silk was a vegetable product, a knowledge of the silkworm not being one of the Roman accomplishments. Delille, and others, it will be noticed, identify Seres with the Chinese. This is not universally allowed. Martyn, in his learned notes on the Georgics, says: "The Seres were a people of India, who furnished the other part of the world with silk. The ancients were, generally, ignorant of the manner in which it was spun by the silkworms, and imagined that it was a sort of down, gathered from the leaves of trees." But Dr. Ure is not satisfied with this statement of the case, and contends that there is no testimony that Seres were silk makers, though he thinks there is evidence that they supplied the world with muslin robes. " But who," he asks, " that ever saw a silk cocoon enclosed in its entangled network of floss, would think of combing it out, or would charge Virgil with the folly of applying the word *depectant* to it, whereas the fleece of cotton wool, waving tress-like from its opened pods, the term *depectant* is most appropriate. The phrase *tenuia vellera,* or delicate fleece, also corresponds to the character of cotton wool as known to the Romans and as described by Pliny, but it is quite inapplicable to the silkworms' coils. The poet and the naturalist probably derived their knowledge of cotton plants from the same source—ambassadors, and other distinguished travellers who came to Rome from Eastern Asia."

The quotation from Virgil and its varying interpretations afford an instructive insight into the theory and practice of translation. Whether the passage will bear all that has been laid upon it may be fairly doubted, but it seems at least certain that Virgil's words contain, not merely an allusion, but a fairly accurate description, so far as it goes, of one variety of cotton ; but, unfortunately, the *Gossypium arboreum* is not the cotton plant which furnishes the raw material of the industry of Lancashire. The real cotton tree is a small herbaceous plant, *Gossypium herbaceum,* which varies from one to four feet in height. It must therefore be acknowledged that the solitary reference to cotton in Latin literature before the Christian era is a very slight one, but it is not without interest in view of the mighty changes that the plant has wrought.

LUXURY, ANCIENT AND MODERN.

BIBLIOGRAPHY.

The literature of luxury is a large one, since there is hardly a moralist, whether ancient or modern, who has not made some deliverance on the subject.

The following modern books and papers may be named as suggestive :

. *" Charicles." By W. A. Becker. English Translation. London, 1866.*

" Gallus." By W. A. Becker. English Translation. London, 1866.

" Quarterly Review." October, 1881.

" Sur la Luxe." Par H. Baudrillart. Paris, 1881.

" Our National Resources." By William Hoyle. Manchester, 1871.

" Luxury, Ancient and Modern." By A. S. Wilkins (Manchester Statistical Society). This contains a criticism of Friedlander's views.

LUXURY, ANCIENT AND MODERN.

WHILST in special instances luxury is at once recognisable, it is not easy to frame a definition of it which shall be entirely just and sufficient. A severe moralist might condemn as luxuries all things which are not absolutely essential to the maintenance of health and strength. This would reduce mankind to the condition of primeval savages, to whom the trees of the forest and the waters of the brook furnish a fare as simple as it is sufficient. Indeed, in many countries and in many ages, men satiated with pleasure, and wearied with the luxuries and enjoyments of life, have withdrawn into quiet hermitages, and, like Timon, have scorned their fellow-creatures as the bond-slaves of superfluity. Yet, as an old divine has pithily observed, " Luxury does not consist in the innocent enjoyment of any of the good things which God has created to be received with thankfulness ; but in the wasteful abuse of them to vicious purposes, in ways inconsistent with sobriety, justice, or charity." The essence of luxury is superfluity, and yet into whatever excesses individuals and nations may have fallen, the desire for superfluities has been the great stimulus by which civilisation has been advanced. The savage, even when so brutalised as to be little more than rudimentary man, has yearnings for something beyond his daily bread. When the imperious demands of hunger have been satisfied, there arises a new set of desires which become a powerful motive to exertion. The pride and vanity of man prompt him to desire the possession of something to distinguish him above the rest of his fellows. To fall below the average of savage riches is a misery which shocks his self-love ; to rise above it is a flattering incense to his pride. If to the desire of acquisition we add that of ostentation, we have the mental fabric upon which luxury is built. It has also a physical basis in the sensuous pleasures and sensual appetites. To these instincts, which the moralists have classed as pride and lust, a recent writer has added the instinct of ornamentation.

This instinctive love of the superfluous may not appear a noble quality, and yet it plays an important part in the development of man. The vanity which makes the savage desire the possession of a plume of feathers may seem ignoble, but it serves a useful purpose if it awakens in him a sense of ambition, stirs him to laborious effort, and makes him take a part—how humble he little knows—in that subjugation of the world by man which is traceable in the progress of many ages. And this vanity in a higher sphere, and with admixture of nobler material, makes the heroism that defies death for the reward of a bit of coloured ribbon. Civilisation is not far removed from barbarism, and works in the same elements, though its fashions are more complicated. In spite, therefore, of the denunciations of writers who have sometimes had more of asceticism in their profession than in their practice, man has not ceased to be possessed by the desire for pleasures beyond the mere satisfaction of animal needs. Thus have arisen the arts of life. Cooking is in this sense a luxury. Architecture is another. Not only the costly *parure* of the lady, but the homelier ornaments on the dress of the peasant girl are arguably superfluous by the logic of the stoics and the moralists. Music and poetry, painting and the drama, all the elegance and refinement of modern life, would come under the same condemnation. Human nature cannot support such prohibitions. The error of the moralists in their denunciations of luxury has been to confound under one name things totally distinct. There is a justifiable and an unjustifiable luxury. History shows us many instances in which the one has degenerated into the other, but their wholesale condemnation is as unwise as to denounce liberty because of the crimes that have been committed in its name. The real luxury of a well-ordered English middle-class home is greater than that of a wealthy Roman one in the days when Rome was the mistress of the world, and yet there is no need to associate the former with the crimes and vices that disfigured the luxury of the City of the Seven Hills. The evil of luxury is dependent upon external circumstances, and is not intrinsic in quality. This will be best seen by a brief survey of its history.

In the dim past

> . . . . Egypt with Assyria strove
> In wealth and luxury.

The religion of ancient Egypt—a strange compound of noble sentiments and gross superstition—was one that lent itself to luxurious adornment. The immense Pyramids, the great funeral monuments of the kings, are witnesses of a grandeur that has passed away. The royal luxury of Egypt was founded upon the forced labour of subjects—and in this particular all the Oriental despotisms are alike. The Great Pyramid erected by Cheops is said to have entailed the labour of 100,000 men for thirty years. Lenormant has truly observed, that "with all the progress of knowledge it would be, even in our days, a problem to solve, to construct as the

Egyptian architects of the fourth dynasty have done, in such a mass as that of the Pyramid, chambers and passages which, in spite of the millions of tons pressing on them, have for sixty centuries preserved their original shape without crack or flaw." The Pyramids are not more remarkable evidences of ancient luxury than is the gigantic Sphinx, the emblem of the ancient goddess of the land, which through so many centuries of revolution has preserved the same inscrutable smile. The temples were also erected upon a vast and magnificent scale. The indulgent Egyptian moralist, whose treatise on the conduct of life still remains to us, advises that the women should be allowed the luxury of decorations and of perfumes. The history of Egypt is one in which we see the structure of civilisation more than once destroyed, and the nation reawaking after long periods of slumber. The splendour of Memphis had lasted for centuries ere it paled before the rising star of Thebes. The decorative art of this period gives a complete panorama of the life of the people, and shows a time when the arts of peace were highly cultivated, and when the ideals of justice and good government were well developed. The great temple was pillaged by Cambyses, but the treasure which remained in the *debris*, after fire and robbery had attempted their worst, was estimated at 300 talents of gold and 2,300 talents of silver. Thebes, Denderah, Abydos are alike witnesses of the skill, the wealth, the artistic talent which was brought to bear on the religious luxury of ancient Egypt.

It would be remarkable if the luxury of the public life of Egypt had found no reflection in the manners and habits of private society. The necessaries of life were apparently within easy reach of all. Some of the Israelites in their long wanderings would have been glad to barter their newly-acquired freedom for the savoury dishes that had been the daily fare of their captivity. This emphatic testimony is conclusive evidence that whatever injustice and oppression the poorer and even servile classes might have to endure, they were at least certain of food, both plentiful and varied.

Menes, the founder of the kingdom, is regarded as the introducer of luxury, and one of his successors inscribed a malediction against him on that score on the walls of the Temple of Thebes. The earlier monarchs had probably, as M. Baudrillart says, less personal luxury in their surroundings than the sacred bulls. The funeral of one of these animals was estimated by Diodorus to have cost £2,000. Its life was as magnificent as its death.

Egypt was both a commercial and a manufacturing nation, and the fineness of its linen was celebrated throughout the ancient world. On the monuments the details of private life show refinement, comfort, and elegance in the furniture. The Egyptian women were not secluded, as in most Oriental countries, but had their place in public ceremonials and amusements, and the desire to please led them into an excess of ornament. " Le progrés, sous ce rapport, n'a guère été qu'apparent ; l'Egyptienne est presque aussi forts sur le fait de la toilette que la Romaine, laquelle ne le cède guère à la Française." The public luxury of Egypt, in its costly temples of religion and vast funereal structures, has never been surpassed, but that of its private life, whatever signs of prodigality may appear, have been far exceeded by that of other nations.

The first Nineveh ended with Sardanapalus, whose life and death alike are marked by the spirit of luxury on its most extensive scale. The descendant of hardy warriors concealed himself in his immense harem, dressed in feminine costume, and aped the weakness but not the virtue of woman; yet when the hour of trial came he showed that, notwithstanding the depth of his degradation, there were elements of nobility in his character which a happier *régime* might have strengthened into the heroic. There is a wild grandeur about his death, when the riches of his palace, his eunuchs, and the women of his harem were all consumed on one gorgeous funeral pyre. If the luxury of his life was unparalleled, not less so was the pomp with which he quitted the world. He was the symbol of the empire around him. Nineveh, enervated by debauchery, ended in flame. But though the seat of the empire was for a time transferred to Babylon, a second Nineveh arose. Seven centuries before Christ, Sennacherib, looking round upon the great city he had built, caused vaunting inscriptions to be placed upon the walls of its palaces and temples : " I have reconstructed the old ways, I have enlarged the narrow streets, and I have made the entire town to be a city shining like the sun." *Now* it is a wilderness, and its buried glories have been disinterred only to enrich the museums of Europe. " To those of my sons who shall come after me, I say this : This palace will grow old and fall into ruins at the end of days. Let my successor rebuild the ruins, and make clear again the writing of my name. Then shall Assur and Istar listen to his prayers. But he who alters the writing of my name may Assur, that great god, the father of gods, treat him as a rebel, and take away from him his sceptre and his throne." The ruin of these grand palaces, built by the blood and tears of so many prisoners of war, was not far off. In less than sixteen years the palace of Sennacherib was in ruins. The sculptures of Nineveh give many evidences of a profuse luxury. The Assyrian stuffs were celebrated in the ancient world ; the artists have shown how varied and how elegant were their embroideries. The relics from private households show that artistic elegance had attained great development. The luxury of ornamentation was highly developed. Not only the women but the men were attired in rich costumes, with costly ornaments, rings, and bracelets. The bottoms of their robes were enriched with agates and cornelians, and the harness of their horses were also decorated with similar costly ornaments.

The outer wall of Babylon the Great enclosed 513 square kilometres, an area as large as the department of the Seine, and the inner wall 290 square kilometres, an area larger than the city of London. The royal city was enlarged by Nebuchadnezzar, whose palace.was an instance of unexampled magnificence. " I laid," he says in one of the inscriptions, " the substructure with brick. I laid on it the foundation stone. I built as high as the level of the waters, and there I firmly fixed the foundation of the palace. I constructed it of bitumen and bricks. For its timber I employed great beams of cedar wood, cased with iron. I employed in it enamelled bricks, forming inscriptions and pictures, and enamelled bricks also formed the doors. I collected there gold, silver, metal, precious stones of every kind and value, valuable objects, and immense treasures." In the grounds of the palace and on the border of the river rose the famous hanging gardens which, by their picturesque arrangement, were intended to recall to the mind of his Queen Amytis the aspect of her far-off Median fatherland. The most ancient

building in the royal city was the Pyramid, which contained
the sanctuary of Nebo, the sepulchral chamber of Bel
Merodach, and the mystic sanctuary of Merodach.   The
cupola was covered with gold, "so it shone like the day."
The Altar of Destinies, which had been constructed of silver
by one of his predecessors, was covered with gold by
Nebuchadnezzar.   Of one satrap we read that the revenues
of four towns were devoted to the maintenance of his Indian
hunting dogs.   Vast spaces were reserved from culture in
order that the rich might have the pleasure of hunting the
savage beasts, which were allowed to retain possession of
them.   The dissoluteness of manners was evidenced by the
coarseness of the matrimonial market, and by the small
regard that was paid to the chastity of women.   Drunkenness and gluttony appear to have been common vices.   The
end of Babylon, rich, magnificent, but corrupt, was even
more tragic than that of Nineveh.

Of Oriental luxury in its worst aspect the Hebrew
monarchy had its share, and the splendour of the empire of
Solomon is not less conspicuous than its departure from the
simpler ideals of the Jewish nation.   The prohibitions in
Deut. xvii. have been amplified and explained by Maimon-
ides, who is, however, curiously silent as to the way in which
they were all violated by the son of David, the ruins of
whose magnificent structures still attest the opulence and
power that raised them.   It may be remarked, in passing,
that a factitious importance may be attached to the apparent
luxuriousness of Oriental nations in the use of gems.   These,
where the complicated banking system of Europe is unknown,
are often the most convenient form of investment.   They
are easier to carry and to conceal than the precious metals.

Even under the despotic sway of a Turkish Emperor or a
Persian Shah, when a man of wealth and importance is struck
by sudden ruin the glittering stones with which he has
adorned his wives will escape the general confiscation that
would overtake any other form of property.   Hence the importance of gems as objects of luxury must be measured by
an entirely different standard in east and west.   The same
remark applies, with some modification, to the status of
women.   Montesquieu has said that in the East women are
not so much luxurious themselves as objects of luxury.   The
prevalence of polygamy led to the possession of a household
of women being regarded as a certain indication of the
possession of wealth.   Hence the harem was a necessity of
pride and vanity, even when sensuality failed to awaken
desire.   The women of the royal household were the symbol
of sovereignty, and in the bloody struggles for power which
were so frequent each contending claimant aimed at their
possession.   This probably affords the true explanation of
the conduct of the rebellious son of David.

In the fifth great monarchy we see the Persians passing
from simple and even abstinent habits to those of greater
licence, until they culminate in the criminal excesses of
Xerxes and his successors.   The old Persian drink of water
was exchanged for wine, and intoxication became under
certain circumstances a ceremonial duty.   Thus, at the feast of
Mithras the king's royal duty was to be drunk.   The custom
of polygamy was general amongst the rich.   They took great
pride in the adornment of their persons, and used cosmetics
for the improvement of their complexions.   So much importance did they attach to this, that a special class of
servants were known as "adorners."   The furniture was

luxurious in its character, and even the horse's harness included a saddle that was as soft as a couch. Their addiction to the pleasures of the table was great. They were eager for fresh dishes, and offered rewards to those who could invent new pleasures.

Amongst the Greeks we are struck by the large quantities of specie devoted to religious uses. The colossal statue of Minerva, in the Parthenon, was draped at a cost of £100,000. The gifts of Gyges to the Temple of Apollo included six golden bowls, weighing 1,700 pounds. The votive offerings of Crœsus to the Temple of Delphi are said to have amounted to seven tons of gold. In the earlier ages the contrast between the simplicity of the private houses and the magnificence of the temples and public edifices was very marked. The expenses of living were exceedingly light, but there are not wanting instances of exorbitant expenditure.

The price which Alexander paid for Bucephalus must appear large even to the most ardent lover of horseflesh, whilst Alcibiades is said to have paid for his dog as much as would have purchased fifty slaves. The philosopher, Gorgias, erected in the Temple of Delphi a statue of himself in solid gold, one evidence amongst many that the teachers of learning and wisdom were able to command high prices for their services. The festivals of the gods were made the excuse for much extravagant display at the expense of the public treasury, and these degenerated into huge bribes by which the mob was sought to be kept in a good humour. What treasure was freely expended upon public works is evidenced by the ruins of structures which even in their decay strike the beholder with delight and admiration. How the arts of Greece were made to minister to the pleasures of the voluptuary is known to the student, who sees in them the degradation and misuse of some of the finest of man's intellectual endowments. Into what profound depths of uncleanness Grecian luxury did at times descend is almost incredible.

The luxury of the ancient world culminated at Rome. "In the presence," says Becker, "of the extravagant splendour of Rome, the most abnormal luxury of any age must appear as miserable poverty." Thus, too, Gibbon: "Under the Roman Empire the labour of an industrious and ingenious people was variously but incessantly employed in the service of the rich. In their dress, their table, their houses and their furniture, the favourites of fortune united every refinement of convenience, of elegance, and of splendour—whatever could soothe their pride or gratify their sensuality." Instances of sensual extravagance so wild and unnatural as to be almost incredible abound in the annals of the empire. The famous letter of Tiberius to the Senate admits the existence of deplorable luxury, but doubts the expediency of attempting to control it by law. "But what is it that I am first to prohibit, what excess retrench to the ancient standard? Am I to begin with our country seats, spacious in their bounds, and with the number of domestics from various countries? or with quantities of gold and silver? or with pictures, statues of brass and wonders of art? or with vestments promiscuously worn by men and women? or with what is peculiar to the women—those precious stones, for the purchase of which our coin is carried to foreign or hostile nations?" The Emperor who thus lamented the prodigality of the time was the same man whose residence at Capri reached a depth of luxurious vice which it may be hoped has never been either exceeded

9

or equalled in after ages. Whatever could be devised to yield pleasure to a sybaritic nature, or stimulate jaded passions to fresh delirium of lust, was put into execution at Capri. So of Nero we have the testimony of Suetonius that he was extravagant and profuse beyond all bounds. During the nine months' stay of Triclates at Rome, 800,000 sesterces daily were spent upon him by the Emperor, who at his departure further presented him with upwards of a million; to a harper and a gladiator he gave the estates of men who had received the honour of a triumph. He never wore the same garment twice, and fished with a golden net drawn by silken cords. The mules of his baggage carts were shod with silver. The same spirit animated him in building. His palace was remarkable not only for the extent which made it like a city, but for the manner in which some of its walls were covered with gold and adorned with jewels and mother-of-pearl. The supper rooms were vaulted, and portions of the ceiling revolved so that flowers and unguents could be scattered from above on the guests below. Of Caligula we are told that he delighted in inventing new dishes; he served up loaves and other foods modelled in gold, and had the poops of his two ships blazing with jewels. In building he aimed at overcoming difficulties deemed to be insuperable. His profuseness is best marked by the statement that in one year he had exhausted the treasure left by Tiberius, and estimated at 2,700,000,000 sesterces.

Roman banquets served to gratify not only the appetite of the guests but the ostentation of the host. Thus of one supper given by L. Ælius Verus, we are told that the cost was 6,000,000 sesterces, although there were but twelve invited, to each of whom, on departure, he presented a mule, and the vessels of gold and silver which had been used at the entertainment. The Emperor Caius is said to have spent in one day more than £80,000. Vitellius expended £7,000,000 during his brief tenure of the imperial purple. Poppæ Sabina, the wife of Nero, is said to have had her mules shod with silver and gold.

The number of the wealthy class, however, was not large. It has been estimated that of the entire population of a million and three-quarters, some ten thousand only belonged to senators and *equites*. The greatest fortunes named are those of Cneius, Lentulus, and Nero's freedman, Narcissus, each of whom is represented as having over £4,000,000. Crassus is said to have left £1,700,000. There are probably in Great Britain fifteen or sixteen peers whose landed property alone would be valued at from £3,000,000 to £12,000,000. There are also various individuals who have acquired or inherited equally immense fortunes, derived from trade and finance. Thus Sir Francis Goldsmid is said to have received £10,000,000 from his father. Astor's wealth was estimated at £6,000,000, Stewart's at £16,000,000. The Rothschilds and other instances might be added.

Instances of individual prodigality might easily be multiplied. We have to remember that most of those upon whose testimony we have to rely respecting the luxury of the Roman world were the disciples of a school which considered that the primary duty of man, or at least his highest wisdom, was to restrict his wants. Riches, they held, consisted not in the extent of possessions, but in the fewness of wants. There is a certain sense in which this is a valuable moral for all ages, but, as we have already seen, its rigorous application would destroy all the arts of life.

Seneca's denunciations of luxury have in them an element
of the grotesque, which almost forbids us to take them
seriously.   The wealthy philosopher denounces the use of
architecture, of shoes, and of shorthand.   He overwhelms
in indiscriminate blame all the arts that make life agreeable,
and is constantly telling us that nature alone will supply all
the legitimate wants of man.   The trees will give him shelter,
the birds and the beasts will find him clothing, with as little
of the contamination of art as may be.   Nature has provided
for all necessities, and cooks and soldiers are alike useless
and detrimental.   Yet, if Seneca's moral fails from want of
perspective and restraint, we must not let its blemishes hide
from us its use and beauty.   His was a voice crying in the
Roman wilderness, and testifying against the cruelty and
prodigality that made its luxury infamous.   In the same
spirit Pliny denounces the culture of the asparagus, and the
methods by which they were made to grow larger and finer
than in a state of nature.

Centuries later von Hutten, whilst accepting the fruits
which then furnished forth the dessert table—which were
once luxuries—attacked the enormity still recent in his days
of the importation of oranges.   Indeed, a modern scholar
has contended against the universal testimony, and insists
that the Roman luxury has been over-estimated.   Fried-
länder's chief contention is that instances cited on account of
their exceptional extravagance have been taken as though
they were the ordinary types.   His argument seems to err in
the opposite direction.   The witnesses are too many to be all
mistaken.   The buried cities of Pompeii and Herculaneum
have also yielded strong evidence that in this, as in other
matters, the Romans aped the Greeks, and like them, though

in an inferior fashion, made art the servant of luxury and voluptuousness.

The Roman sages, who were horror-struck that man should protect his feet from the stones by the luxury of shoes, found their natural successors in the fathers of the church and the preachers of the middle age, who regarded each advance in comfort and decency with a feeling in which dismay and dislike strove for mastery. The introduction of forks was regarded as a striking instance of the corruption of manners. Bed curtains, candlesticks, and bon-bons have alike been cited as types of unbridled luxury.

The stoical sentiment which referred all things to the standard of the shadowy primitive life of man finds an echo in Montaigne, in Charron, and in many other writers of the sixteenth century.

It is, however, foolish to apply such criteria to the luxury of modern times. Our entire society rests upon the development of man's necessities or desires. The increase of these, when legitimate, brings with them the arts of industry and peace; they stimulate to industry, and increase the wealth and well-being of the community. But there are desires which are essentially vicious, and other which are vicious by reason of excess. When an individual or a nation allows these unbridled courses, those evils arise which have led to the indiscriminate condemnation of all forms of luxury. That which may be a harmless luxury in one case may be blameable in another, since the proportion between expenditure and possessions in the one case may be great and in the other small. That which is prodigality in Rutilius may be appropriate for Ventidius. The moral quality of certain personal indulgences depends entirely upon whether the

payment for them will or will not interfere with the performance of specific duties. A representative of the colliers is
said to have asked why they should not drink champagne as
well as others, if they could pay for it. The miner drinking
champagne out of a bucket, and the coal-master indulging in
the same liquid out of vessels formed with elegance and art,
are equally consuming a luxury. It might be an advantage
to the health of both master and man to refrain. It might
be laudable on the part of the master to abstain by way of
example. The difference which justifies the condemnation
of the workman is that the money expended upon bucketfuls
of champagne is abstracted from that which should go to
feed, clothe, and educate the family which he has called into
existence, and towards whom he has certain imperative duties.
Hence the moral quality of luxury depends upon surrounding
circumstances. There are, however, two classes of expenditure,
whether the money be that of a spendthrift or an economist.
It is an old fallacy to assume that so long as money is made to
circulate, the way in which it is expended is a matter of no
consequence. The daring paradox of Mandeville, that
private vices are public benefits, finds few defenders when it
is stated in its naked form. There is an unproductive expenditure upon objects which are at once destroyed and have in
them no seed of wealth or industry. There is a productive
expenditure which creates or extends industries, gives employment to additional workers, and increases the general wealth
and well-being of the nation. If this test be applied to the
expenditure of our nation, there will be found much that the
patriot and the moralist must deplore. Dr. Smiles has
shown what large sums are spent in what he happily calls self-
imposed taxation. Mr. William Hoyle, in 1873, in a similar

way estimated the waste of wealth. He believes that follies of fashion cost £120,000,000; extravagant Government expenditure, £20,000,000; loss from the Game Laws, £20,000,000; loss through costliness of law, £5,000,000; loss through waste of sewage, £30,000,000; waste arising from excess and luxury in food, £20,000,000; cost of tobacco, £14,000,000; direct and indirect cost of drink, £262,000,000. This is a startling sum, the total of which reaches nearly £500,000,000 per annum.

But if we have still

> Luxurious cities where the noise
> Of riot ascends above the loftiest towers,

we may fairly claim that substantial progress has been made. At least there is this great difference between the luxury of the ancient and that of the modern world, that in the old order the enjoyment of the few was purchased by the labourer who had no share in it. The condition of the wealth-producer may still be far from being all that could be desired, but at least it is an improvement on the condition of the proletariat in ancient Rome, where the wealth and magnificence of the few shone in cruel contrast to the misery and degradation of the thousands by whom it was gathered and sustained.

BLINDNESS OR DEAFNESS.

Reprinted from the " Co-operative News," December, 1885.

BLINDNESS OR DEAFNESS.

THERE were enumerated in the United Kingdom at the census of 1881, 22,832 blind and 13,295 deaf and dumb persons.

Which is the greater loss? Not to hear the notes pouring from the throat of the lark and filling all the heaven with a musical delight, or not to mark the track of the bird that "like a cloud of fire" wings through the "blue deep"

> In the golden lightning
> Of the sunken sun.

Which is the greater bliss? To *hear* the voice of those we love whispering tender words of affection and help, or to *see* in their faces the certainty of a love that words can never wholly express? The problem may be stated in a thousand varying fashions. It has been stated and answered by one of the most famous of modern musicians, whose words have attracted much attention. M. Gounod conducted his "Redemption" at the Trocadéro, on Friday, June 6, 1884, for the benefit of the *Ateliers d'Aveugles*, or Blind Workshops of Paris, and in order to show still more his deep sympathy with the inmates of those excellent institutions he published in the programme a letter, of which the *Pall Mall Gazette* gave an English translation. The correspondent who sent it mentioned a conversation on the same subject with Rubenstein, whose sight is well known to be nearly gone, in which the Russian composer urged the same view as Gounod, and confirmed it by remarking how much, in Beethoven's case, his deafness had driven him into himself, and added to the force and individuality of his music.

"If I had to choose," says M. Gounod, "one of these two terrible calamities, deafness or blindness, I do not think that I should hesitate an instant. The deaf are generally said to be less cheerful than the blind; but notwithstanding that, and notwithstanding the fact that loss of hearing would affect me in regard to that which has always been the source of my very keenest and deepest feelings—I mean music—yet, between being deaf and never seeing anything one loves, there is, in my opinion, so vast a gulf as to make that one consideration sufficient to decide the question. One must not forget that a musician can enjoy music to a great degree by merely reading it: and though the actual sensation of the sounds is · necessary to make the impression absolutely complete, yet it is sufficiently strong to convey melody, harmony, rhythm, quality, and all other elements of music— in a word, to give a real mental hearing to the piece, so as to stamp it on the mind without the aid of the external sounds. It is well known that Beethoven wrote many of his master-pieces after he was completely deaf; but he cannot have written them without hearing them in himself, and it therefore follows that the converse can take place, and that music can be heard by merely reading it. Deafness, therefore, does not entirely destroy musical enjoyment. In fact, as far as the sense of hearing goes, every composer when he writes down his ideas is virtually on the same footing as a deaf person, for what he writes is the product of his mind alone. But blind-ness—the privations it implies; the sacrifices it imposes; the virtual imprisonment of not being able to walk alone; the dismal darkness of never beholding the face of nature; the silence and solitude of being unable to read and write! As long as he can read a book, a deaf man remains in close communication with the whole circle of human thought. Historians, poets, philosophers, critics—all are still his companions; the world of painting and sculpture is still open to him. The blind man, on the other hand, is dependent on others for all he wants; he has to ask for everything; he is the prisoner of prisoners. A thousand times rather, then, be deaf than blind."

The case could not be better stated; but is the conclusion the right one? The deaf-mute must live a life apart. He is a citizen of the Silent Land, and even in his native country is but a pilgrim and a stranger. He has a language, but it is a foreign one to most of his countrymen. Considering how readily the manual alphabet may be learned, it is surprising that so few take the trouble to gain possession of a key that would enable them to unlock not only the intellect but the hearts of their deaf-mute brethren. Isolation is the inevitable destiny of those who have lost or never acquired the common method for the communication of thought. It has been urged by the learned inventor of the telephone that the whole course of the education of the dumb, as now pursued, is to intensify this isolation. He even goes so far as to say that by a process of artificial selection a distinct species of humanity is gradually being evolved. Without entering upon the controversial aspect of the subject, it will be sufficient to point out that in the great majority of cases the inability to speak is merely a consequence of the inability to hear. "Reading and writing come by nature," says wise Sancho

Panza, "but speech is the gift of God." It is a gift to the
race, but the individual acquires it purely by the exercise
of the imitative faculties. The absence of the power of
hearing is not at first noticed in the infant, and it may well
happen that the unpleasant truth will not be acknowledged
so long as doubt is possible. When it is definitely certain
that the child is deaf and dumb, its horizon is at once
narrowed. If the parents are wealthy, special teachers are
engaged, and very probably an attempt is made at lip-reading
and articulation. When success is attained it can only be as
the result of long-continued application and the most earnest
attention. For one aspiring to the professions or to the
avocations of the higher walks of life it is an additional
obstacle to be overcome. The difficulty of teaching the
dumb to speak has in this country, until within the last few
years, been regarded as practically insuperable, and the chief
dependence has been upon the method of talking with the
fingers. This at once shuts out the deaf-mute, even when
otherwise qualified and well-educated, from the church, the
bar, and the army; from the teaching profession, from the
House of Commons, from the dramatic and operatic stage, in
short, from all those vocations in which the spoken word
forms an important element. In none of these, except the
army and navy, and perhaps the stage, would blindness be an
irremovable bar. Nay, we might even be reminded of the
blind old King of Bohemia who died on the battlefield. In
stating these disabilities of deafness there is no desire to do
so otherwise than in general terms, and with especial reference
to the educational methods hitherto usual in this country.
Probably no blind troop of actors exists, but a company of
deaf-mutes who had been taught to articulate performed a

play at Milan a few years ago. There have been deaf-mutes who were ecclesiastics, but they preached only to the children of silence.

The voice is still the greatest instrument in the education of the race, and the blind man may feel his way into the tribune where an eager senate will listen with a sympathy that deepens into admiration; he may move the "stormy democracy" from the political platform; he may—behind the lecturer's desk—draw from his hearers the tears that he will never see, or from the pulpit he may denounce the sins of the wicked, and console the sorrows of those that mourn.

It is clear, therefore, that the blind boy of liberal education has an advantage over the deaf-mute of the same social standing. Indeed the only form of intellectual activity from which he is entirely shut out is the artistic. A blind sculptor is a possibility, and one is recorded in the person of Gambasio, but a blind painter is a contradiction in terms. This domain the deaf-mute can claim. The Spanish painter, El Mudo (*i.e.*, The Dumb), is not the only deaf-mute who has attained a certain distinction in the realm of pictorial art. The blind have a great advantage over the dumb in the fact that their want of sight does not isolate them. We find blind children in the ordinary elementary schools, nor are they usually amongst the least advanced. Their affliction is one that commands a ready and easily-expressed sympathy. The man who would gently lead a blind boy across a dangerous street might not have the patience to listen to the attempt of a deaf-mute to explain the nature of the equally necessary help *he* desired to obtain. The great disadvantage of the blind is that the easiest avenue of knowledge is closed. Eyegate is shut and Eargate can only be opened by friendly hands. Sermons and lectures, however interesting or profound, are usually not intended to exhaust the subjects of which they treat, but only to stimulate the hearer to further research in written records. The vast mass of printed literature is accessible to the blind only by the kindly voice of such as may be willing to read aloud to them. It is true that a number of books have been produced in embossed letters, but the literature to be obtained in the types used for the blind, although it has doubtless given mental light to many a darkened hour, is too small in bulk to affect the question very seriously. No one who wanted to take a high place in the work of the world could rely upon it. The blind, then, have to depend upon hearing to countervail the want of sight. Another compensation not infrequently arises, for it leads to fixity of attention and a development of the power of memory that is often remarkable. When books were uncommon the tenacious memory held long narratives both in verse and prose, and the blind man, in the same position as his ancestors ages ago, finds that memory will bear whatever burden may be gradually laid upon her yielding shoulders.

The deaf-mute needs no interpreter to translate messages from the great souls who, being dead, yet speak from the bookcase or library shelf. Nay, the very isolation which has been noted as his chief hindrance impels him to read. He can usually only make known his thoughts or wishes to hearing persons by a slow and perhaps tiresome process. He is shy and sensitive, and for fear of being thought a bore he avoids, as far as he can, all conversation; reserves his social intercourse almost entirely to his own class, but reads with interest, and even with avidity. Dr. Kitto said of lip-reading

—in which he had made some slight progress—that "it offered no adequate recompense to one who felt his time to be very precious, and who knew how to apply his attention to objects in the highest degree useful and interesting." The world of books is open to the deaf-mute with a freedom that the blind can never enjoy. The deaf-mute need only rely upon himself; he can not only pick and choose, but learn the art of skimming, by which the cream can be taken off some books in a very brief space, without the need of reading or hearing them read from *alpha* to *omega*. The blind have perpetual night, but when the darkness gathers round the dying day the deaf-mute is in a deeper gloom. The only avenue to his mind is the eye. Hence, when darkness comes, not only reading but conversation must be suspended. In the badly-lighted streets he is probably subjected to greater inconveniences and dangers than one who is blind.

To the advantage which the deaf-mute possesses as to reading may be contrasted the greater facility of the blind for music and poetry. The very nature of deafness is fatal to all that depends upon harmony of sound, which, on the contrary, is a constant source of pleasure to the highly sensitive and constantly trained ear of the blind. The deaf-mute, notwithstanding his greater familiarity, or power of familiarity, with printed literature, does not always grasp grammatical peculiarities, and hence his words sometimes form strange and inelegant idioms. The higher pleasures arising from the "concord of sweet sounds" are, of course, entirely unknown to him. The blind learn their mother-tongue by the ear alone, and its capacity for melodious expression may well be the subject of day-dreams filling the darkness of their leisure. All metre, whether it be rhymed or only rhythmical, depends upon circumstances beyond the power and experience of the deaf-mute.

The matter may be looked at in a still more concrete form. Let us record the names in either class of those who have done service to mankind or made themselves famous. To the deaf-mutes we may credit Dr. Kitto, "El Mudo," and one or two more painters. There are now living one or two deaf-mute preachers and several persons honourably engaged in teaching.

The blind have a more illustrious company. Without insisting upon blind old Homer or Milton, we must credit them with Euler, Huber, and Saunderson; with Metcalf, the roadmaker; Holmes, the blind traveller; with Salinas, Pesanti, and Carolan, the blind musician. Nor must we omit the honoured name of Henry Fawcett, the blind statesman. If the deaf should claim Beethoven, in his latter life the composer of glorious music that he might never hear, the blind may recall the oratorio of "Samson," composed by Handel when for him had come

> Total eclipse, no sun, no moon—
> All dark amid the blaze of noon.

Why have the contributions of the deaf and dumb to the best work of the world been fewer than those made by the blind? Man is a social being, and the common bond of society is the possession of language. Nepomucene Lemercier, blind in his old age, noticed that the blind are more cheerful than the deaf. "You see," he said, "in speaking to a blind man you make him forget his infirmity; in addressing a deaf man you make him recall his." He who is deprived of speech finds himself shut out from many avocations and destitute of the most powerful instrument by which to reach the sympathies, interests, affections, and prejudices of mankind. Language and thought may be distinct, but they are so closely intertwined in growth and development that practically they are inseparable, and whatever retards or hinders one must injure the other. The vocabulary of the deaf-mute is formed and retained with difficulty, and there are niceties of language which he will perhaps never master. He learns by sad experience that there is something peculiar in his own manner, and, morbidly afraid of ridicule, he shrinks from contact with all but those who are similarly afflicted. The blind are not thus shut out from the ordinary intercourse of life, but find in it an encouragement to exertion and a reward for endeavour. The blind, for the most part, have an even unusual share of the social element. The deaf-mute, on the other hand, is practically incapable of holding converse with the bulk of the world on equal terms. Hence, he must live in a smaller and narrower world of his own. It may be that he struggles against this necessity, and only after repeated failures and rebuffs accepts the inevitable, sees the prizes of life fall to other hands, and the great world recede further and further from his view. The instruments by which the world is shaped from generation to generation acquire their sharpness and power by friction. The deaf-mute stands alone and solitary in the crowd, whilst the pathetic motions of the blind as they grope their way gain them friends even in the wildest mob. Man prospers not by isolation, but by kindly contact with his fellow-men.

THE LEGEND OF THE SIRENS.

BIBLIOGRAPHY.

" *A Philological Examination of the Myth of the Sirens.*" By J. Postgate (*Journal of Philology, vol. ix., p.* 112).

" *Börö Boedoer.*" Par *Wilsen, Brumond, et Leemens. Leide,* 1874 ; *p.* 183.

" *Romantic Legend of Sakya Buddha.*" By Samuel Beal. *London,* 1875 ; *p.* 339.

THE LEGEND OF THE SIRENS.

ONE of the most familiar of the Homeric legends is that which celebrates the charms of the dangerous Sirens. The wise Ulysses is thus warned by Circe to beware of their allurements :—

> Next where the Sirens dwell you plough the seas ;
> Their song is death and makes destruction please.
> Unblessed the man whom music wins to stay
> Near the curs'd shore, and listen to the lay :
> No more the wretch shall view the joys of life,
> His blooming offspring or his beauteous wife !
> In verdant meads they sport, and wide around
> Lie human bones that whiten all the ground ;
> The ground polluted floats with human gore,
> And human carnage taints the dreadful shore.

This passage has been interpreted by Etty in a magnificent painting, of which the Manchester City Art Gallery may be proud to be the home.

The Sirens are described by Homer as possessing a power of enchantment in their song, as having a malevolent delight in the death of man, and an ogre-like taste for human flesh and blood. Ulysses escaped their dangerous influence by filling the ears of his companions with wax, and by causing himself to be lashed to the mast when the vessel approached the dangerous coast whence floated the seductive song of the Sirens. By the classical writers the Sirens were often described as bird-like creatures — sometimes as winged women, and at other times as birds with human heads. From this and the etymological indications supplied by their name Mr. Postgate asks :

" Are we, then, to suppose that this beautiful myth arose from the concurrence of two circumstances on an actual voyage—the singing of birds in the woods of a desert island, and strong currents setting towards its shore, and compelling sailors to lean to their oars if they would escape the ship-wreck of their predecessors ? "

Without attempting any judgment on this terribly ration-alistic suggestion, it may be worth while to point out some hitherto unnoticed analogies to the classical myth which are to be found in the early art and literature of the Buddhists. Thus, in many of the paintings at Börö Boedoer, in Java, we have the figures of the bird-women.   In plate civ. of the great work of Wilsen, Brumond, and Leemens we have what the authors style two of these "celestial gandharvis, beings half-women, half-birds," whose music has attracted the atten-tion of a princely traveller and his suite.

Still more curious is the story of the five hundred mer-chants, translated from the Chinese by the Rev. Samuel Beal.   It narrates the history of five hundred merchants who, under a wise leader, determine on a sea voyage to increase their wealth.   They are wrecked on the shores of a land inhabited by Rakshasis, or demons.   "Now, the Rakshasis, having perceived the disaster and the fate of the five hundred merchants, hastened with all speed to the place, intending to rescue the men and enjoy their company for a time, and then to enclose them in an iron city belonging to them, and there devour them at leisure."   Having transformed themselves from their real shape as hideous ogres into the most lovely women, they first rescued the distressed voyagers, and then cried, "Welcome, welcome, dear youths! whence have ye come so far? But, now ye are here, let us be happy. Be ye our husbands, and we will be your wives! We have no one here to love or cherish us; be ye our lords to drive away sorrow, to dispel our grief! Come, lovely youths! come to our houses, well adorned and fully supplied with every necessary; hasten with us to share in the joys of mutual love."

The merchants, after a period in which to lament for their lost land, responded to these liberal offers. Time passed pleasantly enough, but the suspicions of the chief merchant were aroused by the circumstance that the women always exhorted their husbands to avoid a certain part at the south of the city. Of course he took the first opportunity of visiting the forbidden locality, and there found a number of victims of the Rakshasis still alive, and many more dead, dismembered and mutilated as though gnawed by wild beasts. The unfortunate captives told him that they also had been the lovers of the demon women, who for a time seem to love their companions, but all the while live on human flesh. The chief merchant asks if there is any chance of escape, and is told that once in each year the Horse-King Kesi visits the shore, and cries aloud, "Whoever wishes to cross over the great salt sea, I will convey him over." The chief merchant resolves upon escape, and when the Horse-King appears his aid is invoked. He invites them to mount upon his back.

"Then, mounting into the air, he flew away like the wind. Meantime, the Rakshasis, hearing the thunder voice of the Horse-King, suddenly awaking from their slumber and missing their companions, after looking on every side, at last perceived afar off the merchants mounted on the Horse-King, clinging to his hair, and holding fast in every way, as they journey through the air. Seeing this, each seized her child, and hurrying down the shore, uttered piteous cries, and said, 'Alas! alas! dear masters! why are you about to leave us desolate?—whither are you going? Beware, dear ones, of the dangers of the sea. Remember your former mishap. Why do you leave us thus? What pain have we caused you? Have you not had your fill of pleasure? Have we not been loving wives? Then why so basely desert us? Return, dear youths, to your children and your wives!' But all their entreaties were in vain, and the Horse-King soon carried those five hundred merchants back to the welcome shore they had left, across the waves of the briny sea."

This story is translated by Mr. Beal from the Chinese version of the Abinishkrámana Sûtra, which was done in that language by Djnanakuta, a Buddhist priest from North India, who lived in China about the end of the sixth century of our era. This, however, affords no clue as to the antiquity of the story itself. The Horse-King is referred to in the Vishnu Purana and in the Prem Sagar. Whatever its date may be, the story seems to deserve attention as a curious and close analogue to the Homeric myth of the Sirens.

FACTS AND FANCIES OF LONGEVITY.

BIBLIOGRAPHY.

"*Human Longevity.*" *By James Easton. Salisbury,* 1799. *This is an uncritical record of* 1712 *centenarians between* A.D. 66-1799.

"*Yorkshire Longevity.*" *By William Grainge. Pateley Bridge,* 1864.

"*On Human Longevity.*" *By P. Flourens. Translated by Charles Martel. London,* 1855. *This is an exceedingly suggestive work.*

"*A short Tractate on the Longevity ascribed to the Patriarchs in the Book of Genesis.*" *From the Danish of Professor Rask. London,* 1863.

"*On the Longevity of the Patriarchs.*" ("*Fraser's Magazine,*" *August,* 1870.)

"*On Longevity.*" *By Professor Richard Owen.* ("*Fraser's Magazine,*" *February,* 1872.)

"*Human Longevity ; its Facts and Fictions.*" *By William J. Thoms. London,* 1873. *This and the same author's various articles in "Notes and Queries" are the most valuable contributions to the subject, and in conjunction with Professor Owen's physiological testimony are almost exhaustive of the question.*

"*Comparative Longevity.*" *By E. Ray Lankester. London,* 1870.

The following paper is reprinted from the Companion to the Almanack, 1834.

FACTS AND FANCIES OF LONGEVITY.

THE census of 1881 recorded the existence of 141 persons who were said to be over 100 years of age. The newspaper reader is tolerably familiar with the appearance of paragraphs about centenarians. Sometimes a kindly clergyman appeals for some help to smooth the last days of one for whom a century of toil has not provided a competence; at others the enthusiastic fellow-townsfolk organise a public celebration in honour of one who has eluded death so much more successfully than the bulk of his fellows. On one occasion the parish officer of Chelsea devised an unusual method, for on what was understood to be the hundredth anniversary of Mrs. Hogg's birth he had her sent up in a balloon! Haller collected a thousand cases of longevity, that is, of persons who were believed to have lived between 100 and 150 years. Such statements abound not only in the popular literature of every land, but have, until very recently, been accepted even by medical writers, with but few expressions of doubt. Sir Henry Holland thought there was "sufficient proof" of the occasional prolongation of life to 110, 130, and even 140 years, and was not inclined to reject the claims of Thomas Parr to be considered 152 at the time of his death, and the validity of the claim was admitted also by Flourens.

In our own days a new school of thought has arisen, and their labours have given a fresh aspect to the question. The late Sir Charles Wentworth Dilke, Sir George Cornewall

Lewis, and more especially their friend and disciple, Mr. W. J. Thoms, have altered the scientific if not the popular view of the subject by the simple process of demanding that satisfactory evidence shall in each case be adduced before centenarian claims are admitted. When this touchstone is judicially applied some of the very old people are seen to be conscious impostors, while others, in the senile decay of memory, have begun by adopting the suggestions of those around them as to their great age, and have ended by a firm belief in their truth. "Even as many old men," says Fuller, "used to set the clock of their age too fast when once past seventy, and, growing ten years in a twelvemonth, are presently fourscore ; yea, within a year or two after climb up to a hundred." It is a remarkable commentary upon this tendency to exaggerate age that alleged centenarians abound most in those classes where there is least possibility of documentary disproof. If a superannuated mendicant in a workhouse claims to be a hundred years old, the only positive evidence against his assertion may be its inherent improbability, but in the higher ranks such a statement could be easily tested by reference to the Peerages and other "red books." Thus Sir George Cornewall Lewis points out that in the Christian era "no person of royal or noble rank mentioned in history, whose birth was recorded at the time of its occurrence, reached the age of a hundred years." "I am not aware," he continues, "that the modern peerage and baronetage books contain any such case resting upon authentic evidence." This is all the more notable from the well-known fact that the average mean duration of life is greater in the peerage than in the general population. It is true that Sir Richard Baker asserts that the Earl of Winchester, who died in 1572, was

106, but Camden is content with the more moderate estimate of 97. Lady Mary Bouldby, said to have been 106, is by more reliable annalists set down at 97.

It must not be supposed that any one doubts the possibility of men and women attaining to one hundred years. Neither Mr. Thoms nor any of his followers have made any such assertion. Their contention is that such cases are very rare, and that they are to be examined by the ordinary rules of evidence, and to be accepted or rejected according to the nature of the testimony adduced. In 1790 a young lady of nineteen, Catharine, daughter of Sir John Eden, was selected as one of the Government nominees in the Tontine, and she died in 1872, having more than completed 101 years. These nominees were selected from the aristocracy and the well-to-do classes on account of the ease of keeping them in view in after years. The officials of the National Debt Office also convinced themselves as to the case of David Rennie, a farmer of Dundee, who was born February 28, 1755, and died March 2, 1857. The experience of assurance offices is instructive, for their clients might have been expected to furnish some authentic cases, if centenarians were as common as the general public imagine. In 1872 Mr. A. H. Bailey stated that in the entire experience of life assurance companies, extending from the reign of Queen Anne to the present day, there was but one case of a centenarian—Mr. Jacob Luning. One person had died in the 103rd and three in the 99th year of their age.

Very frequently when the statements as to centenarians are examined, they are seen to be devoid of evidence or based on misapprehension. Miss Mary Billinge, of Liverpool, was said to have attained 112 years. She was born, it was said, at Eccleston, near Prescot, May 24, 1751, and died December 20, 1863. When Sir James A. Picton investigated the case, it was seen to be one of mistaken identity, for the Mary Billinge who died in 1863 was not the Mary who was born in 1751, but was of quite different parents, and did not see the light until 1772. Hence even parish registers, unless carefully scrutinised, may deceive. Another possible source of error is that parents who have lost a child frequently give the same name to another born subsequently. Mr. Thoms mentions a distinguished R.A. who was the third son to whom the name he bore had been given.

"The system of registration of births," observes Professor Owen, "now affords the competent searcher after truth the needful data. Parish registers cover a greater period of time, but both have their sources of fallacy, needing caution. In the case, let us say, of Richard Roe, reported now living at St. Hilda's, Northshire, at the extraordinary age of 120, one writes to the incumbent, respectfully requesting that a search may be made in the vestry for any evidence of said Richard's birth. An answer is duly received that Richard Roe was baptised in November, 1751. This seems straightforward and satisfactory. But the worthy incumbent is again troubled with the request that the parish register may be further searched for the birth or baptism of any other Richard Roe at a later period, and for the entry of the marriage, if perchance such may have occurred in the place of the birth of the Richard Roe of 1751, and of that of any subsequent Richard Roe. It turns out that the Richard Roe of 1751 married early, viz., in 1769, one Margaret, or Margery Doe, of the same parish, and that their eldest son was christened Richard Roe in 1771. Now this Richard Roe, it further appears, wedded at St. Hilda's Elizabeth Bunch, of the same parish ; and surviving Bunches know well that such was the name, and not Doe, of the first wife of the wonderful old man, whereupon it appears that the Richard Roe in question has reached his 100th, not his 120th year." If documentary evidence can sometimes deceive, still less reliance is to be placed on tombstone inscriptions. " To lie like an epitaph " is a proverbial appreciation of graveyard literature, but in many cases it is not at all necessary to assume intentional deception. At Bickenhill, in Warwickshire, an inscription asserts of Miss Ann Smith that she " died a maid and deceased aged 708." This may be the stone-cutter's notation for 78, or some jocular person may have put the 8 as an afterthought to the genuine record. At Brislington, near Bristol, during some repairs, a stone was found inscribed " 1542. Thomas Norman, aged 153," and the parish authorities had it new faced, repaired, and put in a place of honour ; nor did they learn until too late that a wicked wag had inserted the figure 1, and thus given the appearance of patriarchal age to one who died in middle life. The monument of Macklin, the actor, in St. Paul's, Covent Garden, states him to have been 107, but when his coffin, many years after, was brought to light during some alterations, his age, as given on the plate, was seen to be ninety-seven.

Sometimes the generations descended from a person are adduced as proof of centenarian claims, but this is quite inconsequential in the absence of other proof, for it is quite *possible*, though of course very improbable, for a woman to be a mother at eighteen, grandmother at thirty-six, and a great-great-great-grandmother at ninety.

Another source of evidence is the centenarian remembrance

11

of events that happened long ago; but this opens up the question as to the period when memory begins to exercise her functions, and there is some testimony that it may begin at a very early age. Mr. Thomas Cooper, the author of the "Purgatory of Suicides," says that he remembers circumstances that occurred on his second birthday, when he fell into the river, and was rescued from drowning. It must also be borne in mind that there is a tendency to confuse that which has been a matter of personal experience with the impressions derived from conversation and hearsay. This must throw a certain amount of doubt on those who have no documentary evidence for their alleged great age, but calculate it from some historic or notable circumstance that happened in their infancy or childhood.

There are some supposed instances of extreme longevity that are constantly cited as conclusive. Why should we doubt that Catharine Prescot, of Manchester, learned to read when she was over a hundred, and died at the age of 108, when Old Parr died at 152 and Jenkins at 169? Mr. Thoms has carefully examined these typical cases. Henry Jenkins died in 1670 at Ellerton-on-Swale, and the parish register merely states that he was "a very old man," and of that there will be no question. Mr. William Grainge says that "the proofs on which the great age of Jenkins rest have been examined with the greatest severity and care, in order, if possible, to detect the slightest fallacy, but the fact appears to be established beyond reach of reasonable doubt." In fact, Mr. Thoms, in 1870, was the first to utter a historic doubt about the Yorkshire beggarman, and to show that there is really no reason beyond his own unsupported assertion to suppose him to have attained an age so patriarchal. About 1662 or 1663 he told

Miss Anne Savile that he was then about 162 or 163, and could "remember Henry VIII. and the battle of Flodden; that the King was not there, as he was in France, and that the Earl of Surrey commanded." "Being asked how old he was then he said 'I believe I might be between ten and twelve, for,' says he, 'I was sent to North Allerton with a horseload of arrows, but they sent a bigger boy from thence to the army with them.'" He further said that he had been butler to Lord Conyers, and remembered the Abbot of Fountain Abbey very well, "who used to drink a glass with his lord very heartily." Dr. Tancred Robinson adds that Jenkins in the latter part of his life was a fisherman, and used to wade in the stream, his diet was coarse, he was often at the York assizes, and had sworn to 140 years of memory. In 1667 he was a witness in a tithe case, and then gave his age as 157, so that instead of gaining in years he had been growing younger since his interview with Miss Savile, and in his deposition, so far from swearing to 140 years, he was content to say that his knowledge of the matter in dispute extended to "above threescore years," as might very well be the case. Thus the only evidences of the age of Jenkins are his own unsupported and varying declarations. The case of Thomas Parr has acquired still greater celebrity. He is said to have been born in 1483, at Winnington, in Alberbury, and in the year 1635 was seen by the Earl of Arundel, who had him conveyed in a litter to London to be presented to the King. He died in the metropolis, November 15, and a post-mortem examination of the body was made by the famous Harvey, and his gravestone may still be seen in the south transept of Westminster Abbey. John Taylor, the water-poet, wrote an account of "'The Old, Old, very Old

Man," which has often been reprinted. He is said to have been born in 1483, to have been in service from 1500 to 1518, when he entered upon four years' possession of his father's lease, which was renewed to him in 1522 and again in 1543. In 1563, at the age of eighty, he married his first wife, and in 1564 obtained a renewal of his lease, and again in 1585. In 1588 he stood in a white sheet in Alberbury Church for incontinence. In 1595 his first wife died, and ten years later he married a widow. There is not the slightest documentary evidence for any one of the statements as to Parr, about whom the only facts known with certainty are that he was brought before the King as a very old man, and died in 1670. There is, indeed, additional proof that he told the King of the discreditable episode in his life which brought upon him public disgrace in the parish church. The King said to Old Parr, "You have lived longer than other men, what have you done more than other men?" "I did penance when I was a hundred years old." This is not easily reconciled either to probability or to the other statements as to his career. For the pretended descendants of Parr there is no evidence at all, though physiologist and divine have both quoted the apocryphal son aged 113, one grandson aged 109, and another 127, great-grandson aged 124, great-great-grand-daughter aged 103. These are all as mythical as the phœnix. More stress has been laid upon Harvey's autopsy than the facts warrant. The famous physician had brought to him the body of the "poor countryman," and naturally repeated such statements as to the condition of life of the deceased as were made by those who asked him to make the examination. What he says as to the physical condition of the body is carefully written, but the rest is clearly hearsay and gossip.

Another famous centenarian is the Old Countess of Desmond, of whom there is a portrait at Muckross with the following inscription : "Catharine, Countess of Desmond, as she appeared at y° Court of Our Sovraigne Lord King James, in thys present year A.D. 1614, and in the 140th yeare of her age. Thither she came from Bristol to seek Relief, y° House of Desmonde having been ruined by the Attainder. She was married in y° Reigne of King Edward IV., and in y° course of her long Pilgrimage renewed her teeth twice. Her principal residence is Inchiquin in Munster, whither she undauntedlye proposeth (her purpose accomplished) incontinentlie to return. Laus Deo." Sir Walter Raleigh mentions seeing her in 1589, and states that she was married in the reign of Edward IV. Fynes Morison states, in addition, that she was able to go on foot four or five miles to the market town, even in her latest years. Horace Walpole says she danced with Richard III. Now, in 1528, forty-five years after the death of Edward IV., the first wife of Katherine Fitzgerald's future husband was still alive Probably Sir Thomas married her in the following year, when he became Earl of Desmond, and she became the mother of a daughter, who afterwards married Philip Barry Oge. If Katherine Fitzgerald was 140 in 1614 she must have been born in 1464, and would therefore be sixty-six when her daughter was born ! Further than this, the pedigree states that she died not in 1614 but in 1604, and the only mention of her supposed visit to England is in this erroneous inscription. The annalists and pamphleteers would not have left unchronicled so remarkable a person. The probability is that she was a young woman at the time of her marriage, and as her husband died in 1534 she would naturally be known as the Old Countess when seen fifty-five years later by Raleigh. If she were twenty at the time of her marriage she would be ninety-five at her death. In any case her age is far more likely to have been 100 or under rather than 140.

It is not possible in relation to bygone ages to do more than indicate circumstances of doubt, as the data for an exhaustive examination are no longer forthcoming. Most persons interested in the subject have notes of some hundreds of supposed centenarians of the past about whom it would be hopeless to attempt to prove a negative. We can only apply the reasoning suggested by the circumstance that most of the cases now brought forward prove when investigated to be mistakes or deceptions. Joseph Miller, who died in Morpeth Workhouse 25th April, 1872, was believed to be 111 years old. During his latter years he received much extra consideration on this account. "This old man," said one writer, "fought under the gallant Nelson, and, like all old tars, his greatest glory is in repeating the deeds of the bold and the brave. How, when the Pomona frigate was once lying off Boulogne, a live shell was thrown on deck, which he fearlessly grasped and pitched overboard; how he narrowly escaped kingdom-come seventy or eighty years ago; how he laughed when his enemies went by the board; how that his father lived to the age of 119, his sister to 120, and that he hopes to do the same, with an endless variety of characteristic yarns which would lose their pungency by repetition. About twelve months ago he 'astonished' the officers and captain of the gunboat Castor by the agility with which he paced the deck, scanned the rigging, and dived into the cabins." It was said that he was baptised at Whickham, and a certificate was obtained showing that Joshua, the son of Robert Miller and Ann his wife, was baptised there 25th October, 1761. Although the old man said that his mother's name was Thomasina, that clue was not followed up until after his death, when it was found that he was not born until 1783. He entered the navy in 1805, and retired from it in November of the same year. Thus he was really about ninety when he died.

Thomas Geeran's was a case of wilful imposture. He claimed to have been born May 14, 1766, at Scarriff, in the county of Clare, Ireland, and after working as a sawyer enlisted in the 71st Regiment, was at the siege of Seringapatam, was in the Walcheren Expedition, fought in nearly every battle in the Peninsula, and concluded his military career at Waterloo, receiving his discharge in 1819. In his later years he lived upon the contributions of the charitable, and died in the infirmary of the Brighton Union at the advanced age of 105 years. Mr. Thoms's incredulity was the object of much ridicule from medical and other persons, but it was amply justified, for official inquiry showed that Geeran's name was not on the rolls of the regiment to which he alleged he belonged from 1796 to 1819. There was, however, one Michael Gearyn or Gayran, who enlisted 3rd March, 1813, and deserted 10th April, 1813, and this was in all probability the "old soldier" who afterwards gave the rein to his imagination and described the 71st Regiment as being in India and Egypt when it was in England, and said that he was wounded at Salamanca, when the regiment did not take any part in that action. He was about eighty-three at his death, and must often have laughed at the credulity of those who swallowed so readily his contradictory statements. The announcement that a man 108 years of age would preach must often have attracted large congregations to hear "the Venerable George Fletcher," who claimed to have fought at Bunker's Hill, to have been with Abercrombie in Egypt, and in military and other active pursuits to have spent eighty-three years of his life. In reality he was about ninety-two at the time of death. He enlisted in 1785 and deserted in 1792, but was allowed to re-enter under the terms of a Royal proclamation in 1793, and managed to fraudulently add seven years to his claim of previous service, and when he received his discharge in 1803 he made a further addition to his years, and represented himself as forty-nine when he was in reality only thirty-seven. The reason for the deception is obvious. "Fletcher was shrewd enough to know that a man of thirty-seven years of age could not receive credit for twenty-four years and six months' service, as much of that must have been before he was eighteen, and was consequently not entitled to reckon for pension." Edward Couch, who died 30th January, 1871, was believed to be 110, and claimed to have been one of the crew of the Victory at Trafalgar, and to have fought under Lord Howe on the glorious 1st of June, 1794. In reality he was born in 1776, he did not enter the navy until June 30, 1794, and his name is not to be found on the books of the Victory! "Captain" Lahrbush, whose birthday was annually celebrated at New York, made the most absurd mis-statements, and claimed to have had twenty-nine years' service in the British Army, when in reality he entered it in 1809, and was cashiered in 1819. In the same way he added to his age, and distinguished American soldiers and others joined in celebrating the 107th anniversary of a man who in all probability was eighty-seven. The story of Richard Purser, "the oldest man in England," who died in 1868 at the reputed age of 112, was marked by such circumstances of doubt as not only to justify, but to demand scepticism.

So far the evidence cited will convince any reasonable mind that claims of extreme longevity are often made, sometimes with the deliberate intention to deceive and at others in unconscious error, but that few cases can be satisfactorily established. The duty of proof rests on those who make such statements, but they too often appear to think that their assumptions should be regarded as evidence. A person claiming to be 100 should be expected to support his statement by such reasonable evidence as would satisfy a jury in a claim of any other description. The facility with which such statements are accepted is a premium on carelessness and deception. It would be pushing scepticism too far to insist that no centenarians exist. This is a heresy that Mr. Thoms never broached. On the contrary, he recorded several cases where the evidence is satisfactory. Jane, daughter of Francis Chassereau, a French refugee, was born in London, November 13, 1739, and married in 1764 to Mr. Robert Williams, of Moor Park, Herts, and Bridehead, Dorset, where she died October 8, 1841, at the age of 102 years. Her eldest son stated that he had dined with his mother on Christmas Day for seventy consecutive years. She was successfully couched for cataract in the eighty-first year of her age, and when ninety held her great-grand-daughter at the font, and in her ninety-third year addressed her tenantry in reply to the toast of her health. She retained a good memory almost to the last, but her mental powers had otherwise weakened. Mr. William Plank was born November 7, 1767, at Wandsworth, and was for a time a schoolfellow of the late Lord Lyndhurst. He was the "father" of the Salters' Company, and died

November 19, 1867, having lived one hundred years and twelve days. Mr. Jacob William Luning was born at Harvelvörden, in Hanover, May 19, 1767, married at Spalding in Lincolnshire, August 4, 1796, and in 1858, became an inmate of Morden College, Blackheath, and died there June 23, 1870. On his death the case was investigated by the Registrar-General, and it was shown that in 1796 he had insured his life at the age of thirty-six for £200, and had survived that step for seventy-seven years! The evidence in Mr. Luning's case was conclusive, and equally so was that which showed that Mrs. Catharine Duncombe Shafto, of Whitworth Park, had reached the advanced age of 101 years one month and nine days. Her case has already been mentioned, but it may be added that on the day when she completed her 100th year, she appeared at the wedding breakfast of her grand-daughter. A well-authenticated case is that of Frau Forstmeister Johannette Polack, born Genth. She was born June 6th, 1779, and died November 8, 1880, at Wiesbaden. Her photograph, taken on her centennial day, was shown to Professor Owen, who remarked that " it showed all the attributes of extreme old age." " I at length," he continues, " feel consolation for the disappointment in not prevailing on Lady Smith, in her 101st year, to sit to Millais." Lady Smith died in February, 1877, in the 104th year of her age. Mrs. Fanny Bailley, of Worthing, was born at Ferring, August 7, 1777, and died April 6, 1881. The immediate cause of death was a fall by which she broke her thigh. She was 102 years and eight months old. Mrs. Martha Gardner, who died at 85, Grove Street, Liverpool, March 10, 1881, was 104 years and five months old. Her father had entered the ages of his children in a Family Bible, and their baptisms, though performed at home, are all registered in the books of St. Peter's Church, Liverpool. She was a cousin of the Rev. John Wilson, of Trinity College, Oxford, and adminis- tered to his estate when he died in 1873. The lawyers concerned in the matter were somewhat astonished at having to deal with the letters of a lady then in her ninety-seventh year.

From this evidence we have the clear conclusion that in no case of extreme longevity subjected to critical examina- tion has a greater age than 104 been proved. What then is to be said of the ages assigned to the patriarchs and of the "traditions of ancient nations as the Greeks, Babylonians, Egyptians, Hindoos, and others referred to by Bishop Harold Browne ("Speaker's Commentary," vol. i., p. 62.) As to the ages of the patriarchs, Professor Erasmus Rask has suggested that the years were really months, and there is the testimony of Proclus that there was such a method of reckon- ing amongst the Egyptians.

. The physiological aspects of longevity have been clearly explained by Professor Owen ("Fraser's Magazine," February, 1872). He points out that Buffon had said that the duration of the individual life may be measured in some degree by the period of growth. It has been suggested that the period at which the epiphyses of the long bones coalesce with the diaphyses is that at which the growth of the animal is com- plete. This completion of the process of ossification, together with that of dentition, enables a calculation to be made of the full period of human life. Man has but two sets of teeth, and the second set, says Professor Owen, "may do their work under favourable circumstances for thirty or forty years before being worn out and shed." The oldest human remains known exhibit the same characteristics as those of the present day. Professor Owen tells an anecdote which explains how old people are sometimes said to cut a third set of teeth. He was taken to see an old woman of a hundred who was cutting a fresh tooth. She "pulled down a skinny lip and showed a lower jaw toothless save for one black stump, of which the crown had long before been broken away, probably after decay. At fifty the gum had closed over the fang of the decayed and broken-off crown. The absorption which reduces the vertical extent of the jaw by reducing the alveolar part touched not the retained fang, and spared in part its particular socket, when the tooth stump protruded through the subsiding gum." The physiological view is thus summed up by Professor Owen: "The conclusions of Professor Flourens, that, in the absence of all causes of disease, and under all conditions favourable to health and life, man might survive as long after the procreative period—ending say at seventy in the male—as he had lived to acquire maturity and completion of ossification—say thirty years—are not unphysiological. Only under the circumstances under which the battle of life is fought, the possible term of one hundred years inferred by Flourens, as by Buffon, is the rare exception." The causes of this would open out a fresh field of inquiry, and, however tempting the subject, we must refrain. The truth remains, that, as Flourens puts it, most men die of disease, and but few of old age. Why should this be? But even a good constitution and healthy and careful habits of life cannot prolong existence to an indefinite term. The revolutions of the seasons are not more certain than the processes of growth, activity, and decay that every human organism must pass through. "The days of our age are threescore and ten," says the Psalmist, "and though men be so strong that they come to fourscore, yet is their strength then but labour and sorrow, so soon passeth it away and we are gone." This is true for the bulk of mankind, and even of the exceptional mortals we may say with the son of Sirach, "The number of a man's days are about one hundred years."

GEORGE ELIOT'S USE OF DIALECT.

The following address was delivered at a meeting of the Manchester Literary Club, 24th January, 1881. Since then the publication of "George Eliot's Life," by J. W. Cross (Edinburgh, 1885) has added a further expression of opinion as to the literary use of dialect. These will be found at vol. ii., p. 72, and vol. iii., p. 304. They do not modify the views expressed by George Eliot to Professor Skeat.

GEORGE ELIOT'S USE OF DIALECT.

A LITERARY form may be given to the dialectal words and expressions that constitute the folk-speech of a district either from a scientific or from an artistic motive. When Prince Lucien Bonaparte caused the Song of Solomon to be translated into various dialects, his purpose was purely scientific. When Shakspere, Scott, or George Eliot use dialect to give local colour or rustic flavour, the intention is purely artistic. The scientific method aims at the illustration of the dialect itself, with its historical associations and philological affinities. The artistic uses it for the elucidation of character, and by the aid of its minute touches increases the individuality of the portrait. Most dialect writers aim as a first object at the display of the dialect itself, and this not infrequently leads them into exaggeration. Thus Tim Bobbin noted all the uncommon and quaint-sounding phrases that he heard anywhere, and pressed them into his *Lancashire Dialogue*. The effect is that his work cannot be taken as a faithful representation of the common speech of the county at any particular time or place. George Eliot's use of dialect was distinctly artistic. She used just so much of it as was necessary to give point and finish to the personages of rural life who live and breathe in her pages. Thus, in *Adam Bede*, the very opening chapter shows her skill and discretion ; for the men, all engaged in the free and unconstrained talk of the workshop, not only vary in the degree in which they use dialectal ex-

12

pressions, but there is a certain individuality in their way of employing it which marks them off from each other. That George Eliot fully appreciated the value of dialect is shown in the complacent speech of Mr. Casson, the host of the "Donnithorne Arms":—

> I'm not this countryman you may tell by my tongue, sir; they're cur'ous talkers i' this country, sir; the gentry's hard work to hunderstand 'em. I was brought hup among the gentry, sir, an' got the turn o' their tongue when I was a bye. Why, what do you think the folks here says for "hev'nt you?"—the gentry you know says "hev'nt you;" well, the people about here says "hanna yey." It's what they calls the dileck as is spoke hereabout, sir. That's what I've heard Squire Donnithorne say many a time; "it's the dileck," says he.

This delightful passage is suggestive in many ways. The ignorance of Casson is perhaps less due to self-complacency than to want of intellectual grasp, especially in so unaccustomed a field of mental inquiry. The difference between his speech and that of his neighbours has struck him as an interesting phenomenon, but his effort to ascertain the causes of the variance only results in his accepting as a solution what is only a restatement of the problem in a to him scholastic and authoritative form. When Squire Donnithorne says that the country people speak a dialect, he merely tells Casson in an unaccustomed phrase a fact which the former butler's perceptive powers have already ascertained. Casson, however, contentedly accepts the mere word as the key of the mystery. In this he probably resembles many other arrested inquirers who deceive themselves by juggling with mere words, and who fancy they have found effectual answers, when in point of fact they have merely restated momentous problems in unfamiliar words. Casson's perceptive faculty, although equal to noting the broader discrepancies between his own fashion of speaking and that of the rustics around him, is incapable of discriminating between his own style and that of the gentry amongst whom " he was brought up." The departure from conventional English is in this case a note of *caste*. The English gentry as a body have a flavour of public school education and university culture, and yet their household dependants speak in another tongue. The drawing-room and the servants' hall have each their own vocabulary and grammar, and a philological gulf is fixed between the two, though one might at least suppose that the yawning chasm would easily be bridged over by a little educational effort on either side.

With the reticence of genius, George Eliot obtains her effects with the slightest possible expenditure of material. She contrives to give the impression of provincial speech without importing any great number of unfamiliar words into the text. Thus old Joshua Rann stands before us a pronounced Mercian, although not a dozen of his words are unknown to the dictionary :—

"Humbly begging your honour's pardon," said Joshua, bowing low, "there was one thing I had to say to his reverence as other things had drove out o' my head."

"Out with it, Joshua, quickly," said Mr. Irwine.

"Belike, sir, you havena heared as Thias Bede's dead—drowned this morning, or more like overnight, i' the Willow Brook, again' the bridge, right ' front o' the house."

"Ah!" exclaimed both the gentlemen at once, as if they were a good deal interested in the information.

"An' Seth Bede's been to me this morning to say he wished me to tell your reverence as his brother Adam begged of you particular t' allow his father's grave to be dug by the White Thorn, because his mother's set her heart on it on account of a dream as she had ; an' they'd ha' come theirselves to ask you, but they've so much to see after with the crowner, an' that ; an' their mother's took on so, an' wants 'em to make sure o' the spot for fear somebody else should take it. An' if your reverence sees well an' good, I'll send my boy to tell 'em as soon as I get home ; an' that's why I make bold to trouble you wi' it, his honour being present."

"To be sure, Joshua, to be sure, they shall have it. I'll ride round to Adam myself, and see him. Send your boy, however, to say that they shall have the grave, lest anything should happen to detain me. And now, good morning, Joshua ; go into the kitchen and have some ale."

The same method may be seen in the fine portraits of Mrs. Poyser. That emphatic housekeeper thus objurgates the faithful " Molly " :—

"Spinning, indeed ! It isn't spinning as you'd be at, I'll be bound, and let you have your own way. I never knew your equal for gallowsness. To think of a gell o' your age wanting to go and sit with half a dozen men ! I'd ha' been ashamed to let the words pass over my lips, if I'd been you. And you, as have been here ever since last Michaelmas, and I hired you at Treddles'on stattets, without a bit o' character—as I say, you might be grateful to be hired in that way to a respectable place ; and you knew no more o' what belongs to work when you come here than the mawkin o' the field. As poor a two-fisted thing as ever I saw, you know you was. Who taught you to scrub a floor, I should like to know ? Why, you'd leave the dirt in heaps i' the corners—anybody 'ud think you'd never been brought up among Christians. And as for spinning, why you've wasted as much as your wage i' the flax you've spoiled learning to spin. And you've a right to feel that, and not go about as gaping and as thoughtless as if you was beholding to nobody. Comb the wool for the whittaws, indeed ! That's what you'd like to be doing, is it ? That's the way with you—that's the road you'd all like to go, headlong to ruin. You're never easy till you've got some sweetheart as is as big a fool as yourself ; you think you'll be finely off when you're married, I daresay, and have got a three-legged stool to sit on, and never a blanket to cover you, and a bit o' oatcake for your dinner as three children are a-snatching at."

Yet George Eliot does use words that have not found the sanctuary of the dictionary, although the horns of its altar have been grasped by greater lingual offenders. Amongst these we name, at random, the following: Curchey, chapellin, overrun (run away), dawnin' (morning), nattering, plash, coxy, queechy, franzy, megrim, fettle. It is needless to attempt a complete list, as George Eliot's dialect words appear to be all included in the *Leicestershire Glossary** of Dr. Evans, who states that "None of the Leicestershire writers are so rich in illustrations of the Leicestershire dialect as Shakspere and Drayton; while in our own time by far its best literary exponent is the Warwickshire author of *Adam Bede* and *Middlemarch.*" A writer in the *Quarterly Review* (October, 1860), amongst some unjust criticism, bears testimony to the excellence of her presentation of folk-speech.

Thus the most serious characters make the most solemn and most pathetic speeches in provincial dialect and ungrammatical constructions, although it must be allowed that the authoress has not ventured so far in this way as to play with the use and abuse of the aspirate. And her dialect appears to be very carefully studied, although we may doubt whether the Staffordshire provincialisms of *Clerical Life* and *Adam Bede* are sufficiently varied when the scene is shifted in the latest book to the Lincolnshire side of the Humber. But where a greater variation than that between one midland dialect and another is required, George Eliot's conscientiousness is very curiously shown. There is in *Mr. Gilfil's Story* a gardener of the name of Bates, who is described as a Yorkshireman; and in *Adam Bede* there is another gardener, Mr. Craig, whose name would naturally indicate a Scotchman. Each of these horticulturists is introduced into the dialogue, and of course the reader would naturally think one to talk Yorkshire and the other to talk some Scotch. But the authoress apparently did not feel herself mistress of either Scotch or Yorkshire to such a degree as would have warranted her in attempting them; and therefore, before her characters are allowed to open their mouths, she, in each case, is careful

---

* Leicestershire Words, Phrases, and Proverbs, by the late A. B. Evans, D D Edited by Sebastian Evans, LL.D). (English Dialect Society, 1881.)

to tell us that we must moderate our expectations: "Mr. Bates's lips were of a peculiar cut, and I fancy this had something to do with the peculiarity of his dialect, which, as we shall see, was individual rather than provincial." "I think it was Mr. Craig's pedigree only that had the advantage of being Scotch, and not his 'bringing up,' for except that he had a stronger burr in his accent, his speech differed little from that of the Loamshire people around him."

The reviewer's *dicta* are open to some objection alike as to fact and deduction. Mr. Casson, for instance, both uses and abuses the aspirate in his utterances, and the amount of literary material both in "Scotch" and "Yorkshire" would easily have enabled her to become familiar with the general character and structure of those forms of speech. Surely this would have been a small matter compared to her resurrection of a dead age of Italian history.

Whatever uncertainty may have existed as to the varieties of our English folk-speech uttered by the characters of George Eliot must be set at rest by a letter to Professor Skeat, in which George Eliot has expounded her own theories as to the artistic use of dialect.* She says: "It must be borne in mind that my inclination to be as close as I could to the rendering of dialect, both in words and spelling, was constantly checked by the artistic duty of being generally intelligible." This, it will be seen, is the chief distinction between the scientific method which addresses either philological experts or a public—however small— thoroughly familiar with the dialect itself. "But for that check," continues George Eliot, "I should have given a stronger colour to the dialogue in *Adam Bede*, which is modelled on the talk of North Staffordshire and the neighbouring part of Derbyshire. The spelling, being determined by my own ear alone, was necessarily a matter of anxiety,

---

* English Dialect Society: Bibliographical List, Part I., 1873, p. viii.

for it would be as possible to quarrel about it as about the spelling of Oriental names. The district imagined as the scene of *Silas Marner* is in North Warwickshire; but here, and in all my other presentations of life except *Adam Bede*, it has been my intention to give the general physiognomy rather than a close portraiture of the provincial speech as I have heard it in the Midland or Mercian region. It is a just demand that art should keep clear of such specialities as would make it a puzzle for the larger part of its public; still one is not bound to respect the lazy obtuseness or snobbish ignorance of people who do not care to know more of their native tongue than the vocabulary of the drawing-room and the newspaper." This last sentence may be commended alike to those who write in any dialect and to those superfine critics who have not skill to discern the difference between provincial words and mere vulgarisms.

It may be asked why Dinah Morris, the saintly Methodist woman preacher, although on the same social and educational plane as the dialect-speaking characters of *Adam Bede*, is rarely represented as employing any provincial words or phrases. The reason is that such intensely religious English natures, nurturing mind and soul upon the pure English of the Bible, have their entire diction permeated by the influence of its words, which have always a certain dignity and sometimes the truest grandeur and poetic force. Elizabeth Evans*, the original of Dinah Bede, has left an autobiography

---

* How far Elizabeth Evans was the original of Dinah Morris may be seen from George Eliot's letter to Miss Hennell. (*Pall Mall Gazette*, Jan. 6, 1881.)

The likeness between the two had been pointed out by "Guy Roslyn," who gives an abstract of her autobiography. It is remarkable that the incident of the "Face crowned thorns" is not mentioned in it, though it forms so important a part both in the story of Dinah Morris and in George Eliot's own account of her aunt. The provincialism alluded to is in the sentence: "Earth was a *scale* to heaven." The word is not glossed by Dr. Evans. There is a portrait of Elizabeth Evans in *Harper's Magazine*, May, 1881.

extending over several pages, and this narrative, though highly charged with religious fervour, contains only one word that can be regarded as unfamiliar to conventional English. There is another reason why George Eliot would have been justified in not putting dialect words into the mouth of her fair saint.   When we see anyone possessed of and possessed by a spirit of intense religious earnestness and seeking for the good of others, we do not notice the strange or uncouth fashion in which their message may be delivered.   The accidents of speech and manner are burned up like dross in the fire of their zeal, and only the real gold is left behind.   Their mannerisms, whether of action or of speech, do not affect us, and are unnoticed.   We are not conscious of this or that imperfect form of words, but hear only that higher language in which soul calls to soul.

THE ORIGIN OF SUNDAY SCHOOLS.

BIBLIOGRAPHY.

"*Life of S. Charles Borromeo.*" *Edited by Edward Healey Thompson, M.A. London: Burns and Oates. 8vo.*

"*Acta Ecclesiæ Mediolanensis, a Sancto Carolo Cardinali S. Praxedis Archiep. Condita, Federici Cardinalis Borromæi Archiepiscopi Mediolani jussu undique diligentius collecta et edita.*" *Lugduni, 1782, fol., Tomus Secundus.*

"*Geschichte der Pädagogik.*" *Von Dr. Carl Schmidt. Gothen, 1867, 8vo.*

"*Memoir of Miss Hannah Ball, of High Wycombe, in Buckinghamshire.*" *Originally compiled by the Rev. Joseph Cole; revised and enlarged by John Parker, gent. London: Mason, 1839. 12mo.*

"*Memoir of the late Mr. Adam Crompton.*" *By the Rev. Dr. Barnes, in the "European Magazine," vol. xxiv., p. 413.*

"*Rural and Historical Gleanings in South Lancashire.*" *By Joseph Fielding.*

"*Robert Raikes, Journalist and Philanthropist: A History of the Origin of Sunday Schools.*" *By Alfred Gregory. London: Hodder and Stoughton, 1877. 12mo.*

"*A Paper on the Early History of Sunday Schools, especially in Northamptonshire.*" *By the Rev. W. J. Bain. 2nd edition. Northamptonshire, 1875. 8vo.*

"*History and Object of the Sunday School.*" *By James Cowper Gray, London: Stock. 8vo.*

"*Rapports du Jury de l'Exposition International de Paris, 1867,*" *t. xiii., p. 168.*

THE ORIGIN OF SUNDAY SCHOOLS.

Die Sonntagschulen bilden die Grundlage der englischen Volkser-
ziehung: mehr als die Hälfte der Kinder von England und Wales
besucht Sonntagschulen.—*Dr. Karl Schmidt's Geschichte der Pädagogik
b. iv. Gothen*, 1867, *p.* 718.

SUNDAY Schools can claim a much greater antiquity than
has been generally supposed. Saint Carlo Borromeo,
in 1564, instituted Sunday schools, in which instruction was
given to the little folk who were obliged in the week-days to
work for bread, and his example had several imitators in
Italy. The institutions thus originated deserve more attention than has been paid to them in connection with the
origin of Sunday schools. Both the Council of the Lateran
and that of Trent ordered that in all parishes, both on Sun-
days and holidays, the principles of Christian faith should be
taught to the children. In obedience to this injunction,
Cardinal Borromeo, at his first provincial council, directed the
priests under his control to collect the children for catechetical
purposes. He also organised a zealous body of lay-teachers
to help the clergy in this work. Some of these were sent
afterwards in missionary fashion into the different towns and
villages of his diocese. The excellence and importance of
the work done in Milan was recognised by Pope Gregory
XIII. in a letter of indulgence, dated 30th October, 1572.
This is printed in the " Acta Ecclesiæ Mediolanensis," with a
list of similar documents of earlier date. Pope Pius IV. also

testified his approbation by a stamped bull, dated 6th October, 1567.   The rules for the regulation of the teachers, who were formed into a company or society, are numerous, and, as might be expected, the greatest stress is laid upon the necessity of teaching the dogmas and observances of the faith.   There is no allusion to imparting merely secular knowledge, except that writing was to be taught to certain scholars of special ability.   The body of teachers were organised as the " Compania della Dottrina Christiana," and included both ecclesiastics and laymen.   The affairs of all the schools in the diocese were managed by a congregation of teachers, all subject to episcopal supervision.   There were also schools for women under similar regulations.   The school system founded by Borromeo still survives, and the accounts given by travellers show how fully it anticipates many of the characteristics of Sunday schools in our own country.

The Rev. John Chetwood Eustace, writing early in the pre-sent century, pays a deserved tribute to the virtues of St. Charles Borromeo, and remarks that " Many of his excellent institutions still remain, and among others that of Sunday schools ; and it is both novel and affecting to behold on that day the vast area of the cathedral filled with children, forming two grand divisions of boys and girls, ranged opposite each other, and these again sub-divided into classes according to their age and capacity, drawn up between the pillars, while two or more instructors attend each class, and direct their questions and explanations to every little individual without distinction.   A clergyman attends each class, accompanied by one or more laymen for the boys, and for the girls by as many matrons.   The lay persons are said to be oftentimes of the first distinction.   Tables are placed in different recesses for writing."

The same writer, in another part of his work, further remarks : " In the diocese of Milan, or, to speak more properly, in the vast tract of country included between the Alps and the Apennines, and subject to the visitation of the Archiepiscopal See of Milan, in every parochial church the bell tolls at two o'clock on every Sunday in the year, and all the youth of the parish assemble in the church. The girls are placed on one side, the boys on the other ; they are then divided into classes according to their ages and their progress, and instructed either by the clergy attached to the church, or by pious persons who voluntarily devote their time to this most useful employment ; whilst the pastor himself goes from class to class, examines sometimes one, sometimes another, and closes the whole at four o'clock by a catechistical discourse." Such schools were in existence in many places in Italy before the time of Borromeo, but he gave them an extension, activity, and organisation which has lasted to our own day. His friend, Giusano, tells us that there were at one time as many as 740 of these schools in the diocese, with 3,040 teachers and 40,098 scholars.

At Lyons, in 1666, Ch. Demia is said to have commenced Sunday schools for both sexes. The programme appears to have been confined to singing, reading the lives of the saints, and catechetical exercises, quite innocent of any present-world knowledge. Men and women were amongst the pupils, and the object seems to have been rather to keep them away from the tavern and other dangerous places than to impart anything of definite instruction. In 1709 some educational value was imparted to them, for in that year the parish of Saint Sulpice saw a very remarkable experiment. M. de la Salle was concerned in some free schools for poor children, and at the suggestion of M. de la Chétardie, curé of St. Sulpice, he added to them Sunday schools, in which reading, writing orthography, arithmetic, geometry, and design were taught For this purpose he trained the most promising of his day school teachers and pupils to be teachers in the Sunday school, and they soon had 200 young men under their care. Unfortunately the new masters soon became too proud of their newly-acquired learning, and deserted their benefactor. Unable to meet the expense of training a second set of teachers, the school, after only a few years' existence, was discontinued.

It is said that there was a kind of Sunday school at work at Priesthill, in Scotland, in 1680.

Sunday schools are also of considerable antiquity in Germany, for the learned Dr. Schmidt remarks that "Sunday schools supplement primary schools, in order that those children who through home occupation were deprived of a regular school education might receive requisite instruction, and that those who had been already confirmed might have what they had learned at school kept up to the mark. This was the case in Wurtemberg as early as 1695." It will be remarked that Dr. Schmidt makes no allusion to the Sunday school said to have been established by Martin Luther in 1527.

The clergy of the Isle of Man, in a convocation held under Bishop Wilson, 3rd February, 1703, adopted "constitutions" for the establishment of Sunday schools, and these were ratified and made law at a Court of Tynwald, held 6th June, in the same year.

Mrs. Catharine Boevy is recorded upon her monument in Flaxby Church, Gloucestershire, to have been active in "clothing and feeding her indigent neighbours and teaching their children, some of whom every Sunday she entertained at her house, and condescended to examine them herself." She died in 1726.

America sometimes claims precedence with the mother country as the originator of Sunday schools. The German Seventh-day Baptists, who settled at Ephrata, Lancaster county, Pennsylvania, are said to have a Sunday school there founded by Ludwig Hacker between 1740 and 1747.

The Rev. Theophilus Lindsay, who was afterwards so eminent amongst the Unitarians whilst incumbent of Catterick, in Yorkshire, founded a Sunday school, which is said to be still in operation.

There is still existing at High Wycombe a Sunday school believed to have been founded in 1769. Miss Hannah Ball was a disciple of Wesley's, and in a letter to him described her scholars as a wild little company. She took the children to the church. After her death the school was continued by a younger sister, Miss Ann Ball. A relation who had been a Wesleyan rejoined the church, and at the funeral of this re-convert, the Rev. W. B. Williams preached a funeral sermon, in which he was uncharitable enough to say that if an Arminian ever entered heaven, the very angels would cease to sing. Amongst those present were Ann Ball and her scholars. She stood up in her pew, and it was thought she would address the people, but instead of this she marched out at the head of her little flock, and they never re-entered as a body. This was about 1799 or 1800. The school, in 1801, was re-organised on the plan of the other Wesleyan schools then existing.

A Sunday school is said to have been started in County Down, Ireland, in 1770.

In 1778 the Rev. Thomas Stock, M.A., afterwards the zealous co-operator of Raikes, is said to have had a school at Ashbury, in Berkshire. In the same year the Rev. David Simpson was at the head of a large Sunday school at Macclesfield. In 1786 it was handed over to the committee for Sunday schools, and ten years later, under the influence of Mr. Simpson, payment was abolished and voluntary teaching became the rule.

Some years before the date of Raikes' first attempt to gather the children, Mr. Adam Crompton, paper maker, of Little Lever, maintained a Sunday school, which was under the care of one James Heyes. Dr. Thomas Barnes says: "I lived for many years a near neighbour to this poor man, and admired what I then thought to be his disinterested kindness in devoting every Sunday, when by infirmity disabled from attending public worship, to so charitable an office. It was not till long after that I discovered the plan and the support to be the work of Mr. Crompton, who had concealed this, as he wished to do his other charities, even from his nearest friends and relations, among whom I had the pleasure of being numbered." Mr. Adam Crompton died 30th October, 1793, aged 72. Notwithstanding these numerous instances, it is Robert Raikes we must look to as the real beginner of the Sunday school system. The plan which he adopted in 1780 was the starting point of the modern institution. Raikes was very greatly pained by the vice and immorality that made hideous certain portions of his native place. Mr. William King, a benevolent Dissenter, not improbably was the sower of the seed which fructified in the

mind of the Gloucester printer.   They were conversing on
the desecration of the Sabbath, and Raikes asked, "How is
it to be altered?"   The reply was : "Sir, open a Sunday school,
as I have opened one, at Dursley, with the help of a faithful
journeyman ; but the multitude of business prevents me from
spending so much time in it as I could wish, as I feel I want
rest." Mr. Raikes replied : "It will not do for the
Dissenters." "Then," said Mr. King, "why not the Church
do it?"

Raikes having inserted a paragraph in his paper—the
Gloucester Journal—on the new scheme for the reformation
of juvenile morals, it was copied into many papers, and
attracted a great deal of attention.   Amongst others who
wrote to him for information was Colonel Towneley, of
Belfield Hall.   The letter, in reply, gave an interesting
account of the manner in which the idea had suggested itself
to his mind.   It was printed in the *Gentleman's Magazine* for
June, 1784.   Colonel Towneley carried out a similar plan.
Thomas Henshaw, the founder of the Blind Asylum, was
another patron of Sunday schools in Lancashire, and
encouraged writing as a part of the programme.   "They
considered it to be a useful and necessary part of Sunday
school instruction."

The transition from paid to unpaid teachers is the most
important point in the history of Sunday schools.   In Italy,
Borromeo appears to have relied upon voluntary effort. The
school at High Wycombe owes its existence to the unpaid
labours of Miss Ball and her sisters. The schools established
by Crompton and by Raikes were both worked by the
agency of paid teachers. With the immense extension of
the system, the financial arrangements would have been

13

difficult to manage. This is evident from the fact that even in Gloucester the lack of funds to pay the teachers led to a temporary stoppage of the schools in 1811. Whoever was first able to inspire the enthusiasm of volunteers willing to labour without money and without price should be regarded as the second founder of the Sunday school system. This part of the record is very obscure. No doubt this obvious remedy for deficient finances would be applied simultaneously in many quarters. The earliest Sunday school with voluntary teachers of which any account has come under my notice was also in Lancashire. The Wesleyan Methodists of Oldham in 1785 were anxious to establish a Sunday school, and the project was discussed at a class meeting. The leaders were convinced of the utility of the project, but as they were principally operatives the cost was considered to be a fatal bar to the scheme. Mr. Samuel Scholes, of Higher Moor, made this suggestion : " Lads, I'll tell you what we must do ; we must each of us find a teacher ; we must all come and try what we can do ; and if you'll do so we can have a Sunday school." This homely and sensible remark led to the formation of a Sunday school in March, 1785, at the Old Chapel, Bent Brow. In 1787 Thomas Holt and nine others started a Sunday school at Blackley. It was held alternately in each other's houses. In 1790 the Rev. John Griffiths preached a sermon for them, and the collection brought in £28 14s., which enabled them to buy books. In 1794 they were able to erect a building of their own.

Sam Bamford, in his " Early Days," has left an interesting picture of one of these old-fashioned Methodist schools. It was held in the chapel at bottom of Barrow Fields, Middleton. " Every Sunday morning," he says, " at half-past eight o'clock, was this old Methodists' school opened for the instruction of whatever child crossed its threshold. A hymn was first led out and sung by the scholars and teachers. An extempore prayer followed, all the scholars and teachers kneeling at their places; the classes, ranging from those of the spelling-book to those of the Bible, then commenced their lessons, girls in the gallery above and boys below. Desks, which could either be moved up or down like the leaf of a table, were arranged all round the school, against the walls of the gallery, as well as against those below; and at measured distances the walls were numbered. Whilst the Bible and Testament classes were reading their first lesson the desks were got ready; ink-stands and copy-books numbered, containing copies and pens, were placed opposite corresponding numbers on the wall, and when the lesson was concluded the writers took their places, each at his own number, and so continued their instruction. When the copy was finished the book was shut and left on the desk, a lesson of spelling was gone through, and at twelve o'clock singing and prayer again took place, and the scholars were dismissed. At one o'clock there was service in the chapel; and soon after two the school reassembled, girls now occupying the writing desks, as boys had done in the fore-noon; and at four or half-past the scholars were sent home for the week. My readers will expect hearing that the school was well attended, and it was so, not only by children and youths of the immediate neighbourhood, but by young men and women from distant localities. Big collier-lads and their sisters from Siddal Moor were regular in their attendance. From the borders of Whittle, from Bowlee, from the White Moss, from Jumbo, and Chadderton, and Thornham, came groups of boys and girls, with their substantial dinners tied in

clean napkins, and the little chapel was so crowded that when
the teachers moved they had to wade, as it were, through the
close-ranked youngsters." Those who went before him were
content to attempt the cure of a local evil by a local remedy.
Raikes had a keener vision, and to his quiet yet persistent
advocacy it is owing that Sunday schools are now flourishing
in every part of the civilised world.

It is interesting to see the manner in which the great idea of
Raikes was anticipated in different countries and by different
minds. This does not in any sense detract from the credit
that is due to Robert Raikes. He saw the capabilities of the
plan of Sunday schools, and by the publicity he gave to it
paved the way for that great extension which has made it so
remarkable as a social and educational agency.

THE COST

OF

THEATRICAL AMUSEMENTS.

This paper was read before the Manchester Statistical Society, 14th June, 1882, but the figures have been revised and adapted to the year 1887.

THE COST OF THEATRICAL AMUSEMENTS.

A REPORT on the present appropriation of wages and other sources of income was brought before the meeting of the British Association at York in 1881. The committee appointed to consider the subject consisted of Professor Leone Levi, Mr. Stephen Bourne, Mr. Brittain, Dr. Hancock, and Professor Jevons, but the report was the work of Professor Levi alone. In a highly interesting and suggestive fashion, Professor Levi dealt with a variety of topics, and amongst them with the cost of amusements. On this subject it will be well to quote the entire paragraph :—

" AMUSEMENTS.

"In 1877 Mr. Hollingshead gave in evidence that in London there were forty-five theatres licensed by the Lord Chamberlain, and six licensed by the magistrates, with a nightly holding capacity of 76,000, being on an average of twenty per 1,000 inhabitants. Assuming theatrical provision on the same proportion among the 20,000,000 of urban population, there would be provision of 400,000, and at 1s. 6d. each for 200 nights, the total sum would be £6,000,000. The *Era Almanac* gives a list of about 276 theatres, and at an average capacity of 1,400 would give an aggregate capacity of 386,000. The London theatres are considerably larger. Of music halls, the number given in the *Era* is 216. Taking their average capacity at 400 and at 6d. per night, also for 250 nights, the sum so expended would be about £500,000, making, with the theatrical, an expenditure of £6,500,000, only one-fourth of which, viz., £1,600,000, in materials, or in the proportion of 0·12d. gross and 0·03d. net per head per day.

"The Crystal Palace is a type of another order of amusements. By the courtesy of the manager, Major Page, we learn that the average number of visitors who paid for admission in the three years, 1878 to 1880, was 988,760, of whom 833,728 were adults, and 155,032 children, besides nearly as many of season-ticket holders, performers, and others. The ordinary receipt of the company from admissions in 1880 was £40,000, and the amount received from reserved seats and programmes £20,604, making a total of £60,600, giving an average of about 1s. 3d. per person. Add 1s. 6d. for the railway and 6d. for refreshment in excess of the cost at home, we may assume that every visitor pays at least 3s. 3d. There are, however, special days—Boxing Day and Easter Monday, and two other Bank holidays, or equivalent days in the manufacturing districts, in all four days in the year—when a large portion of the population is in quest of amusement. On one such day in London 120,000 find their way to the Crystal and Alexandra Palaces, 72,000 to the different Galleries, and 95,000 to the Zoological, and Horticultural, and Kew Gardens. Assuming that on such days one in ten of the urban population, or about 2,000,000, is bent on amusement, and that on an average 3s. per head is the amount expended, the total for each day would be £300,000, or for the four days £1,200,000.* But there are amusements of quite another order. How shall we estimate the expense incurred on the Derby Day or on racing all the year. There are about 2,500 race-horses, the breeding and training of which cost £300 each, or £750,000. The amount spent in a month's grouse-shooting by a single party is put down at least at £447. Fox-hunting is another heavy source of expenditure. There are 150 packs of fox-hounds kept in England and Wales, the aggregate cost of which, including the cost of hunters, is put down at £700,000. Then there is fishing, coursing, cricket, archery, bicycling,† and numerous other sports, all involving a large expenditure. A total of £6,000,000 a year, of which about one-fourth, or £1,500,000 in materials, or a proportion of 0·11d. gross, and 0·02d. net per head per day, will probably cover all the other forms of amusements in the United Kingdom."

The object of the present paper is to offer a few comments as to the cost to the public of theatres and music halls.

Professor Levi spreads his calculation as to the provision of receipts of theatres over the entire urban population, but

---

* The weekly railway receipts indicate the effect of a holiday on the movements of the people. Taking the entire passengers' receipts of the Great Eastern, Great Northern, Great Western, London and Brighton, London, Chatham, and Dover, London and South-Western, Midland, and London and North-Western for the week before and the week after the Bank holidays in 1880, the excess of receipts amounted to £260,000, but as many take their holiday before the actual day, and many return after the same, the account is not exact. The average receipts per annum for the last three years for traffic to the Crystal Palace by the London, Brighton, and South Coast Railway, was £25,655. On Easter Monday the receipts were £1,084; on Whit Monday, £1,022; on the August Bank Holiday £790, and on Boxing Day £466. [L.L.]

† The Secretary of the Bicycle Union informs us 100,000 may be taken as the number of machines in use, entailing an annual expense of about £500,000, besides the expense of subscription to clubs, uniforms, repairs, and many more items. [L.L.]

the number from whom the Drama draws its patrons must be much fewer.

There are many populous districts in which dramatic amusements have no local habitation at all. The number of theatres estimated to be open at the present date is 258, whilst urban districts are 967 in number. Some of these are however so small that they belong really to the rural half of England. There are, however, 771 urban districts, with a population of more than 3,000.

The inner ring of the population of London may be taken at 3,816,483, and the forty-four metropolitan theatres would therefore mean one theatre for every 86,738. How would this apply to great industrial centres? The population immediately surrounding Manchester is 800,000, and we ought therefore to find at least nine theatres within the district instead of the six that actually exist there. Salford, with a population then of 176,000, opened its only theatre in 1882. Hence, although the proportion given by Professor Levi is perfectly accurate, it must be made up by a number of theatres in the smaller towns. Bath has one theatre and a population of 51,814. Sheffield has two and a population of 284,508. Gorton, with a population of 33,091, has neither theatre nor music hall, whilst Uxbridge with only 7,669 of population has a theatre, and Sandgate with 1,669 people rejoices in a music hall.

The actual topographical distribution of theatres and music halls is shown in the following table, which gives in separate columns the name of the town, its population, and the number of its theatres and music halls.

NAME OF PLACE.	POPULATION.	THEATRES.	MUSIC HALLS.
Aberdare	33,804	0	1
Aberdeen	105,189	1	1
Accrington	31,435	1	2
Airdrie	13,363	1	0
Aldershot	20,155	1	3
Altrincham	11,250	1	0
Arbroath	21,758	1	1
Ashton-under-Lyne	37,040	2	1
Ayr	20,987	1	1
Barnsley	29,790	1	2
Barnstaple	12,282	1	0
Barrow-in-Furness	47,100	1	2
Bath	51,814	1	0
Belfast	207,671	1	2
Berwick-on-Tweed	13,998	0	1
Beverley	11,425	1	0
Birkenhead	84,006	1	2
Bilston	22,730	1	0
Birmingham	400,774	4	8
Bishop Auckland	10,097	1	1
Blackburn	104,014	3	1
Blackpool	14,229	5	0
Blyth	20,974	1	0
Bolton	105,414	1	2
Bournemouth	16,858	1	0
Bootle	27,374	1	1
Boston	14,941	1	1
Bradford	183,032	2	2
Brecon	6,623	1	0
Brighton	107,546	1	2
Bristol	206,874	2	2
Brownhills	11,059	0	1
Burnley	58,751	3	2
Burslem	26,522	1	3
Burton-on-Trent	39,288	1	1
Bury St. Edmunds	16,111	1	0
Bury (Lancashire)	52,213	1	2
Cambridge	40,878	1	0

NAME OF PLACE.	POPULATION.	THEATRES.	MUSIC HALLS.
Canterbury	21,704	1	1
Cardiff	82,761	1	3
Carlisle	35,884	1	1
Chatham	26,424	0	1
Castleford	10,530	1	0
Cheltenham	43,972	1	1
Chester	36,794	1	1
Chesterfield	12,221	1	2
Chorley	19,478	1	0
Coatbridge	10,501	1	0
Colchester	28,374	1	1
Colne (Lancashire)	18,795	0	1
Consett	7,163	1	2
Cork	97,526	1	0
Coventry	42,111	1	1
Croydon	78,953	1	0
Crewe	24,385	1	1
Darlington	35,104	1	1
Darwen	33,557	1	0
Deal	8,500	0	1
Derby	81,168	2	1
Dewsbury	29,637	1	0
Devonport	48,939	1	1
Doncaster	21,139	1	0
Douglas	54,089	3	0
Dover	30,270	2	2
Dublin	273,064	2	3
Dumbarton	13,786	1	0
Dumfries	17,092	1	1
Dundee	140,239	2	2
Dunfermline	17,084	1	0
Durham	15,372	1	0
Earlestown (Lancashire)	10,500	1	0
Eastbourne	22,014	2	1
Edinburgh	228,357	2	1
Elgin	7,388	1	0
Exeter	37,665	1	0
Falkirk	13,170	1	0

NAME OF PLACE.	POPULATION.	THEATRES.	MUSIC HALLS.
Farnborough	9,310	0	1
Farnworth	20,708	1	0
Fleetwood	6,733	0	1
Folkestone	18,816	1	1
Gainsborough	10,873	1	1
Gateshead	65,803	0	1
Glasgow	511,415	5	6
Gloucester	36,521	1	1
Goole	10,418	1	0
Grantham	16,886	1	0
Gravesend	23,303	1	1
Greenock	66,704	1	1
Greenwich	206,651	1	1
Great Bridge	13,690	0	1
Great Yarmouth	46,159	2	0
Great Grimsby	28,503	2	2
Guernsey	35,257	1	0
Halesowen	16,263	0	1
Halifax	73,630	2	1
Hanley	48,361	1	1
Harrogate	14,138	0	1
Hartlepool		0	0
Hartlepool (East)	40,884	0	1
Hartlepool (West)		2	0
Hastings	42,258	1	1
Hereford	19,821	1	1
Huddersfield	81,841	1	1
Hull	161,519	1	2
Hyde	28,630	1	1
Inverness, N.B.	20,000	1	0
Ipswich	50,546	1	1
Ilkeston	9,662	0	1
Jarrow-on-Tyne	25,469	1	1
Jersey	52,455	1	0
Keighley	25,247	1	0
Kidderminster	24,270	1	1

NAME OF PLACE.	POPULATION.	THEATRES.	MUSIC HALLS.
Kidsgrove	3,994	0	1
Kilmarnock	25,844	1	0
King's Lynn	18,539	1	0
Kirkcaldy	23,315	1	0
Kendal	13,696	1	0
Lancaster	20,663	1	1
Leamington	22,979	1	1
Leeds	309,119	2	2
Leek	12,863	1	0
Leicester	122,376	2	2
Leigh	21,734	1	0
Leith	59,485	0	1
Lewes	6,017	1	0
Limerick	48,246	1	0
Lincoln	37,313	2	1
Liverpool	552,508	6	6
London	3,816,483	44	31
Londonderry	28,947	1	0
Longton	18,620	1	1
Lowestoft	19,696	1	0
Luton	23,960	1	1
Macclesfield	37,514	1	1
Maidstone	29,623	1	0
Manchester	393,676	5	4
Margate	16,030	2	2
Merthyr	48,861	1	0
Middlesborough	55,934	1	1
Montrose	14,994	1	0
Morecambe	6,000	0	1
Motherwell, N.B.	17,000	1	0
Neath	10,409	0	1
Newcastle-under-Lyme	17,508	1	0
Newcastle-upon-Tyne	145,349	2	3
Newport	35,313	2	1
Northampton	51,881	1	1
North Shields	20,384	1	2
Norwich	87,842	1	2

NAME OF PLACE.	POPULATION.	THEATRES.	MUSIC HALLS.
Nottingham	186,575	2	2
Oldbury	18,841	0	1
Oldham	152,511	2	2
Oxford	39,186	1	0
Paisley	55,638	2	1
Penzance	12,409	1	0
Perth	28,980	1	0
Peterborough	21,228	1	0
Plymouth	73,794	1	2
Porth	30,250	0	1
Portsmouth	127,989	1	3
Pontypool	5,244	1	0
Preston	96,537	2	1
Ramsgate	22,683	2	2
Ratcliffe Bridge	16,276	1	0
Reading	42,054	1	2
Redditch	9,961	1	0
Richmond	19,066	1	0
Rochdale	68,866	1	2
Rochester	21,307	1	0
Rotherham	34,782	1	3
Runcorn	15,126	1	0
Ryde	28,318	1	0
Salford	176,235	1	0
Sandgate	1,669	0	1
Scarborough	30,504	4	1
Seaham Harbour	7,132	1	1
Sheerness	14,286	0	2
Sheffield	284,508	2	5
Shields (South)	56,875	1	2
Shrewsbury	26,478	1	0
Southampton	60,051	1	2
Southend	7,979	1	0
Southport	32,206	1	1
Spennymoor	5,917	1	1
Stafford	19,977	1	0

NAME OF PLACE.	POPULATION.	THEATRES.	MUSIC HALLS.
Stalybridge	22,785	I	0
Stamford	8,773	I	0
Stirling	16,012	I	0
Stockport	59,553	I	I
Stockton-on-Tees	41,015	I	I
St. Helens	57,403	I	I
Stourbridge	9,757	I	0
Stoke-on-Trent	19,261	0	I
Stratford	26,055	I	0
Stratford-on-Avon	8,054	I	0
Sunderland	116,548	2	2
Swansea	65,597	2	2
Swindon	22,374	I	0
Taunton	16,614	I	0
Todmorden	23,862	I	I
Torquay	24,767	I	0
Trowbridge	11,040	I	I
Truro	10,619	I	0
Tunstall	14,244	I	0
Uxbridge	7,669	I	0
Wakefield	30,854	I	I
Walsall	58,795	I	3
Waltham Abbey	5,368	0	I
Warrington	41,452	2	I
Waterford	28,952	I	0
West Bromwich	56,295	I	0
Weymouth	13,715	I	0
Whitby	14,086	I	2
Whitehaven	19,295	I	I
Widnes	48,194	I	0
Wigan	48,196	2	2
Wigton	3,948	I	0
Windsor	12,273	I	0
Wishaw	13,112	0	I
Wolverhampton	75,766	2	2
Worcester	33,956	I	I
Workington	13,308	I	I
Woolwich	80,782	I	I

NAME OF PLACE.	POPULATION.	THEATRES.	MUSIC HALLS.
Wrexham	10,978	1	0
York	49,530	1	1
Total	15,115,984	302	244

The figures for Douglas are those of the entire island.

From this table it appears that the localities possessing theatres have an aggregate population of 15,115,984. No doubt some allowance must be made for the surrounding populations, who, although not included in this enumeration, would doubtless be at least occasional patrons of the theatres and music halls. Taking 3,000,000 as the population of the metropolis, there will be about 12,000,000 out of the 20,000,000 of urban population in the provinces who are within reach of theatrical amusements.

With the assistance of friends who have special opportunities of accurate knowledge, the theatres in the list for 1881 have been classified according to their probable average yearly receipts. For obvious reasons it would be indiscreet and undesirable to publish this data in full, but no such objection can apply to tabulating the results.

ESTIMATED RECEIPTS OF LONDON THEATRES.

1 Theatre, with average yearly receipts of £100,000	...£100,000
3	,,	,,	60,000 ...	180,000
6	,,	,,	50,000 ...	300,000
3	,,	,,	40,000 ...	120,000
9	,,	,,	30,000 ...	270,000
11	,,	,,	20,000 ...	220,000
1	,,	,,	12,000 ...	12,000
7	,,	,,	5,000 ...	35,000

Crystal Palace
Alexandra Palace 〉 120,000 ... 120,000
Albert Palace

1,357,000

14

ESTIMATED RECEIPTS OF PROVINCIAL THEATRES.

3	Theatres, with average yearly receipts of £30,000	...	£90,000
3	„	„	25,000	... 75,000
6	„	„	20,000	... 120,000
9	„	„	15,000	.. 135,000
· 7	„	„	12,000	... 84,000
4	„	„	10,000	... 40,000
18	„	„	8,000	... 144,000
16	„	„	6,000	... 96,000
15	„	„	5,000	... 75,000
29	„	„	4,000	... 116,000
15	„	„	3,000	... 45,000
18	„	„	2,500	... 45,000
42	„	„	2,000	... 84,000
11	„	„	1,500	... 16,500
62	„	„	1,000	... 62,000
258				1,227,500

Music Halls vary greatly, from the mammoth establishments, which flourish in some of the great cities, to mere extensions of the old-fashioned free and easy. It may fairly be doubted whether the Metropolitan Halls average more than £5,000 yearly receipts, and the places of amusement classed under the same name in the " Provinces " are probably not in receipt of more than half that sum. This agrees with Professor Levi's estimate, which is obtained by a different process. The receipts of the London Theatres are of course exceptionally difficult to estimate with any degree of accuracy, on account of their notable variation in size, quality, and popularity. They cater not only for the resident population of the Metropolis, but for its army of visitors. The success of the season, drawing crowded houses, may be followed by something which fails to hit the public taste, and the nightly receipts fall from three figures to two or even one.

With the reservations which these considerations naturally suggest, the average yearly receipts of theatres and music halls may be thus estimated :—

ESTIMATED RECEIPTS OF THEATRES AND MUSIC HALLS.

258 Provincial Theatres.................................£1,227,500	
31 London Music Halls at an aevarge of £5,000 per annum	155,000
213 Provincial Music Halls at an average of £2,500 per annum	532,500
44 London Theatres	1,357,000
	£3,272,000

Professor Levi estimates the cost of theatres and music halls to the public at £6,500,000. By the method already described in this note, an estimate of £3,272,000 is obtained. There is no great discrepancy between the two, for Professor Levi's estimate includes all the cost of transit to and from the theatre, refreshments, &c., whilst the other is an attempt to gauge the revenue of the theatrical world. Even the smaller sum is sufficiently large to impress the imagination.

The object of this paper is statistical, not ethical. There may be some of us who sympathise with the famous saying of Sir G. C. Lewis, that " life would be tolerable were it not for its amusements." There may be others who regret to see sums, which are certainly large in the aggregate, devoted to what on a superficial examination may appear to be super-fluities. That there is ample room for improvement in the quality if not in the quantity of our amusements few will deny. Amusement for the bulk of mankind is not a luxury but a necessity. Whatever the pecuniary cost of amusement may be it is infinitely cheaper than no amusement at all.

ENGLISH THE DOMINANT
LANGUAGE OF THE FUTURE.

"*A Scheme for making the English Language the International Language for the World.*" *By James Bradshaw. Manchester. 8vo., pp. iv., 73. 1847.*

"*On the Probable Future Position of the English Language.*" *By Thomas Watts. (Proceedings of the Philological Society, vol. iv., p. 207, 1857.) 1850.*

"*The Universal Language; Reasons for a Phonetic Representation of the English Language.*" *By William White. Bath. 8vo., pp. 8. 1854.*

"*Reasons for a Phonetic Representation of the English Language.*" *By William White. Bath. 8vo., pp. 8. 1864.*

"*Histoire des Sciences et de Savants.*" *Par Alphonse de Candolle. Génève, 8vo. 1873.*

"*On the Advantage of a Dominant Language for Science.*" *By Alphonse de Candolle. (Translated by Miss Miers, by permission of the Author. From the "Annals and Magazine of Natural History," 1873. To this is added an interesting Appendix of Notes, by Dr. J. E. Gray, F.R.S.) 1873.*

"*The Future of the English Language.*" *By William E. A. Axon. ("Quarterly Journal of Science," vol. iii., 2nd series), pp. 367-386. 1873.*

"*The Future of the English Language: An argument for a Spelling Reform.*" *By William E. A. Axon, M.R.S.L., F.S.S. (Reprinted [with additions] from the "Quarterly Journal of Science" for July, 1873. London: F. Pitman; Bath: I. Pitman. 8vo., pp. 24.) 1874.*

"*Das Englische als Universal—Sprache der Zukunft.*" *Von Nicholaus Ruffner-Casper. Iter Theil. Bellagio, Lago di Como. 8vo., pp. x., 38. 1874.*

"*On Spelling.*" *By F. Max Müller, Professor of Philology in the University of Oxford. London: F. Pitman; Bath: Isaac Pitman. 8vo., pp. 46. 1880.*

"*The Plough and the Dollar: or the Englishry of a Century hence.*" *By F. Barham Zincke. London: Kegan Paul & Co. 1883.*

"*The English-speaking Populations of the World.*" *By Hyde Clarke (British Association Report, p. 618). 1883.*

"*An International Language.*" *By Malthus Questell Holyoake. London. 12mo. 1884. (This project was extensively reviewed. A letter from Mr. Holyoake appeared in the "Morning Advertiser," 29th November, in reply to a leading article in that paper of 11th October.)*

"*Les langues de la Civilisation.*" *Par W. E. A. Axon. (Revue Internationale.) 1884.*

"*Histoire des Sciences et de Savants.*" *Par Alphonse de Candolle. Nouvelle Edition. Génève et Bâle. 8vo., pp. 594. 1884.*

"*On the Future of the English-speaking Peoples. (A letter written by Right Hon. W. E. Gladstone, M.P., and dated 4th Oct., 1884, although first published in the New York "Tribune," 1st Feb., 1885. It was reprinted in "The Times," 13th Feb., 1885, and commented upon in many English papers at the time.) 1884.*

The following paper was read at the Phonographic Jubilee Celebration Manchester, August 29th, 1887.

ENGLISH THE DOMINANT LANGUAGE OF THE FUTURE.

THE possible future extension of the great languages of the world, although a purely speculative matter, is one of considerable interest, whether regarded from a sentimental or a practical point of view. There is in existence a society for the diffusion of the French language. The Alliance Française has begun its missionary efforts in Tunis, Algeria, and the Levant. The dream of a universal language, once a favourite idea of philosophers, has been abandoned, but it may be confidently asserted that the nearest approach to it is furnished by the English language. There was a time when Europe in a certain sense possessed a universal language, for Latin was the common medium for the thoughts and communications of the scanty portion of mankind to whom culture was then possible. It was the language of the Church and the schools, and therefore the language also of science, law, and diplomacy. But with the growth of popular literatures, the speech of the cloisters fell gradually into disuse. The literary spirit combined with patriotism and religious emotion to give coherence to what had previously been little more than despised dialects. Latin long retained its hold upon science; French became the vehicle by which the diplomats concealed their thoughts; Spanish enterprise led to the extension of that tongue to the New World; and then the colonising force of England planted in every corner of the globe settlements of those who spoke, in at least a modified form, the language of Milton and Shakespeare. The statistics of languages have, perhaps, not yet received the attention they deserve. Amongst savage races, without writing, language is in a continual state of flux. Adelung reckoned the existing dialects of his day at 3,664. Balbi enumerated 860 languages, forming, perhaps, 5,000 dialects. Max Müller thinks the number of languages is not less than 900. The great living languages are, however, comparatively few, and some inquiry as to the numerical strength and other characteristics of the races by whom they are spoken, will enable us to see what chance France possesses of seeing her clear idiom become the common speech of the world. We may leave out of account the Oriental languages, which have, at present, no progressive force. The unknown possibilities of Russia are great, but that empire of millions is said to have at least two dozen languages within its wild boundaries.

The late Thomas Watts, one of the greatest of English linguists, was one of the first to recognise the possible future of the English language. When Rivarol, in 1783, gained the prize of the Berlin Academy for his dissertation on the universality of the French language, he unhesitatingly gave the supremacy to the speech of Gaul. But earlier, David Hume, with a prescient spirit, induced Gibbon, who had contemplated writing his " Decline and Fall " in French, to select rather his native tongue. " Our solid and increasing establishments in America," he said, "where we need less dread the inundations of barbarians, promise a superior stability and duration to the English language." This has become more probable with each succeeding decade. Mr. Thomas Watts, writing, it must be remembered, in 1850, said: " At present the prospects of the English language are the most splendid that the world has ever seen. It is spreading in each of the quarters of the globe by fashion, by emigration, and by conquest. The increase of population alone in the two great States of Europe and America in which it is spoken adds to the number of its speakers in every year that passes a greater amount than the whole number of those who speak some of the literary languages of Europe, either Swedish, or Danish, or Dutch. It is calculated that before the lapse of the present century, a time that so many now alive will live to witness, it will be the native and vernacular language of about one hundred and fifty millions of human beings.

"What will be the state of Christendom at the time that this vast preponderance of one language will be brought to bear on all its relations,—at the time when a leading nation in Europe and a gigantic nation in America make use of the same idiom,—when in Africa and Australasia the same language is in use by rising and influential communities, and the world is circled by the accents of Shakespeare and Milton? At that time such of the other languages of Europe as do not extend their empire beyond this quarter of the globe will be reduced to the same degree of insignificance, in comparison with English, as the subordinate languages of modern Europe to those of the state they belong to—the Welsh to the English, the Basque to the Spanish, the Finnish to the Russian. This predominance, we may flatter ourselves, will be a more signal blessing to literature than that of any other language could possibly be. The English is essentially a medium language—in the Teutonic family it stands midway between the Germanic and Scandinavian branches—it unites, as no other language unites, the

Romanic and the Teutonic stocks.   This fits it admirably in many cases for translation.   A German writer, Prince Pückler Muskau, has given it as his opinion that English is even better adapted than German to be the general interpreter of the literature of Europe.   Another German writer, Jenisch, in his elaborate ‘Comparison of Fourteen Ancient and Modern Languages of Europe,’ which obtained a prize from the Berlin Academy in 1796, assigns the general palm of excellence to the English.   In literary treasures what other languages can claim the superiority?   If Rivarol more than sixty years back thought the collective wealth of its literature able to dispute the pre-eminence with the French, the victory has certainly not departed from us in the time that has since elapsed,—the time of Wordsworth and Southey, of Rogers and Campbell, of Scott, of Moore, and of Byron.”

There were two considerations that gave pause to Mr. Watts.   One was the possibility of the extension of Spanish, and the other the possibility of the foreign immigrants into the United States retaining their own language and forming separate communities.   Neither of these contingencies is now probable.

The extent of the great European languages has several times been estimated.   The figures given in 1873 by Alphonse de Candolle, and which were used, with some modifications and necessary corrections, by the present writer in the *Journal of Science*, were probably not far wrong.   According to this: Portuguese was spoken in Portugal by 3,980,000, in Brazil by 10,000,000—a total of 13,980,000 ; Italian by 27,524,238 ; French in France, Belgium, Switzerland, &c., by 40,188,000 ; Spanish in Spain by 16,301,000, in South America by 27,408,082—a total of 43,709,082 ; Russian by 51,370,000 ;

German by 55,789,000 ; English in Europe by 31,000,000, in America by 45,000,000, in Australia, &c., by 2,000,000, in the Colonies by 1,050,000—a total of 79,050,000.

According to De Candolle, the population doubles in England in 56 years (an under-estimate); in America, among the German races, in 25 ; Italy in 135 ; Russia in 100 ; Spain in 112 ; South America in $27\frac{1}{2}$; Germany in 100 ; France in 140. At this rate we may expect that in the year 2,000 Italian will be spoken by 53,370,000; French by 72,571,000; German by 157,480,000; Spanish, in Europe, by 36,938,338, in South America by 467,347,904—505,286,242. English will be spoken in Europe by 178,846,153, in the United States and British dependencies by 1,658,440,000—a total of 1,837,286,153.

Mr. Barham Zincke, in 1883, made another calculation of the probable progress of the English language :—

	1880.	1905.	1930.	1955.	1980.
United States	50,000,000	100,000,000	200,000,000	400,000,000	800,000,000
Canada	4,000,000	8,000,000	16,000,000	32,000,000	64,000,000
Australia	3,000,000	6,000,000	12,000,000	24,000,000	48,000,000
South Africa, &c..	1,000,000	2,000,000	4,000,000	8,000,000	16,000,000
United Kingdom ..	35,000,000	43,750,000	52,500,000	61,250,000	70,050,000
Total.........	93,000,000	159,750,000	284,500,000	525,250,000	998,050,000

Mr. Zincke says : "The present rate of increase in the population of the United Kingdom is about 3,500,000 in ten years. I have not, however, assumed for it the maintenance of the percentage this gives, but have supposed that this 3,500,000 may safely be added to the increased population of each decennium of the coming century. At this rate the population of the United Kingdom will, a century hence, be double what it is to-day. This will not appear to go beyond what is probable when we recall that in what has now elapsed of this present nineteenth century the population of England and Wales has already trebled itself, whereas we only ask permission to double the amount of the now existing population of the whole country in the next hundred years. As the English of the world beyond these islands has to be supplied by us with a considerable part of the manufactures it requires, its increase implies a somewhat corresponding increase amongst ourselves. Besides, too, our English system of large estates and of large farms appears now to be collapsing through the rapid and peremptory action of economical causes. If this system should pass away, we may expect that an end will be put to the diminution of our agricultural population. This diminution of course involved a corresponding retardation in the increase of our towns ; for were our rural population more numerous a greater number of hands would be employed in the towns for supplying it with the manufactured articles it required. It is, then, not only within the limits of possibility, but, unless something quite unforeseen should arise to hinder the action of the causes now at work, it is as likely as anything prospective can be in human affairs, that the Englishry of 1980 will amount to about 1,000,000,000 souls. As all these people will speak the same language, read the same books, and be influenced by the same leading ideas, it will be found necessary to designate them by a common appellation. The requirements of the language will make this compulsory. The periphrasis of the English-speaking peoples would be sufficiently descriptive, for it would give prominence to the most essential particular of resemblance. What, however, will be insisted on will be a single word. To meet this want I would propose the revival of the word

Englishry, which was originally invented to signify the state and condition of an Englishman, and which I have used in the text above to signify all the people collectively, in whatever part of the world they may dwell, who speak the English language, or any part of them, with the addition in that case of the name of the region it occupies. Using the word in this sense, one might talk of the Englishry of the world, or of a century hence, or of the Englishry of the United States, or of Australia."

Let us now see how the seven great languages stand at the present day. Portuguese can claim 4,348,551 in Europe, and 9,883,622 in Brazil, or say 15 millions. Italian has 28,452,639 in the kingdom of Italy, and has some hold in the Levant and portions of Switzerland—say altogether 29 millions. French may be taken at the estimate of the Alliance Française at 50 millions. Spanish claims 16,625,860 in Europe, and an uncertain number in South America. Taking the latest accessible estimates of the republics of New Spain, we have—Argentine Confederation, 1,736,922 ; Bolivia, 1,957,352 ; Chili, 2,183,434 ; Colombia, 2,951,323 ; Costa Rica, 190,000 ; Ecuador, 1,066,137 ; Guatemala, 1,252,497 ; Honduras, 350,000 ; Mexico, 9,343,470 ; Nicaragua, 350,000 ; Paraguay, 293,876 ; Peru, 2,699,945 ; San Domingo, 300,000 ; San Salvador, 554,785 ; Uruguay, 438,235 ; Venezuela, 2,075,245. If we allow 28 millions for the Spanish-speaking nations of the New World and 17 millions for old Spain, we may estimate the adherents of Spanish at 45 millions. German has not any great currency beyond the boundaries of the Empires of Germany and Austria. It is a language which men of learning cannot do without, but the German emigrants who leave the Fatherland help to strengthen the English-speaking races of the New World rather than to extend the dominion of the speech of Goethe and of Lessing.   We shall therefore not be far wrong if we estimate the German-speaking peoples as 68 millions, made up of 22,144,244 in the Austrian and 45,234,061 in the German Empire.

There remains now only to consider the English-speaking races.   In Great Britain there is a population of 34,884,848. The colonies and dependencies in North America have 4,520,415; Australasia has 2,914,176.   Then there are the settlements and dependencies in South America, Africa, the West Indies, and the English and Eurasian population of India.   It would, perhaps, not be an over-estimate to say that English is spoken by 50 millions of the subjects of Queen Victoria.   To this must be added another 50 millions for the United States.   It may be objected that no deduction has been made for the French-speaking Canadians, but then no credit has been taken for the great mass of English people scattered on the continent and in Russia.   Figures can only be used in a roughly approximative fashion in dealing with a topic so speculative.   In the last ten years Portuguese has risen from 14 to 15 millions; Italian from 28 to 29 millions; French from 41 to 50 millions (if we accept the liberal estimate of the Alliance Française); Spanish from 44 to 45 millions; German from 56 to 68 millions; whilst English has risen from 80 to 100 millions. Moreover, the possibilities of the future are with the English language.   The foreign colonists from the Old World go to increase the English-speaking strength of the American continent.   English has all the prestige that belongs to a conquering race.   It is the speech of the dominant people, and may be expected to find a great increase amongst the 304 millions over whom the Queen holds dominion more or less determinate and direct. The genius of the language is also in its favour. It has a simple grammar, whilst its vocabulary combines in a large measure the best elements of the Latin and Teutonic tongues. A weakness of English is its slovenly and indistinct vocalisation. The greatest difficulty, however, is caused by arbitrary and unscientific spelling. This is probably its greatest drawback, and the best philologists of the present day are agreed as to the necessity of a reform in this direction. The practical difficulties in the way of change are very great, but the advantage would also be very great.

Many proposals have been made for the reform of English spelling. The best known system is that of Mr. Isaac Pitman, which proposes to have one letter for each sound in the language. For the benefit of those who are not prepared for a radical change, Mr. Pitman suggests a progressive reform in three stages, beginning by the omission of some silent letters, and the substitution of one letter for another, as required by the pronunciation, leading gradually to a complete phonetic system. Such a change would be a gain to education and to learning in an extraordinary degree.

De Candolle saw the advantage that would arise to science from a dominant language. The scholar who writes in English now addresses the largest audience. For this reason Professor Thorell, of Upsala, wrote in our language his great work on spiders. Such incidents are becoming commoner, and may be expected to be more and more frequent. Our English language and literature is certainly one of the noblest, and carries with it a heritage alike of intellectual greatness and of

political freedom.   By reason of our wide dominion, by reason of our extensive commerce, by reason of our colonies in
every quarter of the world, the English tongue has attained a
development which no other since the world began ever had,
and the progress which it has made in the past is insignificant
compared with the progress which one may prophesy for it in
the future.   There are millions of Englishmen in India, in
America, in Australia.   They have the inheritance of our
literature and our institutions, and no stretch of imagination
is required to suppose that in the coming ages the subject
races of India will accept the language of their conquerors,
as the subject races of Rome accepted the language of their
conquerors..   Then we have the wide fields of America and
Australia in which to increase and multiply ; and when we
know that even at the present time the English language is
the one spoken by more people than any other on the earth,
we must conclude that at no distant day it will attain to such
gigantic proportions as to overshadow all the rest, and become
the dominant, and, in that sense only, the universal language
of the world.

I may repeat now, with an increased conviction of their
truth, the words I used fifteen years ago on this subject :—

It may appear a sweeping change to alter the form and aspect
of the language, but the change is by no means so violent as
it seems.   Changes in spelling are constantly taking place,
but they are alterations which come about by haphazard and
without system.   If other nations have succeeded in reforming
their orthography—and we know this to be the case with the
Dutch and the Spanish—surely we may hope for success also
in the same undertaking.   And when that day comes on
which we have swept away what Max Müller has so well

called " our corrupt and effete orthography," we shall have
destroyed the last and only barrier which prevents English
from being the language of the world.

Surely that is a future so great and glorious that we need
not hesitate at any trouble which will hasten the day. We
have already achieved much. The flowers that first grew
beside the Avon now bloom alike on the banks of the sacred
Ganges and by the margin of the broad Mississippi. The
lays of merry England are heard alike in the fair Derbyshire
dales and on the plains of the Far West. The thoughts of
our great thinkers, the songs of our poets, are no longer
bounded by the narrow seas that hem in our island home.
They fly to every point of the compass, and find everywhere
audiences not few but fit. In the Australian sheepwalk, amid
the tropical glories of Jamaican scenery, in the glowing valleys
of the Polynesian islands, east, west, north, or south, we find
the restless, energetic Englishman. It is not a thing to be
lightly thought of, this wide extension of our English tongue.

Our language is a beautiful casket shining with gold and
glittering with gems, and enclosing still more precious, still
more costly jewels. Wherever the Englishman goes he carries
with him the energy, the love of order, the purity of home
life, the independence, the freedom of thought, of speech, of
action, which have made England not only great and prosperous, but the "august mother of free nations." The
language is the best test of national capacity. It expresses
not only the exact extent of the nation's knowledge, but also
its spiritual condition and moral aspirations. Apart from all
national vanity, we may rejoice that Shakespeare's language is
going forth to the ends of the earth. It bears with it the
science of Newton and the politics of Adam Smith. It bears

15

with it all that is purest and best in the teachings of the ancient world. It bears with it countless memories of heroic deeds. It bears with it those aspirations after liberty and right which are the most precious possession of our race. May it go forward conquering and to conquer, resistless in its power and majesty, until it becomes a new bond of peace and brotherhood amongst all the nations, until earth's fertile valleys shall glow with fruits and flowers, and the "desert shall rejoice and blossom as the rose."

FOLK-LORE OF ARCHITECTURE.

BIBLIOGRAPHY.

Further details on this subject will be found in "The Antiquary," vol. iii., 8, 188 ; vol. iv., 33, 85, 133, 279; in "Primitive Culture," by Dr. E. B. Tylor, London, 1871, vol. i., p. 94; in "Choice Notes from Notes and Queries: Folk-lore," and in the publications of the Folk-lore Society. These have all been freely used, and especially the suggestive article by Mr. G. L. Gomme, in "The Antiquary."

This paper is reprinted from the "British Architect," February, 1885.

FOLK-LORE OF ARCHITECTURE.

THERE is a varied folk-lore connected with architecture, but for the present it will be enough to indicate briefly the connection of one series of curious building traditions with some of the earlier passages in the evolution of culture.

In 1882 we heard of the sacrifice of a number of young girls by an African potentate in order that their blood might insure the permanence of the barbaric palace he was then constructing. India furnishes another instance. In August, 1880, a correspondent of the *Times* wrote : " A rumour has got abroad, and is firmly believed in by the lower classes of the natives, that the Government is about to sacrifice a number of human beings in order to enforce the safety of the new harbour works, and has ordered the police to seize victims in the streets. So thoroughly is the idea implanted that people are afraid to venture out after nightfall. There was a similar scare in Calcutta some seven or eight years ago, when the Hooghly Bridge was being constructed. The natives then got hold of the idea that Mother Ganges, indignant at being bridged, had at last consented to submit to the insult on the condition that each pier of the structure was founded on a layer of children's heads." The idea underlying this superstition may seem entirely uncongenial to our own soil, and yet in this as in other matters there is good reason to suppose that the present manners and customs of savages reflect or preserve the customs and thoughts of pre-historic ages.

There are many folk-tales which refer to the mysterious removal of buildings, generally churches, from the sites originally intended for them.   Thus there is the story as to Wrexham Church, which would have been built at Bryn-y-ffynnon but for the energetic objections of the fairies, who undid in the night that which the builders had done in the day.   At last a watch was set, and though nothing was seen, there was heard the voice of one crying in the wilderness "Bryn-y-grog."   On hearing this the owner of some land at the spot thus indicated, who had been previously unwilling to sell, expressed his readiness to allow the site to be used for the erection of the church.   The interposition of supernatural agency to decide the precise site of such buildings is a feature common to many folk-tales.   Sometimes when the builders had selected the top of a hill the stones were removed to the valley.   At others, when the human worshippers desired to be in the sheltered vale, the invisible but active spirits of the air decided that it would be more conducive to piety if they had to ascend a mighty hill.   At Denbigh, where Robert Dudley, the favourite of good Queen Bess, began to build on a magnificent scale, the displeasure, we are told, was caused by the vanity and ostentation which impelled him to church building, and the ruins of his intended structure still serve to point a moral and adorn a tale.   If, however, the vanity and ostentation of the founder is to ruin a church, what will be the future of ecclesiastical architecture?   Some of the variants of the story are curious.   Many attempts, we are told, were made to build a church at Godrefarth, near Llandewi, but the walls fell down as soon as they were built until the present site was selected.   Two oxen were employed to bring the stones from the Voelallt rock.   One of them died, and the other made great lamentation for his dead comrade, and then lowed three times, after which the rock was shattered, and there was no further difficulty in obtaining stones for the building of the tower. Various agencies were employed to execute the wishes of the mysterious powers. Thus at Breedon, in Leicestershire, the materials were removed by "doves;" at Winwick, by a pig; at Leyland, by a cat.*

When St. Patrick was building the great church at Cashel the work of the day was undone in the night. St. Patrick watched and saw a great bull—an Irish one, of course—with fire-flashing nostrils, busily engaged in knocking down the stones of the rising church. He set one of his converts to work, and the next time the bull was "on the rampage," Oisin dropped from a rock on to its back, placed a hand on each horn, tore it asunder, and dashed one of the sides so hard against the wall that the impress was left on the wall hardened into stone.

In the parish of Tolleshunt Knights, in Essex, there is an

---

* The church of West Walton, near Wisbech, has a detached tower standing close by the churchyard gate. Of course there is a legendary reason for its present position. When that old church was new the Fenmen made themselves notorious by their special ingenuity in sin, and the Evil One hired "a number of people" to carry the tower away. It is not of course stated why the Devil took special offence at the tower, nor what manner of people they were whom he hired. Apparently they were not of his own household, but sons of the children of men. Probably in this, as in some other matters, he found human cheaper than diabolical labour would have been. He did not show much wisdom in the selection of his instruments, for the "number of people," after getting the tower on their shouiders—a feat that would astonish even a Chicago contractor—were balked by the churchyard wall. They could not get the tower over the wall, and as the gate was not wide enough they finally, after running all round the consecrated circle, "revoked," and dropped the offensive structure close by the entrance. It is impossible not to feel that somewhat hard measure was meted out to the demon on this as on some other occasions. The "number of people" were clearly liable to an action for breach of contract, and their only method of escape would have been the pusillanimous one of pleading that the bargain was void on the ground of its intrinsic immorality. Some towers are, however, so offensively ugly that such a plea would be no valid defence—at least to a jury of taste.

uncultivated field, and at some distance from it an old
manor house known as Barn Hall.   The legend is that the
hall was intended to have been built on the first-named spot,
but the Devil destroyed in the night time all that had been
done in the day.   A knight, with two dogs, was sent to
watch, and when the Evil One came there was a sharp
tussle, but of course Apollyon was vanquished by Greatheart.
The irritated demon thereupon snatched a beam from the
building and hurled it through the darkness, exclaiming—

> Wheresoe'r this beam shall fall,
> There shall stand Barn Hall.

The Devil further declared that on the good knight's death
he would have him, whether he was buried in church or out
of it.   To avoid the penal fires thus threatened, the valiant
warrier was buried in the wall, half in and half out.   In the
latter circumstance we seem to have a distorted reminiscence
of the older custom of sacrificing human life in order to
propitiate the spirits of earth and air.   It is not without
possible relation to this that we find Mr. A. Broughton-
Leigh giving an account of a curious discovery of the
remains of human bodies underneath the walls of a church.

In later times, animals or mere symbols take the place of
men.   German folk-tales speak of empty coffins being
walled up in churches; a Danish story mentions a lamb
walled in under the altar to give stability to the structure.
The Abbey of Sweetheart was so called because the heart of
John Balliol was built into its wall by its founder, his wife,
Devorgilla.   This Mr. Gomme thinks a remnant of the
earlier custom of walling up human beings as a sacrificial
method of securing the safety of the building.   There may

be some doubt on this point, but there need be none as to the existence of such a custom. Geoffrey of Monmouth tells us that when Vortigern was perplexed by the failure of his masons to build a magic tower, which he desired for his own safety, he was told that he must find out a youth that had never had a father, and sprinkle his blood upon the stones. St. Oran, who has been made the subject of a notable poem by Miss Mathilde Blind, was, according to an old mediæval story, actually buried alive in order to secure the stability of the walls of Iona. Three days after the sacrifice (it is uncertain whether it was voluntary or decided by lot), St. Columba had the curiosity to have the earth removed, when the pious Oran amazed them by the heretical assertion : "There is no wonder in death, and hell is not as it is reported." Whereupon St. Columba, with perhaps more worldly wisdom than tolerance, ordered the earth to be thrown again on the mouth of Oran, in order that he might "blab no more." There is an old Roumanian superstition that a human sacrifice is necessary to give stability to any great edifice. Ubicini, in his notes to the ballad of the building of the monastery of Argis, shows the notion in a transition form. Writing in 1855 he says :—" The masons place in the foundations of the houses which they are constructing long reeds, with which they have endeavoured to take the measure of the shadow of some passer-by. This unfortunate person is destined, they believe, to die at the end of forty days, and to be metamorphosed into a *stahic*. The latter is the ghost of a person who has been immured in the walls of the building in order to make it more solid. According to popular tradition, all the important edifices of the country have had their victim."

218   *Folk-Lore of Architecture.*

The Irish peasants believe that the early English settlers built their castles on the slaughtered bodies of their Irish enemies. Mr. Baring-Gould says: "It was the custom in ancient times to bury a dog or boar alive under the corner stone of a church—that its ghost might haunt the church-yard—and drive off anyone who would profane it, *i.e.*, witches or warlocks. In Sweden, the beast which haunts churchyards is called the Kyrkogrim. It is there said that the first founders of Christian churches used to bury a lamb under the altar. When anyone enters a church out of service time he may chance to see a little lamb spring across the quire, and vanish. That is the church lamb. Its appearance in the grave-yard, especially to the grave-digger, is held to betoken the death of a child. In Denmark, the animal is called the Kirkegrim. A grave-sow is often seen in the streets of Kroskjoberg. This is said to be the apparition of a sow once buried alive, and to forbode death. In building a new bridge at Halle, which was completed in 1843, the people wanted to have a child immured in the foundation to secure its stability." Dr. Tylor thus sum-marises some of the evidence as to human sacrifice: "These ideas of church, or wall, or bridge wanting human blood or an immured victim to make the foundation stedfast, are not only widespread in European folk-lore, but chronicle or tradition asserts them as matter of historical fact in district after district. Thus, when the broken dam of the Nogat had to be repaired in 1463, the peasants, on the advice to throw in a living man, are said to have made a beggar drunk, and buried him there. Thuringian legend declares that to make the castle of Liebenstein fast and impregnable a child was bought for hard money of its mother and walled in.

It was eating a cake while the masons were at work, the story goes, and it cried out, 'Mother, I see thee still;' then later, 'Mother, I see thee a little still;' and, as they put in the last stone, 'Mother, now I see thee no more.' The wall of Copenhagen, legend says, sank as fast as it was built, so they took an innocent little girl, set her on a chair at a table with toys and eatables, and, as she played and ate, twelve master masons closed a vault over her; then, with clanging music the wall was raised, and stood firm ever after. Thus Italian legend tells of the bridge of Arta, that fell in and fell in till they walled in the master builder's wife, and she spoke her dying curse that the bridge should tremble like a flower-stalk henceforth. The Slavonic chiefs founding Detinez, according to old heathen custom, sent out men to take the first boy they met and bury him in the foundation. Servian legend tells how three brothers combined to build the fortress of Skadra (Scutari); but year after year the demon (vila) razed by night what the three hundred masons built by day. The fiend must be appeased by a human sacrifice, the first of the three wives who should come bringing food to the workmen. All three brothers swore to keep the dreadful secret from their wives; but the two eldest gave traitorous warning to theirs, and it was the youngest brother's wife who came unsuspecting, and they built her in. But she entreated that an opening should be left for her to suckle her baby through, and for a twelvemonth it was brought. To this day Servian wives visit the tomb of the good mother, still marked by a stream of water which trickles, milky with lime, down the fortress wall."

The custom of burying victims alive has been heard of amongst many savage nations. At Galam, in Africa, a boy and girl were so sacrificed to make the great gate of the city impregnable; in Great Bassim and Yarriba it was a usual custom on the foundation of a house or village. In Poly-nesia the central pillar of the temple at Maeva was planted on the body of a victim. In Borneo the first post of a great house was suspended over a hole in such a manner that when the lashings were cut it fell upon and crushed to death a slave girl selected for the sacrifice. When the fort of Sialkot in the Punjaub was being built the foundations repeatedly gave way. When the rajah applied to the soothsayers, he was assured that the only way to establish it was the sacrifice of an only son. Accordingly the son of a widow was slaughtered.

In the houses of New Zealanders the wall plate of the verandah is often carved to represent the prostrate figures of slaves, on whose bodies the pillars supporting the house appear to stand. This is clearly a connecting link between the real sacrifice and the mere symbolism of later days. The parallels between the building legends of Europe and New Zealand are exceedingly close and curious, and it is only the danger of attributing to native tradition that which may in part be due to missionary influence that leads us to lay less stress upon them than appears to be warranted.

These legends, it will be seen, carry us back to very early stages of thought. In his conflict with nature, man early felt the greatness of the forces opposed to him; hence, probably, arose his fear of the mysterious and unknown powers which appeared to animate the changes of nature. The extremes of hot and cold, the occurrence of catastrophes and cataclysms, would not only impress him with a sense of the power, but also of the malignancy of these invisible agencies. The idea of propitiating them by sacrifice would be the next step forward. The savage keeps an account with his gods, he buys off their vengeance, and he expects their aid in return for service rendered. The sanctity of human life is a conception of a higher plane of civilisation. When this new leaven begins to work the lower animals are slain in place of the lord of creation. Then the sacrifice loses its early meaning ; and after passing through the stage of a mere ceremonial becomes a mere superstition. whose ignorant votaries are unaware of the meaning and significance of the folk-lore in which they believe. Folk-lore is very largely the fossil theology of an earlier age.

THE
GEOGRAPHICAL DISTRIBUTION OF
MEN OF GENIUS.

First printed in the " Manchester Quarterly," October, 1883

THE GEOGRAPHICAL DISTRIBU-
TION OF MEN OF GENIUS.

GENIUS, though not always known or appreciated, is at all events more easily recognised than defined. The distinction between the man of genius and the man of talent may sometimes seem obscure, but usually genius has in it some appearance of inward impulse or possession. The man of talent sets himself to do a definite task, and perhaps as often fails as succeeds; but the man of genius has an indwelling impulse in a certain. direction, and does his work in an unconscious spirit.

For the present purpose we may define or describe a man of genius to be one who has exercised a deep and permanent influence on the thought and destiny of the human race. The history of the world is the history of its great men. It is remarkable how few are the memorable men and women. We know, of course, that there were strong men before Agamemnon, who died unsung and unchronicled, but after every allowance for the activity of the cankered tooth of time incessantly at work in destroying the relics of the past, the fewness of great men is a matter of surprise. The *Dictionary of Biographical Reference*, by Mr. L. B. Phillips, contains one hundred thousand names, and is in effect an index to all the great biographical collections. Amongst the names he registers are those of men who were notable by their official position only, of others who were celebrated merely for their

16

crimes, and of writers who were not in either the first or the fifth rank. Yet the entire number of persons deemed worthy of record in a period of not less than three thousand years is not much greater than the population of Preston. With their wives and children they would not exceed in number the inhabitants of Manchester and Salford.

An attempt has been made to appraise the number and work of the greatest men, and we find then that, instead of one hundred thousand, the men of genius are reckoned but as one hundred and nine. This attempt has had the co-operation, and therefore presumably the approbation, of Emerson, Matthew Arnold, Taine, and others, to whose judgment deference is due. This is a series of eight folio volumes, known as *The Hundred Greatest Men. Portraits of the One Hundred Greatest Men of History.* (London: Sampson Low and Co.) Instead of a hundred, there are a hundred and nine portraits. The names are so arranged that we have groups of poets, artists, philosophers, religious founders, historians, men of science, and politicians, ending with a somewhat miscellaneous assemblage of inventors, discoverers, and philanthropists.

"The great men of the past," says Emerson, "did not glide by any fortune into their high place. They have been selected by the severest of all judges—Time." Even with the aid of this great touchstone, no two men would select the same individuals if asked to name those who had made the history of the world. The personal equation, prejudice of race, patriotic emotion, and religious bias would obscure the judgment of most men in such a task; yet, in spite of the divergence thus caused, there would probably be a substantial agreement in the result. No one doubts the place in literature of Shakespeare's plays, not even the people who think that they were written by Lord Bacon.

One difficulty, almost insuperable, is as to those near to our generation. Time is the perspective of history. The passions and prejudices of the day almost necessarily warp the judgment even of those who strive to be fair and candid in their estimates of those around them. Joan of Arc was condemned as a witch in perfect good faith, and we have no reason to doubt that her judges were incapable of admiration for patriotism. To us Milton is an austere figure that fitly represents the spirit of religious poetry; but to many of his own day he was a daring rebel who had been punished by blindness for disloyalty. To them he was a man who to rebellion added a strong suspicion of heresy, and was thought to be particularly open to the charge of unsoundness on the important subject of divorce. The men who burned Savonarola did not desire the death of a moralist calling men to repentance. For these reasons, in the present inquiry few names are included that come within the present century.

Let us take, then, the section devoted to poetry, which is probably the oldest of the fine arts. The first name is that of blind Homer, "the father of the poets," whose song of Troy was under the pillow of Alexander, and not improbably stimulated that wondrous career of splendid but unhappy conquest. We know that in these latter days the very existence of Homer has been put in question, and the integrity of his *Iliad* denied. Whether he was the first to sing the story of the siege, or was merely one who strung together the ballads of a people, he has become in an almost exclusive degree the type of the Greek poet. We cannot enter into the disputes that have raged as to his place of birth, era, and character.   Until the case is more clearly proved against the common theory, we must hold that he was born in Greece some nine centuries before Christ. The other names are those of Pindar, Æschylus, Sophocles, Euripides, Aristophanes, Menander, Lucretius, Virgil, Dante, Rabelais, Cervantes, Shakespeare, Milton, Molière, Goethe, and Scott.   Such is the list of those selected as the representative poets amongst the hundred greatest men.   As we are not bound by any neces- sity to keep to that centurial number, let us consider who may safely be added to it.   To the Latins let us add the names of Horace and Ovid ; to Dante let us join Petrarch, Ariosto, and Boccaccio, without staying to mark the exact interval that should separate them ; let us claim places for Chaucer, Spenser, Bunyan, Defoe, and Burns ; let us recog- nise that Racine, Corneille, and Lafontaine approached so nearly to the highest greatness that we shall be safer to include than to exclude them ; let us leave undivided the glory of Schiller and Goethe ; and let us, with some doubts, admit to this walhalla the only great man that Portugal has given to literature—Camoens.   Of the poets, whether in prose or verse, Greece claims seven ; Italy, old and new, eight ; France, five ; Portugal, one ; Spain, one ; Germany, two ; and Great Britain, seven.

The artists selected are Phidias, Praxiteles, Leonardo da Vinci, Michel Angelo, Raphael, Correggio, Titian, Rubens, Rembrandt, Bach, Handel, Mozart, and Beethoven.   The men in this list seem to stand on so high a level that it is difficult to make any justifiable additions, and it is not with- out hesitation that the names of Claude Lorraine, Jacques, Callot, Murillo, and Hogarth are added—the latter being more typically English than the more courtly Reynolds. Again summarising, we see that Greece claims two; Italy, five; France, two; Spain, one; and Great Britain, one. Germany has two painters, and in four great names has a monopoly of musical genius.

The next section is one that may be specially open to controversy, for matters connected with theology are apt to generate heat—often indeed more heat than light. Moses, Zoroaster, the founder of the Parsee religion, Confucius, whose philosophical morality is still the state worship of China, Buddha, and Mahomet. Then, turning to the development of the Christian religion, we have the names of St. Paul, St. Augustine, St. Bernard, St. Francis of Assissi, Erasmus, Luther, Calvin, Loyola, Bossuet, and Wesley. This list suffers inevitably from the point of view of the compiler. The name of Lao Tsze, "the old philosopher," is absent. Each of the religions named would claim amongst its adherents men as able and as fateful as Bossuet or Erasmus. Even amongst the names of the great Christians we miss St. Dominic and Thomas à Kempis—assuming for the moment that he really wrote the *Imitatio.* The names of Savonarola, of Wycliffe, and of Swedenborg are also absent. It would probably be wisest to pass over this section as too obviously imperfect; but taking the data for what it is worth, we see that to the development of the Christian doctrine one man of commanding influence came from Palestine, one from Africa, two from Italy, one from Holland, two from Germany, three from France, two from England, two from Spain, and one from Sweden. No existing religion has originated in Europe. Mahomet belongs to Arabia, Zoroaster to Persia, Confucius and Lao Tsze to China, and Buddha to India.

The Europeans have borrowed their religion from another clime and a different race.

Coming now to those whose studies in divine philosophy have echoed through the ages, we have the names of Pythagoras, Socrates, Plato, Aristotle, St. Thomas Aquinas, Francis Bacon, Descartes, Spinoza, Locke, Leibnitz, Bishop Berkeley, Hume, and Kant. Of these four belong to Greece, one to Italy, four to England, one to France, one to Holland, and two to Germany.

To the class of writers who have treated the problems of history and politics belong the names of Herodotus, Thucydides, Demosthenes, Cicero, Tacitus, Plutarch, Montaigne, Montesquieu, Voltaire, Diderot, Lessing, and Gibbon. To these we should surely add the name of Froissart. Of these thirteen, three belong to Greece, three to Rome, five to France, one to Germany, and one to Great Britain.

The men of science are Hippocrates, Galen, Archimedes, Copernicus, Kepler, Galileo, Harvey, Newton, Linnæus, Lavoisier, Bichat, and Cuvier. To these we may add the names of Roger Bacon, Jeremiah Horrox, and John Dalton. Our proximity in time to Darwin and Joule is the only reason for the omission of their names. Of this class, Greece claims three; Germany, two; Italy, one; England, five; France, three; and Sweden, one.

The statesmen and rulers who, whether called by the royal name or not, have had in their hands the destinies of nations are Pericles, Alexander the Great, Hannibal, Julius Cæsar, Charlemagne, Alfred the Great, William the Conqueror, Charles the Fifth, William the Silent, Richelieu, Cromwell, Peter the Great, Frederick the Great, Washington, Jefferson, Nelson, Napoleon I., and Wellington. This list might of course be greatly extended if the mere warriors were added. It is a remarkable circumstance that of all the sovereigns who have reigned in Europe during the last thousand years only five have established their claim to the epithet of great. Taking the list as it stands, we find two Greeks, a Carthaginian, a Roman, four Frenchmen, two Germans, one Dutchman, four Englishmen, and two Americans. The name of Bolivar, who broke the yoke of Spain in South America, may perhaps be added.

The last class enumerated in the work are the inventors and discoverers. These are Gutenberg, Columbus, Palissy the potter, Franklin, who had, however, many claims to remembrance besides his electrical experiments; Montgolfier, James Watt, Sir Richard Arkwright, and Stephenson. John Howard, a preacher of practical philanthropy, is included in this series. This group is not likely to give satisfaction. Far too little is known of the invention of printing. The claims of Arkwright have been warmly contested. The name of Crompton may well be added to the list, for undoubtedly he has exercised a marked influence on the industrial history of the world. There are then one German, one Italian, two Frenchmen, one American, and six Englishmen.

It will be noticed that the actors are left out. The names of Thespis—if he be not a myth—Talma, Garrick, Kean, and Rachel may therefore be added. Of these, two are the children of France and two of England.

The mention of Rachel recalls another curious omission, that of the names of the great women who have figured in history. This may be due to the smallness in literature of work of the very highest class done by women. In public affairs, owing to causes not difficult to surmise, their influence, though real, has oftener been occult than open.   The subject is one of great interest, but it involves many debatable points, and may for the present be put aside.

From the data just laid down, the men who may be said to have given the impulses to the history and civilisation of the modern world are one hundred and forty-two in number. The "Hundred Greatest Men" is originally a French selection, and the additions suggested in this paper are twelve Englishmen, eight Frenchmen, one Greek, six Italians, one German, two Spaniards, one Swede, one Portuguese, and one South American.

The geographical distribution of these names is as follows:

	List in Hundred Greatest Men.	With additions suggested in this paper.
Great Britain	19	31
France	19	27
Greece	22	23
Italy	15	21
Germany	16	18
Spain	2	4
Holland	3	3
United States	3	3
Sweden	1	2
Russia	1	1
Africa	3	3
Portugal	0	1
Arabia	1	1
Palestine	1	1
Persia	1	1
China	1	1
Hindostan	1	1
South America	0	1
	109	143

It is obvious that this list is especially open to criticism in relation to those nations beyond the European circle. Thus, if we take Persian poetry only, the names of Ferdusi, Nizami, Sadi, Hafiz, and Jami would need careful consideration ; and at least one of them would probably have to be added to the list. The omissions in this respect are so striking that we must only take the list as representing those who have exerted a marked influence upon the progress of Europe.

Taking the more notable countries separately, we find that Greece claims seven of the poets, two of the artists, four of the philosophers, three of the historians, three of the men of science, two of the statesmen, and one actor. These all belong to the ancient world, and for centuries past Greece has been an extinct volcano. Now that she has regained her freedom, the arts of peace may once more flourish, and in coming generations the land of Homer again resound with the echoes of immortal song.

There are two Italies, that of Rome and that of the renascence. Without discriminating between them, we see that Italy claims eight of the poets, five of the artists, two of the religious founders, one of the philosophers, three of the historians, one of the men of science, and one of the great discoverers.

France claims five of the poets, two of the artists, three of the divines, one of the philosophers, five of the historians, three of the men of science, four statesmen, two inventors, and two actors.

To Germany we must assign two of the poets, two of the painters, four of the musicians, one of the devotional writers, one of the religious reformers, two of the philosophers, one of the historians, two of the men of science, two of the statesmen, and one inventor.

For England we claim seven of the poets, one artist, two of the religious reformers, four of the philosophers, one of the historians, five of the men of science, four of the statesmen, two actors, five inventors, and one philanthropist. John Howard is rightly placed amongst the inventors and discoverers, for it was he who in the modern world discovered humanity.

All Europe is now either Latin or Teutonic, and it may not be uninteresting to see the proportion of the great men of the two races. The names in the books so often mentioned of the British, German, Dutch, American, and Swedish great men are in number forty-one, whilst those of France, Italy, and Spain are thirty-seven. If we include the names that have been suggested for addition, the result is a still closer approximation, for the Teutons have only fifty-six to boast of against the fifty-four Latins. It would not be wise to assume that these figures represent the possibilities of the coming years. The forces now at work seem to be giving in an increasing measure the near future of the world into the hands of the Teutonic races.

Probably nothing will more readily impress upon the mind the rarity of great men than the study of such a list as this. Admit its incompleteness, and add to it an equal number of those whom the chronicler has omitted, and even then all that can be said is that there have been three hundred men of genius since the dawn of history, and that this small number includes all the greatest of the poets, the painters, the statesmen, and the discoverers of more than three thousand years.

"The population of the British Islands," Carlyle is said to have observed many years ago, "consists of thirty-three million persons — mostly fools." There are, it may be observed, worse beings than fools in the world. The population of the world is now estimated to be about fifteen hundred millions. How many of these will be remembered in the centuries yet to be? How many of them are men of genius?

Man is "the heir of all ages," and reaps where he has not sown. Many climes and many eras have contributed to his intellectual and moral equipment. From the heights of Sinai and Olympus, from the prison cell of Socrates, from the throne of Alfred, from the easy chair of Rabelais, from the observatory of Copernicus, from the printing-office of Franklin, from the gory deck where Nelson died, messages of hope and earnestness will flash forth to successive generations. Emerson says of Carlyle that he "was cognisant of the subtle links that bind ages together, and saw how every event affects all the future. 'Christ died on the tree: that built Dunscore Kirk yonder: that brought you and me together.'" The influence of genius is not bounded by political empires nor circumscribed by time. Even when their names are forgotten, their books lost, their pictures destroyed, even when they have gone to the grave amid despair and the gloom of defeat, the lives of genius have not been without avail. They are not dead, but can still be heard in

> . . . . The choir invisible
> Of those immortal dead who live again
> In minds made better by their presence :
> In pulses stirred to generosity, live
> In deeds of daring rectitude, in scorn
> For miserable aims that end with self,
> In thoughts sublime that pierce the night like stars,
> And with their mild persistence urge man's search
> To vaster issues.

SIR RICHARD PHILLIPS.
A BOOKSELLER AND ·AUTHOR.

"*Memoirs of the public and private Life of Sir Richard Phillips, Knight, High Sheriff of the City of London and County of Middlesex.*" *Impartially compiled from Authentic Documents by a Citizen of London and Assistants. London, 1808. 12mo. This must be regarded as inspired by the knight, if not actually autobiographic.*

"*Biographical Dictionary of Living Authors.*" *London, 1816.*

"*Gentleman's Magazine," Aug.—Sept. 1840, pp.* 212, 360.

"*Royal Society Catalogue of Scientific Papers,*" 1800—1863. *London,* 1870. *Vol. iv.*

"*Budget of Paradoxes.*" *By Augustus de Morgan. London,* 1872.

"*Observations on the Memoirs of his Public and Private Life.*" *Stamford,* 1808. *This I have not seen.*

"*Handbook of Fictitious Names.*" *By Olphar Hamst* [*Ralph Thomas*]. *London,* 1868.

"*Notes and Queries.*" 3rd S., viii., xi., xii.

"*Archibald Constable and his Literary Correspondents ; a Memorial by his Son Thomas Constable.*" *Edinburgh,* 1873. 3 *vols.*

There is a notice of Phillips based on materials communicated by the present writer in "The Ethics of Diet, a Catena of authorities deprecatory of the Practice of Flesh-eating," by Howard Williams. London, 1883. *In this he has reprinted Phillips'* "*Reasons against Flesh-eating.*"

The present biographical sketch first appeared in "The Bibliographer," 1883.

SIR RICHARD PHILLIPS:

A BOOKSELLER AND AUTHOR.

THE biographical dictionaries are for the most part silent
as to the career of Sir Richard Phillips, who was,
nevertheless, a considerable personage at the beginning of
the present century. The materials for a notice of his life are
scattered through various publications, and it may be a useful
task to bring them together.

There is some uncertainty as to the early years of Sir
Richard Phillips. According to one account his real name
was Philip Richards, but no reason is stated for his change of
name, nor is any date assigned at which the transformation
took place. The same authority states that he was born in
London in 1768, and brought up by an uncle in Oxford Street,
a brewer, who sent him to school in Soho Square and in
Chiswick. The boy's tastes were in a different direction
from that opened for him by his uncle's trade. His inclina-
tions being more studious, he entered the teaching profession,
and in 1786 was an assistant in a school at Chester, but in
1788 he removed to Leicester. Before proceeding further
with this narrative it must be pointed out that there is an
entirely different and probably a more accurate account of
Phillips' life up to this point. In the *Memoirs* published
during his shrievalty, it is stated that he was born near
Leicester in the year 1768,* and that his father was a poor

---

* His epitaph, which was written by himself, states that he was born 13th Dec.,
1767.

farmer, who, however, managed to give his children the benefit of education.

Richard's father had looked forward to his eldest son joining him in the labours of the farm, but the young man had no inclination for agriculture, and preferred to try his fortune in the great metropolis. What his plans were precisely are now unknown, but, like many other ardent youths, he found that the streets of London were not paved with gold, and after a brief trial he returned to Leicester.

On his arrival at home he met with the welcome of the prodigal son, though he had no claim to that character. A fatted heifer was smoking upon the table, and Richard ate of it with the rest of the family. It was not until after dinner he learned that the slaughtered animal was one of which, before his removal to London, he had been particularly fond. The thought of having eaten part of his dumb favourite was so revolting to his sensibility, that he resolved never again to make use of the flesh of animals as food. To this determination he adhered during the remainder of a long life. His next venture was of a scholastic character. He placed a blue flag on a pole near the door of a house in which he had engaged a room on the ground floor. Here he gave elementary instruction to such children as were entrusted to him by the good people of Leicester, but at the end of twelve months he gave up the experiment. He determined now to try his fortune in commerce, but in a very humble fashion. The hosier's shop he opened was stocked chiefly by a friendly stocking weaver, who visited the establishment every Saturday in order to ascertain for himself the exact quantity of the week's sales. His business increased, but he now tried fortune in an additional but very different line, by the establishment in 1790 of a newspaper. The *Leicester Herald* was what would now be called a Liberal paper, but it was in those days regarded as revolutionary and incendiary in its tendencies by those who identified the liberties of England with the continued existence of rotten boroughs. Phillips himself was accounted an able political writer, but the chief stay of the paper was the celebrated Dr. Priestley, whose contributions gave it an importance it might not otherwise have possessed. The responsible editor did not escape the perils which then environed advocates of freedom and reform. Richard Phillips was imprisoned in Leicester Gaol. One account says that his incarceration was a punishment for an article in the paper, whilst another attributes it to a prosecution for selling Paine's *Rights of Man*. The term of imprisonment is also variously stated as twelve months and "nearly three years." His jailer was Daniel Lambert, the fat man *par excellence*, who, by his kind treatment of his prisoners, vindicated the common opinion which associates obesity with good humour. The kindness of Lambert greatly alleviated the unpleasantness of imprisonment. Phillips showed a very benevolent spirit in relieving the necessities of some of the poorer prisoners. On his release he sold his interest in the paper, and confined himself to the hosiery business, until a fire destroyed the stock. The prudent tradesman was, however, fully insured. Tired of Leicester, he decided to establish himself as a hosier in London, but he found that trade was not in a flourishing condition. It was in effect cut up by competition and underselling. The success of the *Leicester Herald* probably led Phillips to think of the establishment of a new periodical. On consultation with Dr. Priestley and other friends, he was encouraged to proceed, and

17

the *Monthly Magazine* was the result. This commenced in July, 1796, and had a most decided success. The hosiery shop in St Paul's Churchyard was transformed into a bookshop.

He now married, and the story of his courtship is somewhat out of the common. Phillips, on coming to London, became a lodger in the house of a reputable milliner, who had several respectable girls in her employment. One of these young ladies was a good-looking Welshwoman named Griffiths. Phillips, as a strict vegetarian, found himself compelled to avoid the pastry, often made with lard, exposed for sale at the confectioner's. He mentioned this circumstance one morning to his landlady, who appears to have retailed it to her assistants. When Phillips returned home in the evening he found that the good-natured Welsh girl had prepared for him a pie which was free from the obnoxious ingredients. From this incident arose a friendship between Phillips and Miss Griffiths, which speedily led to a proposal of marriage. They were a handsome pair, and a somewhat precipitate matrimonial alliance was followed by many years of contentment and domestic peace. The old proverb of "Marry in haste, and repent at leisure," was conspicuously falsified in this case.

The *Monthly Magazine* was conducted at first by Dr. Priestley and afterwards by Dr. John Aikin, the author of the *Country round Manchester*. Phillips himself took a part in the management of the periodical, but how much it would be difficult to say. The contributors included Dr. Lettsom, "Peter Pindar," Capel Lofft, Sir John Carr (the pompous but then popular writer of books of travel, who was so mercilessly ridiculed by Edward Dubois), and Mr. Thomas Skinner Surr, an eminent novelist of the period, who became brother-in-law of Phillips. The monthly receipts from its sale amounted to £1,500. A quarrel ensued in 1806 with Dr. Aikin for his share in the arbitration of a dispute between Phillips and one of his authors. He had agreed to pay £200 for a compilation without making any reservation as to the quality of the work. Hence he was held liable for the payment without regard to the merit or demerit of the book. Phillips was so dissatisfied with the performance that, although he paid the money, he never published it. A naturally irritable temper led him to use such intemperate language to Dr. Aikin regarding this unlucky arbitration that the *Monthly Magazine* lost the services of that writer, who was then one of the best-known *litterateurs.* Phillips was not mollified by the appearance of a monthly periodical, " *The Athenæum,* edited by J. Aikin, M.D., late editor of the *Monthly Magazine ;* " and he advertised in the papers that Aikin never had been *the* editor of the monthly magazine, but had merely had a share in its conduct. Phillips was involved in another quarrel. A Mr. Blore and his son had been engaged to illustrate the *Antiquary's Magazine ;* but their performances did not give satisfaction to the publisher, who refused acceptance. This led to an angry wrangle. Nor was the subject of this notice above the tricks of the trade in which he was engaged. The Rev. George Gregory, D.D., was an Irishman, but his mother was a Lancashire woman, and when left a widow settled in Liverpool, where her son became a pupil of Holden, the mathematician, and in 1778 was curate of that town. He removed to London in 1782. Phillips paid him £400 for writing the prospectus of a *Dictionary of Arts and Science* and for allowing his name to appear on the title-page as author. The work was really done by the Rev. Jeremiah Joyce.

Success in business led to a removal of Phillips' publishing house from St. Paul's Churchyard to a much larger establishment in Blackfriars. His home was at Hampstead, where in an elegant villa the opulent bookseller enjoyed domestic pleasures that were commemorated in verse by Mr. S. J. Pratt, who was then celebrated in the domain of poetry, but whose fame has since become hopelessly lost in oblivion. Phillips entered into correspondence with Charles James Fox respecting the *History of James II.*, on which the great Whig statesman was then engaged. Four letters addressed to him by Fox have been printed; but although characteristic, they are not important.

In January, 1804, he wrote to Mr. Archibald Constable the following letter :—

DEAR SIR,—Happening to call this morning upon Longman and Rees, I was told by the latter that he had seen a pamphlet of Mr. Thelwall's in reply to some [*obliterated in MS.*] conduct of the Edinburgh reviewers, advertised as sold by me in London. Now although, dear sir, I feel as great an abhorrence of the scurrilous language and impertinent criticisms which disgraced the early numbers of that review as any man in Britain, yet I consider it my duty to disclaim every sort of connection with a pamphlet to which my name has been affixed without my consent, and, in fact, after my prohibition to the contrary. The temperance of the late numbers of the *Edinburgh Review* proves that the opinion which I entertain of the early numbers has been felt by you and by some of the conductors. You possess too strong a natural feeling of equity (I judge by your urbane manners) to derive any pleasure from the sale of a work on the ground of its scurrility and its disregard of decency, for it may be received as an axiom that the sale of any work of criticism will be, for a time, in the direct ratio of its degree of scurrility. After what I have written, you will perceive that in disclaiming any connection with Mr. Thelwall's pamphlet, I have no view to the favour of the Edinburgh reviewers. As a publisher I am willing to suffer every work of mine to stand or fall on its own merits. Favours from reviews I never seek ; my knowledge of the chicanery and corruption with which many of them are conducted renders me personally indifferent to their crimes of commission and omission. The public, I thank God, do me justice, and I generally find that my name in a title-page is as good a sanction for the respectable execution of a work as the *ipse dixit* of any anonymous critic.—Believe me, dear sir, with unfeigned regard, to be your sincere friend, R. PHILLIPS.

Phillips published in 1805 an *Account of the Early Life of Dr. Johnson*, which was made up of fragments of an autobiography extending with some breaks to his eleventh year, and of letters to and from Miss Hill Boothby. This compilation was denounced by Lord Jeffrey in the *Edinburgh Review* (vi., 436), who asserted that the "present rage for memoirs which infects the public has seldom given birth to a mote barefaced attempt at duping it."

· At Midsummer, 1807, the Livery of London elected the thriving bookseller to the office of High Sheriff for the ensuing year. This gave him an opportunity of showing the reality of his professions as a reformer, and during his tenure of power he introduced many improvements in the management of the prisons under his control, and in the treatment of debtors and others confined in them. He daily visited Newgate and the Fleet, and by personal inquiry made himself acquainted with the actual position of the inmates, and was able to ameliorate their condition in many respects. By his direction also several collecting boxes were conspicuously displayed, and the alms thus collected applied to the relief of the families of destitute debtors. He also insisted that persons whose indictment had been ignored by the Grand Jury should not be detained, as was then the custom, but be immediately released. The benevolent exertions of the High Sheriff made him a very popular man. His acceptance of knighthood was made the subject of some caustic criticisms by his political opponents, who probably thought that all marks of social distinction should be reserved for their own party. The Common Council of London appointed a deputation to present an address to the King; on the 30th of March, 1808, the deputation was received, and, in accordance with custom, some members of it were knighted. Amongst these was Mr. Richard Phillips, " greatly to the astonishment of his republican friends."

When Romilly introduced his measure for the amendment of our then barbarous and bloody penal code, Sir Richard addressed to him a very sensible letter, in which were pointed out some of those defects in the administration of the law with which the official experience of the High Sheriff had made him familiar. He tells us that it was a standing joke of the Recorder Sylvester and Alderman Curtis that when Curtis was sheriff the number hung after every sessions fell together at the New Drop like pounds of candles ! When Mansfield was Lord Chief Justice, Thurlow Chancellor, and Rose Recorder, executions at Tyburn were so numerous that Phillips, on one *hanging* holiday, saw nineteen victims on the gallows, the oldest of whom was not twenty-two.*

Fortune had so far shown herself favourable, but now she played him false. His affairs in 1809 became embarrassed, and a recourse to the bankruptcy court inevitable. Some friends aided him in securing from the general wreck the copyright of the *Monthly Magazine.* The management of this publication was the occupation of his remaining years, and his own contributions, under the signature of " Common Sense," attracted marked attention.

---

* *Million of Facts*, p. 767.

Southey writes to Coleridge bantering him upon the appearance of the numbers of the *Friend*. " Secondly, sir, though your essays appear in so tempting a shape to a lounger, the very fiends themselves were not more deceived by the *lignum vitæ* apples, when

> They, fondly thinking to allay
> Their appetite with gust, instead of fruit
> Chew'd bitter ashes,

than the reader is who takes up one of your papers from breakfast table, parlour window, sofa, or ottoman, thinking to amuse himself with a few minutes' light reading. We are informed, upon the authority of no less a man than Sir Richard Phillips, how 'it has long been a subject of just complaint among the lovers of English literature that our language has been deficient in lounging or parlour-window books,' and to remove the opprobrium from the language, Sir Richard advertises a list, most ending in *ana*, under the general title of *Lounging Books, or Light Reading*. I am afraid, Mr. Friend, that your predecessors would never have obtained their popularity unless their essays had been of the description Ο"μοιον ομοίῳ φίλον,—and this is a light age."*

Tom Moore's diary, under June, 1825, has two entries referring to our knight :—

23rd. Sir Richard Phillips called, and bored me beyond measure. Heard that Lord John Townshend was in Brighton; went and sat some time with him ; promised to drink tea with him and Lady John in the evening. Dined with Sir Richard ([Edward] Moore and I); his daughter a fine woman, brought up entirely on vegetables, like himself, both telling well for this Pythagorean diet. Went to Lord John T.; had much talk with him about Sheridan.

24th. Strolling about Brighton. Mr. —— was to arrive at four: conceived but little expectation from him; evidently a take-in. Dined

---

* *Life and Correspondence of Robert Southey*, vol. iii., p. 261.

in a hurry at the inn, and then set off with Moore to ——'s, who had claret, fruit, and Sir Richard Phillips laid out for us. Just as I thought, a good, vulgar, jolly, ignorant gentleman, [that is Mr. ——] whom Sheridan laid hold of in his latter days, and who was just as fit a recipient for his wit, as a hog trough would be for champagne. Got literally nothing out of him but a few glasses of wine, and escaped with Moore as soon as I could to a raffle at the Library. This is too bad; to come expressly, too, from London for such a bubble! If I had not met Lord John, I should have had just nothing for my pains. - Lord John, by-the-bye, told me that in Sheridan's song, " When 'tis night," it was originally, instead of "Some pretty girl and true" (which Lord John suggested), "Who had his last adieu."*

The following passage from the *Noctes Ambrosianæ* is interesting as giving the opinion of a political opponent who was at all events a good hater :—

North. I have some thoughts, James, of relinquishing animal food, and confining myself, like Sir Richard Phillips, to vegetable matter.

Shepherd. Ma troth, sir, there are mony millions o' Sir Richard Phillipses in the world if a' that's necessary to make ane be abstinence frae animal food, It's my belief that no aboon ane in ten o' mankind at large pree animal food from week's end to week's end. Sir Richard Phillips on that question is in a great majority.

Tickler. North, accustomed all his life to three courses—fish, flesh, and fowl—would think himself an absolute phenomenon, or miracle of man, were he to devote the remainder of his meals to potatoes and barley bannocks, pease soup, macaroni, and the rest of the range of bloodless but sappy nature. How he would be laughed at for his heroic resolution if overheard by three million strapping Irish beggars, wi' their bowels yearning for potatoes and potheen!

North. No quizzing, boys, of the old gentleman. Talking of Sir Richard Phillips, I am sorry he is no longer—to my knowledge, at least—the Editor of a magazine. In his hands the *Monthly* was a valuable periodical. One met with information there that now-a-days I at least know not where to look for; and though the knight's own scientific speculations were sometimes sufficiently absurd, they for the most part exhibited the working of a powerful and even original mind.

---

* *Diary of Thomas Moore,* vol. iv., p. 296.

Shepherd. I agree wi' him in thinking Sir Isaac Newton out o' his reckonin' entirely about gravitation. There's nae sic thing as a law o' gravitation. What would be the use o't? Will onybody tell me that an apple or a stone wadna fa' to the grun' without sic a law? Sumphs that say sae! They fa' to the grun' because they're heavy.

North. I also liked Sir Richard's politics.

Shepherd. Haw!!!

North. He was consistent, James; and my mind is so constituted as always to connect together the ideas of consistency and conscientiousness. In his criticisms on literature and the fine arts, he appeared to me generally to say what he thought the truth; and although sometimes manifestly swayed in his judgment on such matters, like almost all other men, by his political predilections, his pages were seldom if ever tainted with malignity. And on the whole Dick was a fair foe.

Tickler. He was the only editor, sir, that ever saw the real faults and defects of Maga, and therefore, although he sometimes blamed, he never abused her.*

This should be compared with the verdict given by the same authority December, 1822, when we have this reference to Phillips in the *Noctes* :—

O'Doherty. Sir Richard Phillips is another great genius, and yet he does not write a good magazine.

Tickler. Why, Pythagoras, my dear fellow, is one of the most contemptible magaziners in the world. He is a dirty little jacobin, that thinks there is more merit in making some dirty little improvement on a threshing-machine, than in composing an *Iliad.* He is a mere plodding, thick-skulled, prosing dunderpate; and everything he puts forth seems as if it had been written by the stink of gas in the fifth story of a cotton-mill—a filthy jacobinical dog, sir.

North. Poor idiot! he is hammering at Napoleon still; now, indeed, he has taken to exhibiting a twopenny-halfpenny bust of him, in his house in Bridge Street.—Gentlemen and ladies one shilling; children and servants sixpence only!"

The most curious incident in his career as publisher was the refusal of the manuscript of *Waverley.* The author's demands

* *Blackwood's Magazine*, vol. xxii., 1827, p. 125.

were in excess of the value placed upon the novel by the publisher. He says that it was advertised for a time as by W. Scott, and then the name withdrawn, and the work issued as by an unknown author. He also states that he published several works for George III., and a folio on the MSS. of the Herculaneum for George IV. The "first gentleman in Europe" was certainly not the *author* of that book, but George III. may well have been the writer of pamphlets on agriculture, as he is believed to have contributed to the *Annals of Agriculture.*

Cobbett has a characteristic reference to the subject of our notice. "Sir Richard Phillips," he says, "who once rang a peal in my ears against shooting and hunting, does, indeed, eat neither flesh, fish, nor fowl. His abstinence surpasses that of a Carmelite, while his bulk would not disgrace a Benedictine monk or Protestant dean. But he forgets that his shoes and breeches and gloves are made of the skins of animals. He forgets that he writes, and very eloquently too, with what has been taken from a fowl; and that in order to cover the books which he has made and sold hundreds of flocks and scores of droves must have perished: nay, that to get him his beaver hat, a beaver must have been hunted and killed, and in the doing of which many beavers have been wounded and left to pine away the rest of their lives, and perhaps left many little orphan beavers to lament the murder of their parents."*

In *Blackwood's Magazine* for Sept., 1829 (xxvi., 337), there is a long letter from Phillips, who was "meditating to comprise Scotland" in the general tour of the kingdom he was then

---

* Quoted in *Blackwood's Magazine*, 1823, xiv., 318, from *A Year's Residence in America.*

undertaking, and thought it necessary to explain his views on gravitation and other subjects, lest his reception in North Britain should not be of the character to be desired in the interest of his work.

Phillips understood the importance of despatch, and narrates as the most memorable instance of celerity in English typography that effected in the case of D'Amberger's *Travels through Africa*. He received the German volume of the original on a Wednesday morning, at eleven o'clock. Before twelve, thirty-six sheets were divided among six active and able translators. Before one, the map, or finish, and the three engravings were in the printer's hands, and from that time a regular supply was kept up to above twenty pairs of cases of pica type. On Thursday evening 1,500 of several sheets were worked at press, and proofs revised of the engravings, which on Friday morning were in the hands of colourers. On Friday, at two, the thirty-fourth and last sheet was in chase; and at eight the whole was rapidly drying. On Friday morning was written a translator's critical preface of twelve pages. At two o'clock on Saturday morning the binders brought in perfect volumes. At half-past two the clerks were subscribing the volume through the trade; and on Saturday evening, at half-past six, not one copy remained on hand. The 1,500 were all sold.

Phillips was a friend and correspondent of the famous Edinburgh publisher, Archibald Constable, and the following letters addressed to him are published by his son:—

LONDON, *20th Feb.*, 1817.

DEAR SIR,—Will you exchange with me for a set of the *Encyclopædia Britannica*? That amount of my wares would soon be vended in N.B. I would soon extend it to a set of the *Edinburgh Review*, clean or used. I want both for my own library, and not for sale, and my frequent consequent reference to both would serve as valuable advertisements. I would send you, per sea, a fair and equal assortment of my books, and if you desired it, a set of the *Monthly Magazine.* I have been diverting the melancholy of a man of enterprise, who lives in bad times, by a piece of downright authorship (I don't mean my old trick of bookmaking), and in a few days it will see the light, under the title of *A Morning's Walk from London to Kew.* What a rare subject for your inimitable Jeffrey—a bookseller in the press, and playing the philosopher! What an exquisite subject for wit and raillery! Made the most of, it might raise the *Review* 1,000! Every author would enjoy the jokes, and every bookseller would feel a keen interest. A copy shall find its way to Edinburgh, but whether in the shape of a provocative to your great critic, or for a place in the library of Scotia's great bibliopolist, I have not determined.—I am, dear sir, yours truly, etc.,   R. PHILLIPS.

HOLLOWAY, *March 17th,* 1817.

DEAR SIR,—I received your delightful case of books, and I bear a willing testimony that they are among the best in the English language. They reached my Tusculum on Saturday evening; on Sunday City friends engaged me, but this morning I availed myself of the dawn of day to unpack the case, and like a glutton at a great feast, I tasted of every volume with greediness. I take up my pen to address a few lines to you in consequence of my ambition to see my *Walk to Kew* treated in the *Edinburgh Review.* I care not for praise—I am either above it or below it; if the author and his book are condemned, I shall be taught, and I am willing to learn; and in either case praise or censure will serve the public. I' truth, my dear sir, I have long had in my head certain crotchets to which I am partial, and some of them I have displayed at various lengths in that volume of the *Walk to Kew.* One of these is a theory of the cause of *gravitation.* I published it first in the *Monthly Magazine* in October, 1811, and I enclose the sheet. I have repeated it briefly in the *Walk to Kew*, page 329, etc., but on cutting open the pages of the *Edinburgh Review,* I find in vōl. x., " On the Provost's Le Sage," and in vol. xiii., " Vince on Gravitation," something so like my theory, that a hasty and superficial reader would conclude that I had been pillaging and disguising Le Sage! I write then for the eye of the able, learned, and candid author of those articles, and I invite his attention to what I have done at page 329, *Walk to Kew*, and in the enclosed sheet. I never saw or heard of Le Sage till this day. Since I published in 1811 I have been told of Vince's book, but I never could get it; and I am anxious to invite the comparison of your learned critic between both my articles and my system and that of Le Sage. He will see that, though alike, they are essentially different; and I persuade myself that my theory is less complicated and artificial than that of Le Sage, and not liable to the strong objection at the foot of page 148. The same learned critic will not fail likewise to be struck with an observation at page 187, like another idea of Le Sage's, and he will observe a further coincidence at pages 352-3, but without any likeness. I pray of you to do me the favour and the justice to show him this letter, and invite his attention also to my analysis of the doctrine of Prediction at page 243, etc. I conclude you and my agent will pleasantly arrange the exchange, and I am, dear sir, with increased regard, yours, etc., R. PHILLIPS.

P.S.—As an excuse for not reading or seeing these numbers of the *Edinburgh Review*, I beg to explain that I was sheriff in 1807-8, and too much engaged in other matters.

———

HOLLOWAY, *October 17th*, 1818.

DEAR SIR,—I have just been engaged in transferring your wonderful list of books in the press to my Varieties. Your spirit of enterprise is ably directed, and every one of the works is most creditable to your taste and intelligence. Methinks you do not allow me to be as useful to you as my sense of your great merits would lead me to be if I saw more of your works as they appear. Most of them would command a column of my Proemium, and in general my warmest eulogies. I trust you now begin to know enough of me to be aware that I am the slave of no selfish feelings, and much disposed to do justice to merit wherever and however it appears. Can you ascertain for me whether your illustrious Playfair and your professors and societies received the copies of my essay which I addressed to them? I *defy* their objections, and *demand* their just concessions.—I am, dear sir, very truly yours, R. PHILLIPS.

P.S.—After I had wafered my letter I met with the essay on "Probabilities" in No. 46, and was surprised at page 333 to see an argument and a series of inferences about the uniform direction of the planetary motions. Now this uniformity, the learned critic will observe, is *on my system* a necessary consequence of the motion of the sun round its own centre of action. That motion is produced by the motion of the planets, while it also produces the motions of the planets, which of necessity are governed in their direction by the direction of the uniform cause. To the acute and candid mind of the critic I need not observe on the gratuitous hypothesis of Le Sage's moving atoms, and on the absurdity of their producing their effects by impinging against the planets. The doctrine of an elastic medium, quiescent till disturbed by the foreign or novel bodies of the planets, is, I humbly conceive, far more probable, and equally applicable to all the phenomena.   R. P.

————

October 24th, 1822.

DEAR SIR,—In a recent visit which I made to Captain Parry at Castlebeare, I found that you had returned to Edinburgh, and in better health. It was my purpose to have called upon you on the subject of a letter which I had received from your representative in Edinburgh, which betrayed very angry and foolish feelings, and to have urged a word for that liberty of discussion of which you and your friends have made such free and profitable use. On my part I must be regarded as a friend of the *Edinburgh Review* and its interests, but, on the other hand, I have not interfered in every case between the opinions of my correspondents and that work in the *Monthly Magazine.* I have often done so, but on some occasions it is inexpedient and impracticable. I learn, however, that a war or petty fire has been opened upon me in your magazine. I am too busy to run after such things, though I always endeavour to amend from the observations of enemies. A fact, however, has come across me this morning—if it be fact—which displays an excessive malignity. A Mr. Campbell persuaded me last spring to bring out for him an edition of *Ossian.* Such a thing was not much in my way, and I do not covet miscellaneous works, or, as you may easily suppose, I could deluge the world with books. I could do all I pleased in this way, but it does *not* please me. Campbell, however, has been showing a letter, written, as he says, by Mr. Jeffrey, or by some one in his name or by his authority, in which it is pointedly said that his *Ossian* cannot be reviewed in the *Edinburgh Review,* because it has my name on the title-page—that nothing of mine will ever be noticed there— that my name has damned the work, etc., etc. The impudence of this libel speaks for itself, and as words are cheap, might be retorted, but I am for peace, and the object of this note is to appeal to your urbanity and good sense, and to arrive at a better understanding of existing differences.—I am, very truly, etc., etc.,   R. PHILLIPS.

To this the following reply was sent :—

EDINBURGH, *November 6th,* 1822.

DEAR SIR RICHARD,—I have received your note of the 24th October. I returned to Edinburgh with improved health about three months ago. I should have been very happy to have seen you had you come to the neighbourhood of Castlebeare before I left it, and to have talked over literary projects. I knew very little, however, of what had been passing in the literary world for the last two years, excepting the publications of my own house, which have been, you are aware, both numerous and popular. My state of health did not permit of my giving myself the trouble to know more. I have certainly not observed anything in the *Edinburgh* or *Scot's Magazine* of the offensive nature as to your undertakings which you point at, and if such has appeared, I hope I may venture to assure you that it cannot have proceeded from any malignant feeling, but from some accidental effusion of an occasional contributor. The *Monthly Magazine,* which originated with yourself, has always been a great favourite of mine; it possessed for many years an unrivalled place of excellence in British monthly literature, and even now, in spite of all contending opposition, still maintains its own rank in utility. With regard to the *Edinburgh Review,* you have not at this time to learn that it has ever been placed above the partiality and influence of booksellers. Works from your press, from our learned fathers in the Row, Tom Tegg in Cheapside, and those from my own, all experience the same independent treatment. I assure you that neither the name of author nor bookseller has the least sway with the editor in regulating praise or censure in the pages of the *Edinburgh Review;* it was begun on that principle, has been most usefully and successfully conducted on it, and must continue for the present generation to be so. We cannot, you know, answer for those who may succeed us, more than we can at present for the foolish misrepresentations to which the projects, the conduct, and the motives of all of us are every day exposed. I have not kept any enumeration of the publications reviewed, but my impression is that there is a very fair proportion on the whole of works with your name on the title-page; this is my idea. But I am quite sure the letter which you point at, insinuating their total exclusion, was quite unauthorized by any person connected with the *Edinburgh Review*, and altogether unworthy of notice. I think, however, my good sir, you have sometimes been in the habit of attacking the *Review* in the *Monthly Magazine.* I don't mean to approve of this in estimating the character of your work; and although, on the whole, I have always considered it excellent as preserving a vast mass of useful information, yet has it not been sometimes illiberal and even reckoned unjust? Perfection, you know, is not attainable.—I am, dear Sir Richard, your faithful and obedient servant,

ARCHIBALD CONSTABLE.

When the crash came that overwhelmed the house of Constable, Sir Richard wrote a sympathetic letter.

74, ST. PAUL's CHURCHYARD.

DEAR SIR,—I have more than once within the last nine months taken up my pen to express my sympathy towards you, and in my own doleful story claim yours for me. I had retired to Brighton, leaving good working stock, which had cost me £70,000, in the hands of Whittaker, when in December last all my dreams of ease and comfort were violently disturbed, my stock blocked up, and engagements of all kinds reverting back on me. . . Enough of myself, however. I wish you would put me in the way of proving my esteem for you. We have been contemporaries, and your talents have always extorted my admiration. I am qualified to judge of them, and I cheerfully testify in regard to your superiority, not only as a man of business, but as a valuable pioneer of literature and a patron of genius. You have added to the glory of Scotland, and through its genius and industry have advanced the human race. On this point there is but one opinion; but how the sentiment can be made available to your future fortunes is a difficulty which ought not to be insurmountable. If it could be well directed, you would soon be among the most prosperous men of your time. I write in the dark, and perhaps my observations are unnecessary, and may be ill-timed. I claim credit only for the best of motives, and for being, dear sir, truly and devotedly yours,   R. PHILLIPS.

Of his later years we have no particulars, but his literary works show that he was not inactive. The following is the completest list I have been able to compile of the various publications which came from his pen; but in addition to these, he is known to have compiled or edited several school-books, which formed a profitable part of his trade. He tells us himself that all the elementary books under the names of Rev. James Adair, Rev. David Blair, Rev. J. Goldsmith, Rev. S. Barrow, M. l'Abbé Bossut, Miss or Mrs. M. Pelham, were his productions between 1798 and 1815. Mr. Thomas believes that he also wrote some of the books which pass as the productions of. Rev. C. C. Clarke, George Hamilton, Rev. John Robinson, and D. Robinson. Quérard attributes to him some of the works issued as by William Mavor :—

On the Practices of Anonymous Critics. 1806.

A Letter to the Livery of London relative to the Duties and Office of Sheriff. London, 1808. 12mo.

A Letter to the Livery of London relative to the Views of the Writer in executing the office of Sheriff. Second edition. By Sir R. P. London : Gillet, 1808. 8vo. He states the cost of serving the office at 2,000 guineas (p. 268).

Treatise on the Powers and Duties of Juries and on the Criminal Laws of England. London, 1811. 12mo. This was translated into French by M. Comte, and from French into Spanish by Antonio Ortiz de Zarate y Herrara (Madrid, 1821).

Communications relative to the Datura Stramonium as a Cure for Asthma. London, 1811. 8vo.

Social Philosophy, or a New System of Practical Ethics.

Golden Rules for Jurymen. London, 1814. Printed on a sheet.

A Morning's Walk from London to Kew. London, 1817. 8vo.

18

In this last (p. 213) he mentions his school-days at Chiswick, and the Sunday service at the church: "I saw with the mind's eye the widow of Hogarth and her maiden relative Richardson walking up the aisle, dressed in their silk sacks, their raised head-dresses, their black colashes, their lace ruffles, and their high-crook'd canes, preceded by their aged servant Samuel, who, after he had wheeled his mistress to church in her Bath-chair, carried the prayer-books up the aisle and opened and shut the pew! There too was the portly Dr. Griffiths, of the *Monthly Review*, with his literary wife, in her neat and elevated wire-winged cap! And ofttimes the vivacious and angelic Duchess of Devonshire, whose bloom had not then suffered from the cankerworm of pecuniary distress, created by the luxury of charity! Nor could I forget the humble distinction of the aged sexton Mortefee, whose skill in psalmody enabled him to lead the wretched group of singers whom Hogarth so happily portrayed; whose performance with the tuning-fork excited so much wonder in little boys; and whose gesticulations and contortions of head, hand, and body, in beating time, were not outdone even by Joah Bates in the commemorations of Handel!" (p. 214).

A Million of Facts of Correct Data and Elementary Constants in the Entire Circle of the Sciences and on all Subjects of Speculation and Practice. London, 1832. 8vo.

Letter on the Theory of Education. London, 1835.

The Importance of Educating the Poor, a Sermon by John Evans, to which is added the interesting letter of Sir Richard Phillips, Sheriff of London, on the present state of the prisons of the metropolis. Second edition. Canterbury, 1808.

Phillip's letter is addressed to George Cumberland.   He states in it that on a certain memorial from a hundred and fifty-two of the criminals, in Newgate, twenty-five signed in a fair hand, twenty-six in a bad and partly illegible hand, and the remaining hundred and one were marksmen, having never learned to write.   "At the present time, of the men in the condemned cells, under sentence of death, five can neither read nor write."   Three women under the same sentences were also illiterate.

It may, perhaps, be guessed from several of the titles here to be given, by those skilled in paradoxical literature, that Sir Richard was an opponent of the Newtonian system of astronomy.   He attempted to convert Professor De Morgan in 1836, and although he did not succeed, the latter has given his writings a place in his *Budget of Paradoxes.* The pension given to defenders of current science all appeared jobs to Phillips, who regarded the " present philosophy " as "a system of execrable nonsense by which quacks live on the faith of fools."   De Morgan's judgment on these writings is terse and worth quoting: "Sir Richard Phillips had four valuable qualities : honesty, zeal, ability, and courage.   He applied them all to teaching matters about which he knew nothing, and gained himself an uncomfortable life and a ridiculous memory."*

The Phenomena called by the Name of Gravitation proved to be Proximate Effects of the Orbicular Rotary Motions of the Earth.   In *Tilloch's Philosophical Magazine,* xlx., 1817, pp. 430—442.

Further Considerations on the Doctrine that the Phenomena of Terrestrial Gravitation are occasioned by Known Terres-

---

* De Morgan, *Budget of Paradoxes.*   London, 1872.   P. 145.

trial Motions. In *Tilloch's Philosophical Magazine*, l., 1817, pp. 101—105.

On the New Theory of the System of the Universe. *Tilloch's Philosophical Magazine*, l., 1817, pp. 219—224.

Popular Abstract of the New System of Philosophy, a folio chart.

Essays on the Proximate Mechanical Causes of the General Phenomena of the Universe. By Sir Richard Phillips. London: Adlard, 1818. 12mo. Second edition, 1821.

Electricity and Galvanism explained on the Mechanical Theory of Matter and Motion. London, 1820. Pp. 393—397. *Tilloch's Magazine,* lvi., 1820, 195—200.

Protest against the Prevailing Principles of Natural Philosophy, with the Development of a Common Sense System. No date. 16 pp. Another edition, 1830. 8vo. Pp. 71. The copy in the British Museum has an autograph letter of the author.

The Proximate Causes of Material Phenomena, and the True Principles of Universal Causation, considered and illustrated. By Sir Richard Phillips. 2nd edit. London, printed for the author, 1821. 8vo.

Four Dialogues between an Oxford Tutor and a Disciple of the Common Sense Philosophy relative to the Proximate Causes of Material Phenomena. By Sir Richard Phillips. London: Sherwood, 1824. 8vo.

Golden Rules and Social Philosophy, or a New System of Practical Ethics. By Sir Richard Phillips. London, printed for the author, 1826. 8vo. Pp. 363. In the dedication to Simon Bolivar, he mentions that he had known Miranda, whose tragic fate did not deter the great liberator. This work contains some of his pieces which had been separately published. *The Golden Rules for Electors and Jurymen* had reached nearly half a million copies. In 1823 he had retired to Brighton on a moderate competency, but suffered great losses in the panic of 1825.

Natural Philosophy [then on p. 2 *Principles of Natural Philosophy developed and proposed for Adoption*]. By Sir Richard Phillips. [Dated on p. 16, Park Row, Knightsbridge, August 4th, 1827.] 8vo. Pp. 16.

Protest against the Prevailing Principles of Natural Philosophy, with Development of a Common Sense System. By Sir Richard Phillips. London. 8vo. Pp. 72. In the British Museum copy there is a MS. letter to Captain Kater, dated 10th April, 1830.

Popular Abstract of the New System of Physical Philosophy proposed by Sir Richard Phillips, vide his Essays and the "Monthly Magazine" for 1817 and 1818 (a broadsheet sold at 6*d.*).

A Dictionary of the Arts of Life and Civilization. By Sir Richard Phillips. London: Sherwood. 14*s.* 8vo. The dedication is dated December 13th, 1833. "The author in early life acquired a taste for such subjects in a great London brewery, which carried mill work machinery, etc., and the arts of fermentation to their limit" (p. vi.).

A Century of Original Aphorisms on the Proximate Causes of the Phenomena of Nature. London, 1835. 12mo.

A Personal Tour through the United Kingdom, describing Living Objects and Contemporaneous Interests. London: Horatio Phillips. 8vo. Number 1. Bedfordshire, Northamptonshire, Leicestershire. Number 2. Derbyshire, Nottinghamshire. (No more appears to have been published.) He gives an interesting sketch of his visit to Leicester, where most of his contemporaries of 1790 were dead.

It is by the *Million of Facts* that Phillips is now best known. It is an immense collection, and although many of the "constants" have already become obsolete, it may still be examined with interest. The Newtonians come in for reprobation. The plan of the work is that of a classified collection of scraps on all the arts and sciences. It was so popular that five large editions were published in seven years. His preface to the stereotyped edition is dated December, 1839. He remarks that "his pretentions for such a task are prolonged and uninterrupted intercourse with books and men of letters. He has, for forty-nine years, been occupied as the literary conductor of various public journals of reputation; he has superintended the press in the printing of many hundred books, in every branch of human pursuit; and he has been intimately associated with men celebrated for their attainments in each of them."

Occasionally there are autobiographical notes of interest. Thus he says that early in 1825 he suggested the first idea of the Society for the Diffusion of Useful Knowledge to Dr. Birkbeck, and then, by his advice, to Lord Brougham. His idea was that of a fund, for vending or giving away books and tracts, like the Religious Tract Society. From another paragraph we learn that amongst his pictures was a Madonna de la Seggia, said to be the one formerly at Woodstock in the collection of King Charles.*

To avoid the immense expenses of railway viaducts, embankments, and removal of streets, Sir R. Phillips proposed suspension-roads, ten feet above the house-tops, with inclined planes of 20° or 30°, and stationary engines to assist the rise and fall at each end. Cities might be traversed in this

---

* *Million of Facts*, p. 630.

way on right lines, with intermediate points for descent and ascent.*

"Sir Richard Phillips," says Dr. Smiles, "was one of the few who early recognised the important uses of the locomotive, and its employment on a large scale for the haulage of goods and passengers by railway. In his 'Morning's Walk to Kew' he crossed the line of the Wandsworth and Croydon Railway, when the idea seems to have occurred to him, as it afterwards did to Thomas Gray, that in the locomotive and the railway were to be found the germs of a great and peaceful social revolution :—

"'I found delight,' said Sir Richard, in his book published in 1813, 'in witnessing at Wandsworth the economy of horse labour on the iron railway. Yet a heavy sigh escaped me as I thought of the inconceivable millions of money which have been spent about Malta, four or five of which might have been the means of extending double lines of iron railway from London to Edinburgh, Glasgow, Holyhead, Milford, Falmouth, Yarmouth, Dover, and Portsmouth. A reward of a single thousand would have supplied coaches and other vehicles, of various degrees of speed, with the best tackle for readily turning out; and we might, ere this, have witnessed our mail-coaches running at the rate of ten miles an hour drawn by a single horse, or impelled fifteen miles an hour by Blenkinsop's steam-engine. Such would have been a legitimate motive for overstepping the income of a nation, and the completion of so great and useful work would have afforded rational ground for public triumph in general jubilee.'" †

---

* This looks very like an anticipation of the elevated railways of New York, though even these have not reached the height that Phillips thought desirable.

† *Life of George Stephenson.* By Samuel Smiles   P. 66.

He was equally interested in steam navigation. While
Fulton was in England, converting a speculation into a reality,
he was in friendly intercourse with Sir R. Phillips, to whom
he despatched a triumphant letter on the evening of his first
voyage on the Hudson. This letter was shown to Earl
Stanhope and four or five eminent engineers, but treated with
scorn, as descriptive of an impossibility. Sir R. Phillips then
advertised for a company, to repeat on the Thames what had
been done on the Hudson; but he obtained only two ten-
pound conditional subscriptions, after expending some pounds
in advertising! He then printed, with commendation,
Fulton's letter in the *Monthly Magazine*, and his credulity
was generally reprobated! Then, for several years, the
American accounts were treated as falsehoods, till a man
ruined himself by launching a steam-vessel on the Clyde,
though afterwards a Clyde vessel was brought round to the
Thames. In her first voyage to Margate none would trust
themselves, and Phillips, three of his family, and five or six
more, were the first hardy adventurers! To allay alarms he
published a letter in the newspapers, and ere the end of that
summer he saw the same packet depart with three hundred
and fifty passengers.*

The stereotyped edition of the *Million of Facts* contains a
good portrait of Sir Richard Phillips, from a drawing by
Turnerelli.

The *Athenæum* for July 16th, 1853, contains an advertise-
ment, filling a column, of Phillips' works for schools. One
of these is Phillips' *Five Hundred Questions, forming an
Interrogative System of Instruction, applied to all the Educational Works*, published by Sir Richard Phillips, post 4to,

* *Million of Facts*, p. 797.

2s. each. A key to each set, 9d. each. Whittaker & Co., Ave Maria Lane.

The literary abours of the veteran author had apparently a preservative influence upon his health. The success of the *Million of Facts* must have been very gratifying to him. The final edition of the work appeared in 1839, and in the following year, on the 2nd of April, he died at Brighton, in his seventy-third year. On his tomb in Brighton Old Churchyard is this epitaph, which, with the exception of one date and the concluding paragraph, was written by the knight:

HERE REST THE REMAINS OF

SIR RICHARD PHILLIPS, KNIGHT.

[*Born December 13th, 1767 ; died April 2nd, 1840.*]

He lived through an age of remarkable events and changes, and was an active and anxious contemporary.

He was Sheriff of London and Middlesex in 1807-8, and an effective ameliorator of a stern and uncharitable criminal code.

He was, in 1798, the inventor and promulgator of the interrogative system of education, by which new impulses were given to the intelligence of society.

He also placed natural philosophy on the basis of common sense, and developed the laws of nature on immutable principles, which will always be co-extensive with the respect of mankind for truth ; in the promotion of these objects, and a multitude of others, he wrote and published more original works than any of his contemporaries, and in all of them advocated civil liberty, general benevolence, ascendency of justice, and the improvement of the human race.

As a son, husband, father, and friend, he was also an example for imitation, and left a mourning family little to inherit besides a good name.

He died in the enjoyment of that peace which is the sweet fruit of the Christian religion, and which the world can neither give nor take away.

FIRST BALLOON ASCENT IN ENGLAND.

BIBLIOGRAPHY.

"*An Account of the First Aërial Voyage in England.*" By Vincent Lunardi. London, 1784.

"*Astra Castra, a History of Aërostation.*" By H. Turner. London, 1865.

This paper first appeared in the "Manchester Guardian," 15th Sept. 1884.

THE FIRST BALLOON ASCENT IN ENGLAND.

THE accounts that reached this country in 1784 of the aerial ascents in France were received with mingled interest and incredulity. John Bull was just a little disposed to think that his lively neighbours were romancing, and he was perhaps also, when admitting the truth of the discovery, a little inclined to regret that the invention had not arisen upon his own domain. There have been several projects for aerial locomotion, for, not to mention the myths of Icarus and Daedalus, or the oriental fables of Solomon's carpet, there was the suggestion, made in the seventeenth century by the Jesuit Lana, who thought that metallic globes might be exhausted of air, and so made to ascend. The experiments of Cavendish, who in 1766 discovered the remarkable lightness of hydrogen gas, or inflammable air as it was then called, and the further experiments of Cavallo, seemed to point in the direction of aerostation ; but the actual discovery of the balloon was due to the genius of Etienne and Jean Montgolfier. Their attention was called to the subject by a passage in Cavendish's book, and as far back as the middle of 1782 they made experiments. The first person to ascend in a balloon was Pilâtre de Rozier, who lost his life in a subsequent aerial voyage. He made two or three expeditions. The Montgolfier balloons were fitted with a gallery and a grate, as they were fire balloons. The first balloon in which "inflammable air" was enclosed was that of MM. Roberts and Charles. When they ascended,

Dec. 1st, 1783, their departure was watched by a great crowd. A pamphlet on the "Air Balloon" went through three editions, and the subject was a general theme of conversation. Amongst others who took an interest in the subject was a young Italian, Vincent Lunardi, who was secretary to the Neapolitan Embassy at London. He was then only 25, and had the ardour befitting his age. One of his compatriots, Count Zambecari, had projected an aerial ascent, but the affair came to nothing. Lunardi felt the undertaking was hazardous in many ways, and he thought that public opinion would be conciliated if the first experiment were made in behalf of charity. He therefore applied to Sir George Howard for permission to ascend from the gardens of Chelsea Hospital, and offered to devote the profits to the funds of that institution. With the King's approbation, consent was given, and the matter publicly announced. The balloon itself was exhibited at Exeter Change, but did not excite so much attention as the speculative diplomatist had expected.

But whilst Lunardi was maturing his plans, a Frenchman named Moret announced that he would ascend at no great distance from Chelsea Hospital, and at an earlier date than that which Lunardi had fixed upon. But Moret's attempted ascent was an ignominious failure, and the enraged mob, regarding him as an impostor, tore the balloon to pieces and did much injury in the neighbourhood. The authorities of Chelsea Hospital now took the alarm and rescinded their permission, nor could all the entreaties of Lunardi induce them to risk the possibility of a riot in case of failure. After looking about for some alternative, he applied to Sir Watkin Lewis, M.P., who was then colonel of the Honourable Artillery Company, for permission to use their grounds in

Moorfields for the ascent.   Lunardi further offered to pay
100 guineas to a fund then being raised for the family of Sir
Bernard Turner, a deceased member of the corps.   There
was great difference of opinion, and at two courts of the
company the proposal was only carried by the casting vote
of Sir Watkin Lewis, who had made himself master of the
details, and was untouched by the apprehensions felt by
many of his officers. ~ Lunardi had next to overcome some
difficulties with the keeper of the place where the balloon
was being shown, and, indeed, did not recover possession of
the " machine " until the intervention of the law had been
invoked.

When Wednesday, the fifteenth of September, arrived, the
apprehension of a tumult had prevented many from being
present, and only those were admitted who had previously
bought tickets, which were sold at a guinea, half a guinea,
and five shillings each.   But the streets were thronged with
spectators, and the householders whose windows commanded
a view of the Artillery Grounds had made the most of the
opportunity by letting them to sightseers.   The Prince of
Wales, Charles James Fox, Lord North, Edmund Burke,
R. B. Sheridan, and many other famous personages were in
the enclosure to witness the novel enterprise.   There was
some delay in filling the balloon, and the populace became
impatient and suspicious.   When " the gallery " was annexed
to the globe, it was found that there was not force enough to
take both Lunardi and Mr. George Biggin, who had intended
to accompany him.   The latter relinquished his position, and
Lunardi was next driven to distraction by the announcement
that there had been an accident which would prevent the
balloon from ascending.   Fortunately, he found that the

injury was trifling, and he determined to risk all. "I threw myself into the gallery," he says, "determined to hazard no further accidents that might consign me and the balloon to the fury of the populace, which I saw was on the point of bursting. An affecting, because unpremeditated, testimony of approbation and interest in my fate was here given. The Prince of Wales, and the whole surrounding assembly, almost at one instant took off their hats, hailed my resolution, and expressed the kindest and most cordial wishes for my safety and success. At five minutes after two the last gun was fired, the cords divided, and the balloon rose, the company returning my signals of adieu with the most unfeigned acclamations and applauses. The effect was that of a miracle on the multitudes which surrounded the place, and they passed from incredulity and menace into the most extravagant expressions of approbation and joy. At the height of twenty yards the balloon was a little depressed by the wind, which had a fine effect; it held me over the ground for a few seconds, and seemed to pause majestically before its departure. On discharging a part of the ballast, it ascended to the height of two hundred yards. As a multitude lay before me of a hundred and fifty thousand people, who had not seen my ascent from the ground, I had recourse to every stratagem to let them know I was in the gallery." His sensations he has described in a very graphic manner. The city lay beneath him, but so reduced that he could find no simile to describe it. "I had not the slightest sense of motion from the machine; I knew not whether it went swiftly or slowly, whether it ascended or descended, whether it was agitated or tranquil, but by the appearance or disappearance of objects on the earth. I moved to different parts of the gallery, I adjusted the furniture and apparatus, I uncorked my bottle, ate, drank, and wrote just as in my study. The height had not the effect which a much lesser degree of it has near the earth—that of producing giddiness." At about half-past three he descended in a cornfield, on the common at South Mimms, but re-ascended amidst the cheers of those who had witnessed his arrival. One of Lunardi's objects had been to test the value of oars as a means of descent. One he lost almost at the beginning, but the remaining one he continued to use; and at twenty minutes past four, some labourers in a field at Standon, near Ware, in Hertfordshire, were amazed by calls for assistance from an odd-looking structure that had apparently dropped out of the clouds. They declined to have any dealings with this "devil's horse;" but a young woman, Elizabeth Brett, endowed either with more courage or greater compassion, boldly took hold of the cord, and incited the men to help her. The example was contagious, and Lunardi descended to earth, having safely accomplished the first aerial ascent ever made in this country. General Smith, who had followed on horseback the course of the balloon from London, with others, now rode up; and after resting at the Bull Inn, at Ware, Lunardi was introduced to Mr. William Baker, M.P., who took him to his seat at Bayford Bury, and entertained him with characteristic English hospitality.

Lunardi was now the hero of the day. Dining with the judges at the Lord Mayor's table, two incidents were mentioned as indicative of the general interest. He had taken two oars, but one of these fell from the balloon early in the ascent. A lady amongst the spectators mistook this, in its descent, for the body of the aeronaut, and the horror which

19

the sight inspired had such an affect upon her that she died in a few days. This story was "capped" by one of the judges who said that a jury, rather than miss the spectacle, promptly acquitted the prisoner before them, and the court as promptly adjourned in order to witness the ascent. Thus, if he had been the cause of the loss of a life, he had also been the cause of one b ing saved. The King was interested in the matter. There was a Cabinet Council at the time that Lunardi was passing over London. "We may resume our deliberations on the subject before us at pleasure," said the King, "but we may never see poor Lunardi again." The council broke up, and the King, with Pitt and the other Ministers of State, watched the balloon till it passed out of their sight. On the Wednesday following Lunardi was presented at Court, and was much pleased by the fact that the King talked to him for about five minutes on the subject of his ascent.

Lunardi soon had imitators. Messrs. Blanchard and Sheldon ascended from Chelsea, 16th October, 1784; and Blanchard and Jeffreys crossed the Channel from Dover to Calais, 7th January, 1785. Sir Edward Vernon and Count Zambecari, with a young lady, whose name is not given, ascended 23rd March, 1785, and sailed from London to Horsham. On May 3rd, 1785, Blanchard and Miss Simonet ascended. Lunardi had a second trial 13th May, 1785, when he rose from the Artillery Grounds, but the balloon soon burst, and he descended in Tottenham Court Road. Mr. Thomas Baldwin has written a very circumstantial narrative of his ascent in Lunardi's balloon from Chester, 8th September, 1785. The first ascent from Manchester was on the 12th May, 1785, when Mr. Sadler ascended from a garden behind the house now known as the "Manchester Arms," Long Millgate. This appears to have been the first provincial ascent. Lunardi's portrait was painted by Sir Joshua Reynolds. He died in 1799.

Ballooning has not yet justified the high hopes of its earlier days, but it would be rash even now to speculate how far the true spirit of prophecy was in him who "dept into the future," and

Saw the heavens fill with commerce, argosies of magic sails,
Pilots of the purple twilight, dropping down with costly bales;

Heard the heavens fill with shouting, and there rained a ghastly dew
From the nations' airy navies, grappling in the central blue;

Far along the world-wide whisper of the south wind rushing warm,
With the standards of the peoples plunging thro' the thunder-storm

Till the war drum throbb'd no longer, and the battle-flags were furl'd
In the parliament of man, the federation of the world.

A CENTURY OF THE COTTON TRADE.

BIBLIOGRAPHY.

"*Manchester City News*" *Notes and Queries, vol. v., p.* 149-152. *(The Chronological Table, p.* 287, *is taken from this source.)*

"*Facts of the Cotton Famine.*" *By John Watts. Manchester,* 1866.

"*History of the Cotton Famine.*" *By R. Arthur Arnold. London,* 1864.

"*Historical Data respecting the Cotton Manufacture.*" *By Henry Ashworth. Manchester,* 1866.

"*The Cotton Manufacture.*" *By Andrew Ure. London,* 1836.

"*Woman as an Inventor.*" *By Martha J. Gage. ("North American Review,*" 1884.)

The following paper appeared in the "Companion to the Almanac for 1886."

A CENTURY OF THE COTTON TRADE.

THE cotton trades of America and England, in their organised form, are only the growth of about a hundred years; but they have roots far deeper in the soil of antiquity. It is an amazing circumstance, that although the cotton plant is indigenous to Syria and Egypt, its use as a substitute for linen does not appear to have been thought of, and the cotton manufacture was long insulated in India. Cotton clothing is mentioned by Herodotus, Strabo, and Pliny, and is alluded to by Virgil in the Second Georgic. Spain appears first of any European country to have encouraged the cultivation and manufacture of cotton; and this was doubtless owing to the influence of the Mahometan conquerors. It is said that cotton cloth woven on the coast of Guinea was imported to London from the Bight of Benin in 1590. It may be safely asserted that the tropical countries of Asia, Africa, and America made clothes from cotton long before it was known in Europe. When the passage to India by the Cape of Good Hope was discovered, cotton goods and muslins were brought home. The Dutch and the Italians are also doubtfully said to have had some small home cotton industry. Towards the end of the fifteenth century cotton came to England in the tall ships of the Genoese. At the beginning of the seventeenth century it was imported from Sicily, the Levant, and Lisbon. There are various casual references to the English cotton manufactures in the sixteenth century; but it must be confessed that the word is very loosely applied. A statute of Edward VI., in dealing with woollen manufactures, mentions, among them all, "Manchester, Lankastershire, and Cheshire cottons." Camden also employs the word in the same manner. Captain Robert Hitchcock, the entertaining author of "A Politic Plat," published in 1580, observes: "At Rouen, in France, which is the chiefest vent, be sold our English wares, as Welsh and Manchester cottons, northern kerseys, whites, lead, and tin." This is one of the earliest instances in which the name of Manchester is associated with cotton; and it is half a century earlier than the often quoted passage in Lewis Roberts's "Treasure of Traffic." From the last named, it appears that Manchester wove linen yarn, which it brought from Ireland, and imported cotton wool from Cyprus and Smyrna to work into fustians, vermillions, and dimities. The word cotton is from the Arabic *Qutn, Qutun,* but it has come to us by the intermediation of the French language.

The influence of the religious refugees from the Netherlands upon the trade of Lancashire can only be surmised—though it must have been considerable. A prosperous home industry sprang up. Every farmhouse, and almost every cottage had its loom or loom-house; but the product of this primitive industry was a very coarse fabric of cotton weft and linen warp. The demand exceeded the supply; and thus invention was stimulated to quicken production. The inventions of Hargreaves, Kay, Arkwright, Cartwright, and others led to a prodigious increase of the cotton manufacture, and of course to an enormous increase in the demand for the raw material. A new field of supply was now to open. In 1784 eight bags of cotton were imported from the United States to Liverpool; and a blundering Custom House official detained them—as he was confident they had not been grown in America. They were consigned to the firm of Messrs. William Rathbone and Son, who for several months were unable to find buyers, and eventually disposed of them to the Strutts, of Derby. Since that date the cotton trade of Liverpool has probably been continuous; though in its earlier years it was comparatively insignificant. The year 1784 was not, however, the date when cotton first began to be received in England from America. In 1770 the port of Liverpool received three bales from New York, four bags from Virginia and Maryland, three barrels from North Carolina, and three bags from Georgia. It is, of course, possible, though certainly improbable, that this cotton had first been taken to those States from the British West Indies. The cultivation of the cotton plant was early introduced into what were then English colonies. In 1666 a writer says of the Cape Fear Settlement, that they have "indico, tobacco, very good, and cotton-wool." Dr. Hewitt says that cotton "was not of importance enough to have occupied the whole attention of the colonists" of South Carolina and Georgia. In 1682 it is mentioned that "cotton of the Malta and Cyprus sort grows well in Carolina, and plenty of the seed is sent thither."

Mr. Spalding, of Sapelo Island, near Darien, Georgia, is said to have been one of the first to cultivate the long-staple or Sea Island cotton in 1787, growing it from seed received from the Bahamas. The upland cotton is the variety produced by the different climate and culture of Georgia. Thomas Jefferson, in his "Notes on Virginia," written in 1781, says that "during this time we have manufactured within our families the most necessary articles of clothing. Those of cotton will bear some comparison with the same kinds of manufacture in Europe." The state of affairs during the Revolutionary War, and immediately after, led to an increase in the home-making of clothes. The yarn was spun at home, and sent to the nearest weaver. The cotton for spinning was prepared in general by the field labourers, who were each expected to pick 4 lbs. weekly in addition to their other labours. In 1792, the year preceding the introduction of the saw-gin, the cotton exported from the United States was 138,328 lbs., and the amount retained for domestic consumption about five and a half millions. The amount exported in 1794 was 1,601,700 lbs; in 1795, 5,276,300 lbs.; and in 1800, 17,789,803 lbs. The first cotton mill built in the United States is said to have been that erected at Rhode Island, 1791, under the management of Samuel Slater, who had been an apprentice of Jedediah Strutt, of Belper. Earlier than this the jennies had been in use for the manufacture of home-spun cloth. The importance of America in relation to the cotton trade has, however, been agricultural, and not manufacturing.

The development of the factory system in England has led to an increase of demand which the old methods of cultivation could not supply. A revolution was effected by the invention of the saw-gin in 1793. The Whitney cotton-gin enabled one farm hand to separate the seed from 300 lbs. of cotton-fibre daily, whilst only 11 lbs. could be accomplished by hand. It came at a moment when the inventions for carding, spinning, and weaving had caused an enormous demand for the raw materials; it decided the future of the agriculture of the Southern States; and it had a marvellous effect upon the industrial condition of England. Who can estimate the results, social and political, that have flowed from the introduction of this single labour-saving machine? In the Southern States the very primitive method employed had been of separating the seed with the fingers. In India beating was the fashion. In Georgia a long bow was fitted with numerous strings, which were set vibrating by the blows of a wooden mallet, and, being held at the same time in contact with a bunch of cotton, thus shook out the seed and dust. About the year 1742, Dubreuil, a wealthy planter of New Orleans, invented a cotton-gin which gave some impetus to cultivation in Louisiana; but forty years later the importation of Indian cleaning machinery was recommended by the Parisian colonial authorities. Various forms of roller-gins were invented by Borden, Bisset, and others; but they were found to injure the staple, and had, therefore, to be abandoned. Martha J. Gage, writing in the "North American Review," has claimed the Whitney gin as the invention of a woman. The famous ex-Quaker, General Nathaniel Greene, who had taken his share in the War of the Revolution, settled in Georgia as a planter, but soon died, and his widow, Catherine Littlefield Greene, was left to manage the estate. The difficulty of separating the seed from the pod was a frequent matter of observation and comment, for the entire family joined in the work each evening, and it was often observed that a "fortune would reward whoever could invent a machine to do the work." After a conversation of this character between some guests at her house, Mrs. Greene conceived the idea of such a machine, and entrusted its construction to the hands of Eli Whitney, then boarding with her, and possessed of the usual New England faculty for the use of tools. The wooden teeth

at first tried not doing their work well, Mr. Whitney wished
to abandon the machine altogether; but Mrs. Greene, whose
faith in ultimate success never wavered, would not consent,
and suggested the substitution of wire. "Within ten days
from the first conception of Mrs. Greene's ideas, a small
model was completed, so perfect in its construction that all
subsequent gins have been based upon it." To the very
natural query as to why Mrs. Greene did not take out the
patent in her own name, the reply is returned, that to "have
done so would have exposed her to the ridicule and contumely
of her friends, and a loss of position in society, which frowned
upon any attempt at outside industry by a woman." It
would take too long to record the excitement and litigation
which followed the patent granted to Whitney in March, 1794;
and the statement as to Mrs. Greene's share of the credit would
probably not be accepted without controversy. At the end of
1801 the Legislature of South Carolina purchased the patent
right for that State at a cost of 50,000 dols., and threw it open
to the public. The manufacture of cotton-gins is now in itself
an important industry. We have already mentioned that the
Rathbones sold their eight bags of cotton, in 1784, to the
Strutts, of Derby. This firm is said to have manufactured
the first goods of English make, of which the warp was
cotton, in 1773. After a quantity of these English calicoes
had been made, it was discovered that they were subject to
double the duty that was charged upon mixed fabrics of linen
and cotton, and that their sale was illegal in the home
market. In 1774 an Act was passed (13 Geo. III., c. 72),
which sets forth that, "Whereas a new manufacture of Stuffs,
wholly made of Raw Cotton Wool (chiefly imported from the
British Plantations) hath been lately set up within this King-

dom, in which manufacture many hundreds of poor persons are employed; and whereas the Use and Wear of printed, painted, stained, or dyed Stuffs, wholly made of cotton, ought to be allowed under proper Regulations, it is therefore ordered that no higher duty than 3d., for every yard in length, shall be imposed upon such English 'callicoes;' and that all persons may wear them if so disposed, any previous Acts of Parliament to the contrary notwithstanding." The duty on calicoes was abolished fourteen years later. The first purchase of Sea Island cotton is credited to the sagacity of Robert Owen, afterwards the apostle of Socialism. This is said to have happened in 1791, when he was the manager of the Bank Top Mill, Manchester. The cotton imported into England in 1787 was reckoned at 22,600,000 lbs. ; and none of it is set down as derived from American sources. If we compare this with the figures of the present consumption, it will be seen how great is the increase commemorated by the Cotton Centennial. Instead of the tiny cotton culture, which aimed chiefly at supplying coarse home-spun clothing for the plantation hands, the Southern States are now the great source of cotton supply for the entire world; and not less than 17,322,388 acres of land are devoted to the cultivation of cotton.

Amongst the papers of Mr. George Walker, F.R.S., are some data respecting the cotton trade, which have been printed by the Manchester Literary and Philosophical Society. One memorandum is a calculation that in 1790 112,400 packages of cotton were imported into Great Britain ("99,000 B. and P. West India, supposed 160 lbs. each; 13,400 bales Turkey, supposed 260 lbs. each"). It was supposed that the manufactories had used 80,000 West India at

160 lbs. nett each, 12,800,000 at 15½d. = £827,000 ; 12,000 Turkey at 260 lbs. nett each, 3,120,000 at 10½d. = £136,500. Then reckoning 15,920,000 lbs at 6s. 8d., the value of the cloth, when finished and for sale, is £5,310,000, leaving £4,346,500 for wages and profit. It is remarkable that in this estimate none of the cotton is described as coming from America. Another table, however, shows clearly the great change that was taking place. From 1806 to 1812 there were importations to Liverpool of cotton from America, Brazil, Portugal, Demerara and Berbice, Surinam, Trinidad, Dominica and Grenada, Tortola, Antigua, St. Vincent, Nevis, &c., St. Thomas, Jamaica, Bahamas, St. Lucia, Ireland, Mediterranean, Azores, &c., and St. Croix, sometimes in very small quantities. The total imported in the seven years was 1,366,309 packages, or an average of 3,753 per week. The number that came from America was 665,196, and of these 107,123 were from New Orleans. The business facilities of that day may be imagined from the circumstances that in November, 1774, Mr. Walker paid £4 10s. 3d. for sending a letter by express from Manchester to Glasgow, by way of Wetherby, Newcastle, and Edinburgh, and that an express to London cost £2 15s. 3d. The London letter was delivered in 36 hours, and that to Glasgow in 66 hours.

The following chronological memoranda will show some of the more important events recorded by the annalists of the cotton industry. In regard to the earlier periods there is considerable obscurity, and therefore room for controversy. With the beginning of the eighteenth century matters became clearer. It is not until the organisation of the factory system that the cotton industry became of national importance.

A.D.

1253. Linen first made in England by Flemish hands.

1298. Cotton used in England for candle wick.

1330. Manufactures of Flanders introduced into Manchester.

1530. Spinning wheel invented at Brunswick.

1631. Printed calicoes imported from India.

1641. Fustains and dimities introduced in England.

1641. Cotton yarn imported from the Levant.

1670. Muslins first worn in England.

1675. Calico-printing introduced into England.

1676. Introduction of the Dutch loom engine.

1677. East India calicoes to the value of £160,000 consumed in England.

1690. A small printworks established on the Thames, at Richmond.

1698. First steam engine brought into successful operation, by Savery.

1701. Value of cotton goods exported, £23,000.

1720. Act prohibiting the use or wear of printed calicoes, whether printed in England or elsewhere, under a penalty of £5 the wearer, and £20 the seller.

1736. So much of the Act of 1720 repealed as forbade the wear of mixed printed goods—that is, goods not all cotton.

1738. Invention of the fly-shuttle by John Kay, of Bury.

1738. Machine for spinning with rollers invented by John Wyatt and Lewis Paul.

1753. A cotton reel invented by Mr. Earnshaw.

1756. Cotton velvets first made in England.

1757. Duty of 4d. per lb. on yarn imported from India.

1760. Value of cotton manufactured in Great Britain, £200,000 per annum.

1760. Warping mill invented.

1763. Muslin and cotton quiltings first made in England.

1763. Bleaching generally introduced.

1764. James Hargreaves' invention of the spinning jenny to spin eleven threads at once.

1764. Calico-printing first practised in Lancashire.

1765. English printed calicoes exported to Holland.

1765. Calicoes (so-called from their resemblance to Indian manufactures brought from a province of Calicut) first attempted in England.

A.D.

1766. Value of cotton goods made in Great Britain, £600,000.

1767. Spinning by machinery (the water frame).

1769. Drawing rollers patented by Arkwright.

1770. Spinning jenny patented by Hargreaves.

1772. Arkwright and Co. successfully accomplish the manufacture of calicoes.

1772. First English cotton goods made with cotton warps, by Messrs. Strutt, of Derby.

1774. Chlorine discovered by Scheele.

1775. Mule spinning invented by Samuel Crompton.

1776. First cotton mill erected at Stalybridge.

1777. First cotton mill erected at Preston.

1777. Green dye for calicoes introduced by Dr. R. Williams.

1780. The finest cotton brought from Berbice. Price of cotton: Berbice, 2s. 1d.; Demerara, 1s. 1d.; Surinam, 2s.; Cayenne, 2s.

1781. Brazil cotton first imported from Maranham.

1782. A panic in Manchester, in consequence of 7,012 bales of cotton being imported between December and April.

1783. Brazil cotton first brought to Manchester.

1783. Arkwright's machinery for spinning and carding cotton by steam used in Manchester.

1784. Machinery for spinning open to the trade.

1784. Bleachers, printers, and dyers compelled to take out licenses under an annual tax of £2, by Pitt.

1785. Cotton first cultivated in Georgia and South Carolina, from seed from the Bahamas.

1785. Cotton imported from America—one bag from Charlestown, one from New York, and twelve from Philadelphia.

1785. First steam engine for cotton mill, by Watt.

1785. Cylindrical printing invented by Mr. Bell, and greatly improved by Mr. Lockett, of Manchester.

1786. A small quantity of cotton received from the Isle of Bourbon, sold at 7s. to 10s. per lb.

1786. Bleaching with acid introduced into the bleach works of Mr. M'Gregor, near Glasgow, by James Watt.

1787. First copyright for printers.

A.D.

1787. Excise duty of 3¼d. per square yard imposed on calicoes made and printed in England, and foreign calicoes charged with a duty of 7d. per yard when printed and died in Great Britain.

1787. Previous to this year the supply of cotton was principally from the West Indies.

1787. 108 bales of cotton imported from America.

1787. Power-loom invented by Dr. Cartwright.

1787. Forty-one spinning factories in Lancashire.

1788. Acid first used for bleaching in Manchester.

1791. First cotton mill erected in United States.

1793. First attempt to spin yarn from 100's and upwards by power.

1793. First importation of consequence of cotton from America.

1793. Whitney's saw-gin invented for cleaning cotton.

1798. Chloride of lime for bleaching patented by Mr. Tennant, of Glasgow.

1801. Discharge work in printing accomplished by Messrs. Peel.

1801. First construction of a fire-proof cotton mill, Messrs. Phillips and Lea, of Manchester, first applying cast-iron beams to this purpose.

1802. The first Factory Act passed. It was promoted by the first Sir Robert Peel, and limited the labour of apprentices in cotton mills to twelve hours, prohibiting night-work after June, 1804, and provided for their instruction and clothing.

1802. Import duties on raw cotton re-imposed, slightly higher than those of 1798.

1803. A power-loom patented by H. Horrocks, of Stockport.

1804. Invention of the dressing machine by Thomas Johnson, of Stockport; it supplied the missing link in power-loom invention, for want of which the looms had failed to achieve any decisive success.

1808. New method of engraving with dies for calico-printing introduced by Mr. Lockett, of Manchester.

1809. Parliament granted Dr. Cartwright £10,000 for his invention of the power-loom.

1810. Turkey red first introduced into calico printing.

1812. Between four and five million spindles at work in Great Britain.

20

A.D.

1813.   H. Horrocks, of Stockport, made important improvements in the power-loom, 'and his machine eventually came into general use. The handloom weavers took the alarm, as the spinners had done in 1799, and power-looms were extensively destroyed by mobs.

1815.   Eight pounds of cotton twist sent to India on trial.

1815.   Robert Owen, of New Lanark Mills, on the Clyde, advocates a ten hours bill.   The Act of 1802 was evaded by the employment of non-apprenticed children.   Sir Robert Peel advocated Owen's views in Parliament.

1816.   Yarn trade opened with the Continent.

1817.   Number of spindles in use in the United Kingdom estimated by Mr. John Kennedy at 6,645,000.

1819.   Second Factory Act, commonly called Peel's Act, prohibiting the employment of children under nine years of age, and limiting the labour of all young people under sixteen to twelve hours a day.

1821.   First regular exportation of twist to India.

1823.   Cotton first imported from Egypt.

1825.   Richard Roberts, of Sharp and Roberts, Manchester, patents his self-acting mule.

1827.   De Jongh's self-acting mule patented.

1831.   Third Factory Act, promoted by Lord Morpeth and Sir John Hobhouse.   It shortened the hours of labour in cotton mills of young persons under eighteen to eleven and a half hours a day, and eight and a half on Saturdays, in all sixty-nine hours a week.

1832.   Duty on printed calicoes repealed.   Spindles in the United Kingdom, 9,300,000 ; power-looms, 203,000.   Ninety-six cotton factories at work in Manchester and Salford.

1833.   William Graham, of Glasgow, invented the self-acting temple, which kept the cloth constantly stretched by the action of a pair of clippers.   Afterwards superseded by the use of roller temples.

1834.   Fourth Factory Act, originated by Lord Ashley, but carried through by Government.   It limited the employment of persons under eighteen to twelve hours in one day, and sixty-nine hours a week ; and of children under eleven to nine hours a day, and forty-eight hours a week.   Under this Act Inspectors of Factories were appointed for the first time.

A.D.

1835. In Lancashire there were 683 cotton factories at work, and in Great Britain and Ireland 1,263, employing in all 108,886 males and 120,283 females.

1836. J. C. Dyer, of Manchester, invented the cardmaking machines.

1845. Duty on cotton repealed.

1847. The Ten Hours Bill passed.

1851. Muslin shown at the Great Exhibition, manufactured from yarn of the extraordinarily fine count, 700's, spun by Mr Thomas Houldsworth, of Manchester and Reddish.

1858. Mr. Evan Leigh, of Manchester, invented revolving flat cards for carding, and loose boss top rollers for spinning.

1861-4. The Cotton Famine, caused by the Civil War in the United States.

The founder of the modern cotton industry is Richard Arkwright. The originality of his inventions have been warmly contested, and the patent granted to him in 1769 for spinning with rollers was set aside in 1785 for want of novelty. It would take too long to examine in detail the evidence for and against his claims, nor is it at all necessary, for even those who deny his mechanical genius do not doubt the wonderful sagacity and power of organisation by which he not only reaped a large fortune for himself, but laid the foundation of a trade which has added so greatly to the wealth and prosperity of the nation. The invention of the fly-shuttle, the various improvements in carding, and the patenting of Hargreaves' spinning jenny in 1770, prepared the way for the use of the spinning frame or throstle, which, whether the invention of Arkwright or not, was effectively introduced by him. The cotton trade as a home industry was now gradually transformed by the factory system.

The year 1775 witnessed the completion by Samuel Crompton of his "mule jenny." No more important invention has been made in relation to the cotton industry. It is a melancholy fact that Crompton, a man of genius and of sensitive and refined nature, was treated with conspicuous ingratitude by the people whom he had helped to enrich. His mechanical talent was not accompanied by business capacity, as in the case of Arkwright. Parliament eventually made a grant of £5,000, a sum ludicrously small in comparison with the wealth that his invention had brought to the country. The character of Crompton was a fine one: modest and sensitive, honourable in his dealings, deeply religious, with a tendency to mysticism, and with something of the artistic temperament, he was little fitted for a struggle with the coarse and unfeeling generation amongst whom his lot was cast. His life was made poor by the ingratitude of those who became rich by the plunder of his brains. The contrast between Arkwright and Crompton in character and fortune is striking.

The next great mechanical innovation was the "power-loom." The inventor was not one interested in the cotton trade, but was a Suffolk clergyman. How the Rev. Edward Cartwright came to turn his attention to this matter he has himself told in an interesting passage :—

" Happening to be at Matlock in the summer of 1784, I fell in company with some gentlemen of Manchester, when the conversation turned on Arkwright's spinning machinery. One of the company observed that as soon as Arkwright's patent expired so many mills would be erected, and so much cotton spun, that hands never could be found to weave it. To this observation I replied that Arkwright must then set his wits to work and invent a weaving mill. This brought on a conversation on the subject, in which the Manchester gentlemen unanimously agreed that the thing-was impracticable ; and in defence of their opinion they adduced arguments which I certainly was incompetent to answer, or even to comprehend, being totally ignorant of the subject, having never at that time seen a person weave. I controverted, however, the impracticability of the thing by remarking that there had lately been exhibited in London an automaton figure which played at chess.

" Some little time afterwards, a particular circumstance recalling this conversation to my mind, it struck me that, as in plain weaving, according to the conception I then had of the business, there could only be three movements, which were to follow each other in succession, there would be little difficulty in producing and repeating them. Full of these ideas, I immediately employed a carpenter and smith to carry them into effect. As soon as the machine was finished, I got a weaver to put in the warp, which was of such materials as suit cloth is usually made of. To my great delight a piece of cloth, such as it was, was the produce. As I had never before turned my thoughts to anything mechanical, either in theory or practice, nor had ever seen a loom at work, or knew anything of its construction, you will readily suppose that my first loom must have been a most rude piece of machinery. The warp was placed perpendicularly, the reed fell with a force of at least half a hundredweight, the springs which threw the shuttle were strong enough to have thrown a Congreve rocket. In short, it required the strength of two powerful men to work the machine at a slow rate, and only for a short time. Conceiving in my great simplicity that I had accomplished all that was required, I then secured what I thought a most valuable property by a patent, 4th April, 1785. This being done, I then condescended to see how other people wove; and you will guess my astonishment when I compared their easy mode of operation with mine. Availing myself, however, of what I then saw, I made a loom, in its general principles nearly as they are now made; but it was not till the year 1787 that I completed my invention, when I took out my last weaving patent, August 1st of that year." Parliament made a grant to Cartwright of £10,000.

The next great improvement was due to the genius of Richard Roberts, a man who it has been rightly said could "invent to order." It was in 1825 that he invented the self-acting mule, and thus completed the remarkable series of inventions which have contributed to the cotton trade of the last hundred years.

The growth of the cotton trade was coincident with the growth of the factory system. The demand for labour was great, and by a system of apprenticeship the mills of Lancashire were largely supplied by pauper children imported into the county. There were no safeguards against overwork, and no sanitary regulations. The first Sir Robert Peel was instrumental in passing the first Factory Act, that of 1802 (42 Geo. III, c. 73). This limited the labour of children to twelve hours daily, and prohibited their employment in night work. The next legislative enactment passed in 1819 (59 Geo. III., c. 56), which forbids the employment of children under nine years of age in cotton factories, whilst between nine and sixteen they could only be employed for twelve hours. By Lord Althorpe's Act of 1833 (3 and 4 Wm. IV., c. 103) the principle of half-time was introduced. Inspectors were appointed, and the Acts thus became something more than a dead letter. The agitation for a Ten Hours Bill was carried on with great vigour, and under the lead of Lord Ashley (afterwards Lord Shaftesbury) gained an increased support. He carried the proposal for limiting the work of women and children to ten hours, and Peel agreed to a twelve hours' limit by way of compromise. Thus the Factory Act became law in 1844 (7 and 8 Vict., c. 15). Its provisions were that the working hours of children under thirteen should be diminished to six and a half hours per day; that the time during which they were to be under daily instruction in schools should be extended from two to two and a half hours in winter, and three in summer; that the labour of persons between thirteen and eighteen, and of adult women (now first brought under the Factory Acts), should be limited to twelve hours a day; that a certificate of baptism should be produced, if demanded, to prove that the child was really of the age required by the law; that the amount of the fines imposed for the violation of the law should be diminished, but that they should be inflicted for each person improperly worked, instead of for such offence, which might include several persons; and that machinery should be guarded to prevent accident. Inspectors were appointed to carry out the Act. In 1847 Mr. John Fielden, member for Oldham, introduced and carried a bill which limited the labour of young people between the ages of thirteen and eighteen to twelve hours a day, allowing two hours out of the twelve for meals; and he further proposed that the same restriction should apply to females above eighteen years of age. The principle of State regulation of the labour of women and children was thus fully recognised.

The American war was a terrible blow to the prosperity of the cotton districts. Thousands of decent working people had to part with their little earnings to keep the wolf from the door, and those who had been Sunday-school teachers and scholars were reduced to begging in the streets. At first the public mind did not realise the magnitude of the evil, and it was thought that the millowners were not doing their duty. This was a mistake, for many of them made great sacrifices, and saw the source of their prosperity dried up by a quarrel in which they had no concern. After a period of short time the cessation of the cotton supply led to the stoppage of many of the factories. In July, 1862, a relief fund was started, and the generosity of the British public saved the Lancashire artisan from starvation. Many emigrated, and many turned their hands to other labour; but cotton manufacture has its own needs and characteristics, and it was not always that those who had acquired skill and deftness in it could adapt themselves to other kinds of work. The total raised for the relief of the distress caused by the cotton famine was £2,000,000; but this does not represent by a long way all that was done by private philanthropy. The famine came to an end in the summer of 1865. Some fortunes were made by running the blockade of the Confederate ports and bringing out cotton. It was remarkable that whilst the aristocratic classes sympathised to some extent with the slave holders, the working people of the north were enthusiastically in favour of the Free North. This was emphatically the case in Lancashire, where the artisans saw almost the destruction of the social fabric. It had been said "cotton is king," but the sentiment of freedom was stronger than sordid interest.

The civil war in the United States gave increased urgency and importance to the question of cotton supply. In India many attempts had been made to improve the quantity and quality of cotton, but not with conspicuous success. The highest quantity exported to Great Britain was in 1857, when it amounted to 680,000 bales (£5,458,426), but the stoppage of the American supply led to a great increase, and in 1866 the figure was 1,847,760 bales (£25,270,547). This quantity has not been maintained, but after the United States the most important place is now taken by India in the growth of cotton, and the efforts made for its improvement are not fruitless.

Cotton has been known in Egypt from a remote period, but its cultivation did not attain any great importance until about 1820, when some seeds brought from Ethiopia by Maho Bay were successfully grown in his garden at Cairo. The plant was recognised by M. Jumel, who was in the service of Mehemet Ali. That quick-witted despot gave great encouragement to the culture, and in 1823 exported 5,623. Jumel became the director of the Viceroy's cotton plantation, and the cultivation of the plant has since greatly extended in Lower Egypt. The gross misgovernment of that unhappy country is, perhaps, the chief hindrance to the development of the natural advantages which for cotton growing are said by competent judges to be as great as those of the Southern States of America. The advantages of Turkey as a source of cotton supply are not so great, but official corruption and misgovernment have greatly hindered its possible development.

The "cotton famine," caused by the struggle in America, led many countries to experiment in cotton growing, and it is not impossible that if the Slave War had been continued the new sources of supply would have eventually proved adequate to the needs of the manufacture. In 1862 there was held at the International Exhibition a conference of representative cotton-growing districts, and Brazil, Peru, Africa, and West Indies, New South Wales, Queensland, Italy, Greece, Turkey, Egypt, and India all showed great activity. Thirty-five countries exhibited samples, but ten years later most of these had been beaten out of the field. The success of the Federal Armies; the generous terms given to the vanquished by Grant; and the renewal of industry in the Southern States put an end to the hopes of competitors. "Let us have peace" was the aspiration of the great citizen-soldier, and with peace America once more took the foremost position in the production of cotton. The marvellous manner in which the devastation of the war has been repaired and the ruined fortunes of the South built up again is a matter of history. The disappearance of slavery, as costly from an economical point of view as it is wicked from an ethical standpoint, has removed the greatest hindrance to the greatness and prosperity of the American nation.

Since the end of the cotton famine improved machinery has greatly increased the productive power of the industry, but progress has not been uniform, and more than one crisis has interfered with its prosperity. At the present moment it is suffering from the long-continued general depression of trade, and eager eyes are being turned in the direction of possible new markets. If we look at the immense advances of the cotton trade in the past century, there is little reason to fear any permanent check of its growth and importance. This record can most clearly be expressed statistically.

The quanttiy of raw cotton imported into the United Kingdom in 1815 amounted to only 99,000,000 lbs.; it rose to 152,000,000 in 1820; to 229,000,000 in 1825; to

264,000,000 in 1830; to 592,000,000 in 1840; to 663,576,861 lbs. in 1850; and to 1,390,938,752 lbs. in 1860; it fell to 669,583,264 lbs. in 1863. The subjoined table gives the total cotton imports, exports, and the home consumption.

Years.	Total Imports of Cotton.	Total Exports of Cotton.	Retained for Home Consumption.
	lbs.	lbs.	lbs.
1860	1,390,938,752	250,339,040	1,140,599,712
1861	1,256,984,736	298,287,920	958,696,816
1862	523,973,296	214,714,528	309,258,768
1863	669,583,264	241,352,496	428,230,768
1864	893,304,720	244,702,304	648,602,416
1865	977,978,288	302,908,928	675,069,360
1866	1,377,129,936	388,952,368	988,177,568
1867	1,262,536,912	350,626,416	911,910,496
1868	1,328,084,016	322,620,480	1,005,463,536
1869	1,220,809,856	272,928,544	947,881,312
1870	1,338,305,584	236,630,576	1,101,675,008
1871	1,778,139,776	362,234,160	1,409,905,616
1872	1,408,837,472	273,005,040	1,135,832,382
1873	1,527,596,224	220,000,256	1,307,595,968
1874	1,566,864,432	258,967,632	1,307,896,800
1875	1,492,351,168	262,853,808	1,229,497,360
1876	1,487,858,848	203,305,872	1,284,552,976
1877	1,355,281,200	169,396,304	1,185,884,896
1878	1,340,380,048	147,257,936	1,193,122,112
1879	1,469,358,464	188,201,888	1,281,156,576
1880	1,628,664,576	224,577,360	1,404,087,216
1881	1,679,068,384	207,710,618	1,471,357,776
1882	1,784,111,168	264,998,160	1,519,113,008
1883	1,734,333,552	247,228,800	1,487,104,752
1884	1,749,169,184	251,661,648	1,497,507,536

The population engaged in the cotton industry has greatly increased. The check caused by the American War has been overpassed. The following table will show the statistics of cotton factories at intervals in the last quarter of a century :—

No. of Factories.

Cotton Factories.	1856.	1861.	1868.	1880.
England and Wales ...	2,046	2,715	2,405	2,579
Scotland..................	152	163	131	89
Ireland	12	9	13	6
United Kingdom	2,210	2,887	2,549	2,674

No. of Spinning Spindles.

Cotton Factories.	1856.	1861.	1868.	1880.
England and Wales ...	25,818,576	28,352,125	30,478,125	42,640,309
Scotland	2,041,129	1,915,398	1,397,546	1,487,853
Ireland	150,512	119,944	124,240	78,528
United Kingdom	28,010,217	30,387,567	32,000,014	43,206,690

No. of Power Looms.

Cotton Factories.	1856.	1861.	1868.	1880.
England and Wales ..	275,590	368,125	344,719	489,960
Scotland..................	21,624	30,110	31,864	22,265
Ireland	1,633	1,757	2,746	2,686
United Kingdom	298,847	399,992	379,329	514,911

No. of Persons Employed.

Cotton Factories.	1856.	1861.	1868.	1880.
England and Wales...	341,179	407,598	357,052	451,508
Scotland..................	34,698	41,237	39,809	29,775
Ireland	3,345	2,734	4,203	1,620
United Kingdom	379,213	451,569	401,064	482,903

The following Table will show the production and exportation of yarn :—

Years.	Yarn Produced.	Exported.	Consumed at Home.
	Yards.	Yards.	Yards.
1819	98,566,200	18,085,410	80,480,790
1824	148,656,600	33,605,510	115,051,090
1834	270,186,876	76,478,468	193,708,408
1844	445,577,480	138,540,079	307.037,401
1854	693,659,000	147,128,000	546,531,000
1861	899,902,000	177,848,000	722,054,000
1862	373,352,000	88,554,000	284,798,000
1863	404,979,000	70,678,000	334,301,000
1864	432,629,000	71,951,000	360,678,000
1874	1,120,525,000	220,599,000	899,926,000
1884	1,411,000,000	270,904,600	1,140,095,400

The result of the cotton trade in recent years may be gauged by the figures as to the exports of cotton piece goods in successive years.

Years.	Exports of Cotton Piece Goods.	Years.	Exports of Cotton.
	Yards.		Yards.
1863	1,710,962,072	1874	3,606,639,044
1864	1,751,989,300	1875	3,562,462,166
1865	2,014,303,716	1876	3,669,404,374
1866	2,575,698,138	1877	3,837,220,850
1867	2,832,023,707	1878	3,618,665,300
1868	2,977,106,551	1879	3,724,648,800
1869	2,868,630,125	1880	4,495,645,000
1870	3,266,998,366	1881	4,777,273,300
1871	3,417,405,811	1882	4,349,391,000
1872	3,537,985,311	1883	4,538,888,500
1873	3,483,735,585	1884	4,417,280,000

We have thus traced in outline the progress which from small beginnings has in a single century become one of the most important of English industries. The products of the looms of the cotton districts go through many hands and ands. The nations of the earth are bound together by the prosaic processes that go on from morn to night in a Man-

chester warehouse. The swarthy Hindoo receives her packages
in the Ghauts of the Ganges, and the swarthier negro unloads
them by the Niger.   At this moment she may watch the
caravans toiling over the Asiatic plains ; the fighting Pindarees
forcing their way through the passes of Hindostan; the indolent
Turk sitting cross-legged in his bazaar, smoking the pipe of
unthoughtfulness, and selling his wares to those who choose to
buy.   In every clime there are the ambassadors of those
whose mission has been said to " cottonize " the world.

ON THE INCREASE OF WEALTH AND POPULATION IN LANCASHIRE.

The following Paper was read before the Economic Section of the British Association, at Manchester, Sept., 1887.

ON THE INCREASE OF WEALTH AND
POPULATION IN LANCASHIRE.

THE growth of the wealth and population of Lancashire within the last century and a half has been exceedingly rapid. When the British Association visited Manchester in 1842 some particulars as to the increase of wealth in the county were submitted by the late Mr. Henry Ashworth; and as the progress made since that date has been very remarkable, it may be useful to examine the subject once more from a statistical point of view.

The name of the county of Lancaster does not occur in Domesday Book, but the 188 manors in the district now known by that name are valued at £120, a sum which Baines, in his *History of Lancashire*, estimates as equivalent to £13,200.

When the Great Council or Parliament of Westminster, 1352, was held for the purpose of "settling the staple" or manufactures of the kingdom, the county sent only one representative. The list of decayed towns of Lancashire in 1544 includes Lancaster, Preston, Lyrepool, and Wigan. In the military muster of 1553, Lancashire was called upon for 2,000 men, and in 1559 there were 1,919 "harnessed men" and 2,073 without armour. In 1574 it furnished 6,000 able men, 3,600 armed men, 600 pioneers and artificers, 12 demi-lances, and 90 light horse—standing amongst the most important of the counties in a military sense.

In the same year the gross produce of the tenth and fifteenth taxes was recorded as £376 11s. 11½d. The figures for the hundreds were : Leyland, £36 10s. 4d. ; Blackburn, £48 8s. 6d. ; Salford, £48 7s. 4d. ; West Derby, £125 8s. 7d.; Amounderness, £66 17s. 0d.; Lonsdale, £50 18s. 2d. The levy for ship money in 1636 shows the estimate as to the relative wealth of various places. The contribution of Lancashire was one ship of 400 tons, 160 men, and £1,000. Preston contributed £40 ; Lancaster, £30 ; Liverpool, £25; Wigan, £50; Clitheroe, £7 10s. ; Newton, £7 10s. Yorkshire contributed two ships of 600 tons and £12,000. Hull was assessed at £140; Leeds at £200; Bristol at one ship of 100 tons, 40 men, and £1,000. London contributed seven ships, 4,000 tons, 1,560 men, and six months' pay.

Mr. Ashworth calculated the value of Lancashire from the land tax in 1692, and compared it with that of the rateable value in 1841. This is the starting point of the following calculations. The increase of both population and of rateable value has been due to the immense development, in the first instance, of the cotton trade, and to the impetus given by it to other forms of industry. The increase of population in Lancashire may be thus stated: 1801, 672,731 ; 1811, 828,309 ; 1821, 1,052,859 ; 1831, 1,335,800 ; 1841, 1,667,054; 1851, 2,031,236; 1861, 2,428,744; 1871, 2,819,495; 1881, 3,454,441. The rateable value of the six hundreds into which the county is divided may now be stated. The figures for 1692 are those calculated by Mr. Ashworth, and the later dates are the official estimates for the county basis or standard of rating :—

Rateable Value of the County of Lancaster.

The first column calculated from the land tax returns; the remainder from the basis or standard for county rates.

Hundreds.	1841.	1853.	1866.	1872.	1877.	1884.
	£	£	£	£	£	£
Lonsdale	8,500	291,963	298.275	423,665	514,402	767,630	1,010,772
Amounderness	10,288	364,994	414,691	525,239	592,544	718,018	896,956
Leyland	5,774	199,884	199,038	950,663	1,159,472	1,432,206	1,738,740
Blackburn	11,131	498,286	574,607	248,795	282,236	321,114	370,946
Salford	25,907	2,703,291	3,051,347	4,082,799	5,269,222	6,848,754	7,791,862
West Derby ..	35,642	2,124,925	2,375,115	3,798,806	4,734,124	5,539,168	6,789,222
	95,242	6,183,343	6,913,073	10,029,967	12,552,000	15,626,890	18,598,498

If we take the townships forming and adjoining the city of Manchester and the borough of Salford, the increase is shown to be very marked. It is notable that the increase of wealth has been progressive, notwithstanding the complaints of trade depression.

Name of Place.	Value in 1692.			Value in 1841.	Value in 1866.	Value in 1884.
	£	s.	d.	£	£	£
Chorlton-on-Medlock	256	4	2	137,651	162,952	266,848
Hulme	152	10	5	75,733	180,073	252.034
Ardwick	175	0	0	46,471	69,171	128,928
Salford	809	19	7	162,847	189,587	382,904
Cheetham	215	18	4	38,933	75,470	137,920
Manchester	4,025	0	0	721,743	882,998	1,579,552
Broughton	230	6	8	33,956	70,551	158,896
Pendleton	363	12	11	48,150	84,497	192,420
Crumpsall	95	6	3	13,237	19,895	40,018
Rusholme	146	13	4	15,281	33,906	63,110
Moss Side	61	9	2	4,958	21,691	102,744
	6,531	0	10	1,298,960	1,780,791	3,305,374

These figures measure the industrial progress of Lancashire. Whilst each hundred has had its share of prosperity, the greatest increase of wealth has been in the Salford Hundred, which comprises the Manchester district, and West Derby,

BOOKS AND PAMPHLETS

WILLIAM E. A. AXON, M.R.S.L.,

MANCHESTER,

Miembro Corrisponsal de la Sociedad de Ciencias Fisicas y Naturales de Caracas; Foreign Corresponding Member of the Numismatic and Antiquarian Society of Philadelphia.

BOOKS.

1870—Folk Song and Folk Speech of Lancashire.

1877—Handbook of the Public Libraries of Manchester and Salford.

1878—Architectural and General Description of the Town Hall, Manchester.

1883—Lancashire Gleanings.
Contents: Nanny Cutler, a Lancashire "Dinah Bede." The Mosley Family. The Extraordinary Memory of the Rev. T. Threlkeld. Sunday in the Olden Time. Tim Bobbin as an Artist. Ann Lee, the Manchester Prophetess. Master John Shawe. Traditions collected by Thomas Barritt. Did Shakspere visit Lancashire? The Lancashire Plot. Sherburnes in America. Curiosities of Street Literature. Thomas and John Ferriar. Turton Fair in 1789. Story of the Three Black Crows. Lancashire Beyond the Sea. Murders Detected by Dreams. The Black Knight of Ashton. Robert Tannahill in Lancashire. Population of Manchester. Prince Charles Edward Stuart's supposed Visit to Manchester. Congregationalism at Farnworth, near Bolton. Church Goods in 1552. The Estates of Sir Andrew Chadwick. Early Art in Liverpool. The Story of Burger's "Lenore." Manchester in 1791. Early References to the Jews in Lancashire. Whittington and his Cat. "Fair Em." The Father of Thomas de Quincey. Origin of the Word "Teetotal." Robert Wilson and the Invention of the Steam Hammer. Ralph Sandiford. Elias, the Manchester Prophet. Westhoughton Factory Fire. Peter Annet. Some Old Lancashire Ballads, Broadsides, and Chap-books. George Fox's First Entry into Lancashire. The Legend of Mab's Cross. The Lindsays in Lancashire. The Liverpool Tragedy. Lancashire Proverbs.

1884—Cheshire Gleanings.
Contents: Dean Stanley and Alderley. The Northwich Demoniac. "Warning for Fair Women." John Critchley Prince. Richard Ramsey. William Hornby's Scourge of Drunkenness. Did Harold die at Chester? The Word Bachelor in Cheshire. Was Marat a Teacher at Warrington? The Botanist's Funeral. The Cheshire Man called Evelyn. The Wizard of Alderley Edge. Was John Smith a Cheshire Man? Sir John Chesshyre's Library at Halton. The Brereton Death Omen. The Fool of Chester. The Thin Red Line. A Birkenhead Newspaper in 1642. J. C. Prince and K. T. Korner. Joseph Rayner Stephens. On the Stalk as a Sign of Contract. The Genius of Avernus. Tennyson's "Northern Cobbler" a Cheshire Man. The King of the Cats. Mary of Buttermere. Old Easter Customs of Cheshire. The Chester Plays. Sunday Observance in Cheshire. Early References to the Jews in Cheshire. Dr. Moffat as a Cheshire Gardener. Joseph Mowbray Hawcroft: In Memoriam. A Fragment of the Chester Plays. Sion y Boddiau. Mark Yarwood. The Fight of the Thirty. Old Mynshull of Erdeswick. Nixon, the "Cheshire Prophet." Cheshire Marling. Cheshire Proverbs. The Earthquake of 1777. The Suspected Spy. Sir Gawayne and the Green Knight. Book Rarities of the Warrington Museum. The Undutiful Child Punished. Dr. John Ferriar. Cheshire and Lancashire Dialects in the Earlier Part of the Nineteenth Century. Samuel Hibbert Ware. A Cheshire Chesterfield. Riding the Stang. William Broome, LL.D. Dean Arderne. Sir Thomas Aston. A Cheshire Lord Chief Justice. Cheshire Ballad.

1888—Stray Chapters in Literature, Folklore and Archæology.

EDITED.

1873—Nixon's Cheshire Prophecies.
1875—Mechanic's Friend.
Harland's Genealogy of the Pilkingtons.
1874—Guide to Manchester and Salford.
1878—Nixon's Cheshire Prophecies. 2nd Edit.

1882—Mother Shipton : A Collection of the Prophecies.
Field Naturalist.
1883—English Dialect Words in Bailey's Dictionary.
Procter's Barber's Shop.
Caxton's Game of the Chesse.
1886—Annals of Manchester.

PAMPHLETS.

1867—Co-operation and Partnerships of Industry.
1869—Poetry of the Bibliomania.
1870—Hints on the Formation of Small Libraries.
Literature of the Lancashire Dialect.
Legend of the Disguised Knight.
Black Knight of Ashton.
1872—The Strassburg Library.
A Plea for Free Speech.
Juvenile Smoking.
Tobacco and Disease.
Tobacco Question.
Smoking and Thinking.
On the Extent of Ancient Libraries.
1873—Future of the English Language.
Physiological Position of Tobacco
1874—Notice of the Rev. Thomas Threlkeld.
On the Relative Proportion of the Sexes.
1875—Book Rarities of Manchester Free Library.
Bibliographical List of Books in Lancashire Dialect.
Defects in Statistics of Books and Libraries.
Statistics of the Deaf and Dumb.
1876—Biblioteche Antiche e Moderne.
Smallest Books in the World.
Exotica.
1877—On a Printed Catalogue for the British Museum Library.
Notabilia Bibliothecæ Chethamensis
Glance at the Westminster Free Library.
Statistics of the English Publishing Trade.
1878—Song of the Nightingale.
British Museum in Relation to National Culture.
Book Rarities of the Warrington Museum.
Good and Evil of Tobacco.
1879—Bolton and its Free Library.
Sunday Opening of Libraries and Museums.
The One Legged Robin.
1880—Sunday in Manchester.
Libraries of Lancashire and Cheshire.
1881—Legislation for Public Free Libraries.
George Eliot's Use of Dialect.

1881 -Plague of Caterpillars at Clitheroe.
Pronunciation of Deaf Mutes who have been Taught to Articulate.
John Ruskin : A Bibliographical Biography. 2nd Edit.
Relation of Archæology to Art.
Corn or Cattle.
On an Epidemic of Tricophyton Tonsurans.
Literary History of Parnell's " Hermit."
1882—List of the Leading Public Libraries in the United Kingdom.
Did Shakspere visit Lancashire ?
Milton's " Comus" and Fletcher's " Faithful Shepherdess " Compared.
Sunday in Lancashire and Cheshire.
Cost of Theatrical Amusements.
1883—Education in Salford.
1884—Art in Lancashire.
On Fritz Reuter's Story of the " Ganshandel."
Byron's Influence on European Literature.
Wardley Skull-House.
1885—Hugh of Manchester.
1886—Books and Reading.
Social Results of Temperance in Blackburn.
The Holy Mountain.
Buddhism and its Founder.
1887--Ten Sonnets.
Vegetarismus und litterarische Arbeit.
A Gossip about Old Manchester.
Provision of Cheap Meals for School Children.
What was the first Book printed in Manchester ?
Who was Mistress Joyce Lewes of Manchester ?
Wordsworth in London.
1888—Possibilities of Co-operation in Temperance Work.
Significance of Kufic Coins in Northumbria.
Berber Folk-Tales.
In Memoriam Adolph Samelson.
Thomas Lurting : A Liverpool Worthy.

John Heywood, Excelsior Printing and Bookbinding Works, Manchester.